# ADVANCES IN CONSCIOUSNESS RESEARCH

ADVANCES IN CONSCIOUSNESS RESEARCH provides a forum for scholars from different scientific disciplines and fields of knowledge who study consciousness in its multifaceted aspects. Thus the Series will include (but not be limited to) the various areas of cognitive science, including cognitive psychology, linguistics, brain science and philosophy. The orientation of the Series is toward developing new interdisciplinary and integrative approaches for the investigation, description and theory of consciousness, as well as the practical consequences of this research for the individual and society.

## EDITORS

Maxim I. Stamenov (*Bulgarian Academy of Sciences*)
Gordon G. Globus (*University of California at Irvine*)

### EDITORIAL BOARD

Walter Freeman (*University of California at Berkeley*)
T. Givón (*University of Oregon*)
Ray Jackendoff (*Brandeis University*)
Stephen Kosslyn (*Harvard University*)
George Mandler (*University of California at San Diego*)
Thomas Natsoulas (*University of California at Davis*)
Ernst Pöppel (*Forschungszentrum Jülich*)
Richard Rorty (*University of Virginia*)
John R. Searle (*University of California at Berkeley*);
Geoffrey Underwood (*University of Nottingham*)
Francisco Varela (*C.R.E.A., Ecole Polytechnique, Paris*)

Volume 2

Ralph D. Ellis

*Questioning Consciousness*

# QUESTIONING CONSCIOUSNESS

## THE INTERPLAY OF IMAGERY, COGNITION, AND EMOTION IN THE HUMAN BRAIN

RALPH D. ELLIS
*Clark Atlanta University*

JOHN BENJAMINS PUBLISHING COMPANY
AMSTERDAM/PHILADELPHIA

TM The paper used in this publication meets the minimum requirements of American National Standard for Information Sciences — Permanence of Paper for Printed Library Materials, ANSI Z39.48-1984.

**Library of Congress Cataloging-in-Publication Data**

Ellis, Ralph D.
 Questioning consciousness : the interplay of imagery, cognition, and emotion in the human brain / Ralph D. Ellis.
   p.    cm. -- (Advances in consciousness research, ISSN 1381-589X ; v. 2)
 Includes bibliographical references and index.
   1. Consciousness. 2. Apperception. 3. Human information processing. I. Title. II. Series.
BF311.E485      1995
153--dc20                                                                              95-10923
ISBN 90 272 5122 3 (Eur.) / 1-55619-182-0 (US) (Pb; alk. paper)                          CIP

John Benjamins Publishing Co. • P.O.Box 75577 • 1070 AN Amsterdam • The Netherlands
John Benjamins North America • P.O.Box 27519 • Philadelphia PA 19118-0519 • USA

# CONTENTS

# ACKNOWLEDGEMENTS

As an epistemologically eclectic theorist who is willing to welcome any reliable source of information — be it empirical, analytic, or phenomenological — I am indebted to many and diverse people. In particular, Eugene Gendlin's views on the implicit in conscious processes and the roles of embodiment and symbolic explication have crucially influenced my thinking ever since I first read Gendlin 25 years ago. A crucial turning point also was the discovery of Natika Newton, who introduced me to the 'sensorimotor theory of cognition,' to the central role of proprioceptive imagery, and to a wealth of related work. Important contributions to the development of this book also came from Gordon Globus, Maxim Stamenov, John Bickle, Irwin Goldstein, Nicholas Georgalis, Marcelo Dascal, Terry Horgan, and Tom Nenon, who provided valuable criticisms and suggestions. Bill Bechtel, Elizabeth Behnke, David Carr, John Sallis, Lester Embree, John Tienson, Larry Lacy, and Bob McCauley each confronted me with the need to rethink certain issues in the course of this work. Marvin Minsky, Thomas Natsoulas, Michael Posner, Carl Aurell, Eleanor Rosch, Francisco Varela, and William Lyons were also decisive in their influence. I believe all the people just mentioned are forces in the shaping of an important new direction for cognitive theory and the philosophy of mind.

# INTRODUCTION

## Differences between Conscious and Non-conscious Processing: Why They Make a Difference

There is an old story about a gathering of scientists for the purpose of awarding a prize in special recognition of the most significant achievement of the twentieth century in the area of cognitive theory. After some discussion, a well-known artificial intelligence worker stood and said, "I believe there can be little doubt as to the most important breakthrough of the century: Obviously, it is the thermos bottle." After a dramatic pause, he continued, "If the liquid is hot, it keeps it hot; if cold, it keeps it cold. My friends, I ask you! — How does it *know*?"

This story well illustrates the major shortcoming of recent cognitive theory as far as the understanding of human consciousness is concerned. Equivocal usages of terms like 'know,' 'see,' 'learn,' 'remember,' etc., are now so commonplace that it is no longer possible even to meaningfully *ask* whether a given theory or hypothesis has any relevance to the study of the corresponding conscious processes or not. By 'equivocal usages,' I mean the use of the main terms that are available to talk about conscious processes to denote functions which obviously do not involve consciousness, but with the implicit suggestion that, if only we could learn enough about how computers, thermostats or thermos bottles 'know,' 'see,' and 'remember' things, this would somehow help us to understand how it is that the *conscious* processes called 'knowing,' 'seeing,' 'remembering,' etc., are produced. Human cognition involves both conscious and non-conscious processing, and it is important to understand both kinds.

The purpose of the present book is to distinguish 'knowing,' 'seeing,' 'remembering,' etc., in their metaphorical or non-conscious senses, from knowing, seeing, remembering, etc., in their conscious senses, with a view toward understanding how and why conscious cognitive functions are associated with the brains of living organisms, and often are structured quite differently from non-conscious cognitive functions. In order to understand *how* and *why* conscious cognition occurs, we must also understand *what* consciousness is.

By contrast to much of what is being done in contemporary cognitive theory, I shall argue in support of both the truth and the importance of the following hypotheses:

1. Consciousness is a process, brain function is its substratum, and this does not necessarily mean that consciousness is *caused by* the actions of its substratum (the contrary arguments of Searle 1984, Smart 1959, and other epiphenomenalists notwithstanding). In living organisms, the form of the process often determines what happens to the substratum rather than the other way around. (On this point, I am in essential agreement with Merleau-Ponty 1942-1963, and with Varela *et al* 1993, although my reasons for this conclusion are a little different from theirs.) I shall argue that the central difference between conscious and non-conscious cognition is the presence of emotional intensity, which gives the process the motivational force needed to appropriate, shape, and even reproduce elements of its own substratum.

2. Imagination (as Rosch 1975 and Newton 1993 have suggested) is the basic building block of all consciousness. I. e., all contents of consciousness involve a subjunctive and imaginative element. They involve in one way or another imagining what would happen if something were other than the way it is. Even the perceptual consciousness of an infant, according to Piaget (1928-1965, 1969), involves imagining what could be *done* with the object *if* the infant *were* to reach out, grasp it, throw it, beat on it, etc. This idea that identifying an object involves imagining how it could be manipulated has been supported in more recent developmental research by Becker and Ward (1991), and by Streri, Spelke and Rameix (1993), confirming in humans the same principle that Held and Hein (1958) found for cats: When deprived of the

opportunity to manipulate and interact with the objects they were looking at, kittens ended up being functionally blind.

Even perceptual consciousness, then, is in part imaginative and subjunctive. This means that attentive consciousness always involves an implicit or explicit process of 'imaginative variation' as described by Husserl in his *Lectures on Phenomenological Psychology*, which is equivalent with saying that it involves counterfactuals in the same straightforward sense discussed by David Lewis in *Counterfactuals*. A being which registers only the presence of objects as they actually are, or reacts behaviorally only to actual stimuli, is not a conscious being. To consciously *see* an object requires not only that light impinge on the retina, and that a nerve impulse travel through the thalamus to stimulate the primary projection area of the occipital lobe (Posner and Petersen 1990; Aurell 1983, 1989; Luria 1973), thus causing stimulation of the 'feature detectors' in the columns of neurons in the primary projection area (Hubel and Wiesel 1959). None of this yet results in *consciousness* of the object, as we know from PET scans and other measures of electrical activity in localized brain areas (Posner and Rothbart 1992; Aurell 1983, 1984, 1989; Posner 1980). Seeing occurs only when we *attend to* (i.e. *look for*) the object on which we are to focus. And *looking for* involves asking the question about a concept or image, 'Is this concept or image instantiated by what is in my visual field right now?' But the forming of an image or a concept requires a much more complex, active and global brain process than merely to receive and react to data from the senses. One reason for the importance of this point is that, even though some learning without awareness does occur, as documented by 'blindsight' and 'priming' experiments (Bullemer and Nissen 1990; Cohen *et al* 1990; Weiskrantz 1986), there are many kinds of learning and information processing that do *not* occur except with the help of conscious attention (Cohen *et al* 1990; Posner and Rothbart 1992; Hillis and Caramazza 1990).

This implies another main difference between conscious and non-conscious processing: In conscious processing the imaginative act *precedes* the perceptual one as part of the arousal and attentional mechanism (Bruner 1961; Ausubel 1963; Neely 1977; Broadbent 1977; Logan 1986). This is confirmed in more recent empirical studies by Mele (1993), Rhodes *et al* (1993), Lavy *et al* (1994), Sedikedes (1992), Higgins and King (1981), and Wyer and Srull (1981). A desire or interest originating in the midbrain leads to limbic activity and general increase in arousal (Hebb 1961), at which point the prefrontal cortex translates the emotional feeling of desire or interest into the formulation of questions (Luria 1973: 188-189, 211, 219ff, 1980; Sperry 1966), which entail images (requiring parietal activation), concepts and abstractions (Ornstein and Thompson 1984: 41-60) which often also involve symbolic activity (entailing interaction of left temporal syntactic and right parietal semantic functions, as discussed by Miller 1990: 78ff; Tucker 1981; Springer and Deutsch 1989: 309ff.; and Dimond 1980). Only at the point when the whole brain knows what it is 'looking for' in this sense does the occipital activity resulting from optic stimulation become a conscious registering of a perception, an attentive seeing of the object. This means that a conscious registering of a perceptual object leads to much more extensive processing of the data than the non-conscious registering of it could possibly lead to. It means that I am much more likely to remember the data, act on it, think about its further significance, and, if it is significant, look for recurrences of the object in the future. This last point is confirmed empirically by Higgins and King (1981), Wyer and Srull (1981), and many others whom we shall discuss later.

3. I shall argue (notwithstanding the contrary arguments of Fodor 1975, 1981, 1983, the Churchlands 1979, 1986, and Dennett's earlier work — for example, see 1969) that the difference between conscious and unconscious cognition *makes* a difference, and that conscious cognition is structured completely differently from unconscious cognition. Neurophysiology corresponds to *both conscious and unconscious* cognition, not only to unconscious cognition. As Thomas Natsoulas (1994) has argued, we cannot simply regard consciousness as an 'appendage' which has been superadded to processes which could also have occurred on an unconscious basis. Nicholas Georgalis (1994) argues for a similar distinction between conscious and unconscious processes on epistemological grounds: The sheer fact that information gets processed somehow or other does not mean by definition that consciousness of that information occurs, yet clearly the consciousness in many instances is needed to facilitate the processing. When consciousness is involved, what is happening neurophysiologically is fundamentally different from the way the brain functions when information is processed on a non-conscious basis. But many things about consciousness cannot be learned through objective methods;

they also require a (rigorous) phenomenological method. And many of the questions we answer through objective methods would never be asked if not for subjective concepts — as Dennett (1991) grants in his chapter on 'heterophenomenology' (notice the change here from his earlier thinking). As Posner and Rothbart (1992) point out, "The use of subjective experience as evidence for a brain process related to consciousness has been criticized by many authors. . . . Nevertheless, if one defines consciousness in terms of awareness, it is necessary to show evidence that the anterior attention network is related to phenomenal reports in a systematic way (98)."

4. A great deal of confusion and fruitless argument results from failure to understand the ontological status of consciousness. Oversimplified reactions against 'dualism' are now so commonplace that many neuroscientists feel compelled to ignore the role of consciousness on pain of being labelled as 'dualists' and therefore as 'dewy-eyed metaphysicians.' It is often assumed that the only alternatives to a metaphysical dualism (or what Popper and Eccles 1977 called 'interactionism') are (i) causal epiphenomenalisms, which posit that consciousness is a byproduct of (and cannot itself cause) brain processes, and (ii) theories of strict psychophysical identity, which posit that 'consciousness' does not *mean* anything other than 'brain functioning.' In my view, this oversimplification of the theoretical options constitutes a false limitation of alternatives; if we were to confine ourselves to these options, then there would indeed be an inexorable logic which leads from this starting point to the conclusion that consciousness plays no role in facilitating or producing cognitive functions. It seems to most neuroscientists today that, if one causal antecedent for a phenomenon (a physical one) is both necessary and sufficient to explain the phenomenon, then no other antecedent (say, a conscious one) can be either necessary *or* sufficient to explain that same phenomenon. If consciousness is neither necessary nor sufficient to explain cognitive functioning, then it plays no role in bringing it about. And if consciousness can play no role in bringing about cognitive functioning, then certainly neuroscientists should ignore it in their work. This is the essential basis of both 'reductive' and 'eliminative' materialisms (for example, see Smith and Jones 1986). I shall argue, however, that the premise of this inexorable logic is false. Metaphysical dualism, psychophysical identity, and causal epiphenomenalism are not the only three possible conceptualizations for the

relationship between consciousness and its physiological correlates. Neuroscientists therefore need not accept the harmful conclusion that they must avoid all references to the important role of consciousness in cognitive processes. Many puzzling questions can be answered only if we correctly understand the ontological status of consciousness. For example, the paradox of 'memory traces' is solvable when we realize that the *continuation* of a process can include an almost infinite variation of combinations in the patterns of electrical and chemical change in all the neuronal circuits involved — a complex pattern of changes which in essence is a *behavior* which can be triggered by a cue, much as a conditioned response can be triggered by a stimulus (as Merleau-Ponty 1942-1963 suggests). To ask how we 'remember' how to re-enact this complex pattern is like asking how someone with a nervous twitch 'remembers' to twitch the muscle. To ask where the memory is 'stored' is like asking where a thermostat 'stores' its tendency to return to the temperature that has been set. And to ask how it is that there are so many more memories stored in the brain than there are neurons or even neuronal connections (Coulter 1983) is like asking how it is that an infinite number of melodies can be played on an instrument with only twenty-six keys. But if we try to think of 'memory traces' as quasi-permanent spacial configurations of substances or thing-like entities in the brain, we will never find them. To recall a memory is to re-enact an efferent behavior, accompanied by a 'feeling of recognition' or 'feeling of familiarity' (the terms used by Mandler *et al* 1990; Jacoby and Kelley 1992; and Mayes 1992, with regard to the subjective conviction that we remember something, as opposed to merely performing behaviorally as though we knew it). I shall discuss this issue in detail in Chapter 6.

5.   As soon as the above theses have been established, it will then be possible to show that all consciousness is permeated and directed by emotion (in agreement with Edelman 1989 and Gray 1990). But here again we must distinguish between feelings in their conscious and non-conscious senses. There are 'desires' in the non-conscious or metaphorical sense (as when an ion 'wants' to neutralize its electric charge). And there are 'representations' in the non-conscious sense (as when information about the appearance of an object is projected onto the 'primary projection area' of the occipital lobe, where

columns of neurons record the lines, angles and colors of the object, but with no *conscious awareness* of the object). But 'desire' becomes *desire* in the conscious sense only when it becomes a process which is capable of and motivated toward *appropriating and reproducing elements to be used as its own substratum* by growing to include a representation of the missing elements, or at least a representation of contents ideationally related to the missing elements. For example, the 'desire' for cellular sustenance grows to include proprioceptive images of oneself eating (Newton 1994), and then imaginary representations of edible objects which finally find matching patterns of activity in the primary projection area if sensory input from such an object in the environment is received. A desire which is conscious, even to a minimal extent, is one which is capable of controlling, appropriating and reproducing elements of its own substratum in such a way as to form within itself a representation (however vague and approximate) of that of which it is a desire. Without this primacy of the process over its own substratum, an event cannot qualify as a conscious event.

The reason for this (I shall argue) is that the mind-body problem can be solved only on the condition that consciousness is a higher-order process which takes lower order processes, such as electrical and chemical events, as its substrata. Consciousness, as we shall see, is like a wave which takes a material medium as its substratum. There are important senses in which the movement of the medium does not simply cause the wave to have the pattern that it has, but just the reverse is true. The wave, originating elsewhere, causes the medium to vibrate or oscillate in the pattern that it does.

By saying that the wave 'causes' the particles to oscillate in certain patterns, I do not mean to imply that the particles do not also 'cause' *each other* to oscillate, but they do so in a different sense. Let me briefly and preliminarily suggest the difference between these two senses. In one sense, we say that the reason people engage in sexual behavior is because they enjoy it; and we can even explain this enjoyment in terms of chemical reactions in the reproductive and nervous systems. This would be a 'mechanistic' explanation — an explanation of a total situation in terms of the behavior of the elements of its substratum. But in another sense, we say that the reason people engage in sexual behavior is that reality is such that, in an ecological situation like ours, beings that enjoy sexual behavior are more likely to reproduce themselves. This would be an explanation of the behavior of the substratum elements in terms of the nature of the overall situation — an explanation in terms of 'process.' The fact that beings that enjoy sexual behavior are more likely to reproduce themselves is a statement about a process that characterizes our ecosystem, and there is a sense in which this process partly determines the behavior of any particular substratum elements which enter into it (Neisser 1967, 1976, 1994). But this does not contradict the fact that the same behavior can be explained mechanistically. Which type of explanation we use depends on whether we are trying to understand one element's behavior in terms of a previously established understanding of another element's behavior, or whether we are trying to understand why the whole situation is patterned in such a way that any elements which enter into it will inevitably behave in certain ways.

What I am suggesting is that, when the pattern governing a substratum originates to a great extent outside of the system to be explained — for example, when a sound wave, originating elsewhere, causes a wooden door to vibrate — it is misleading and even false to say that the substratum of the system causes that pattern to occur. And I am suggesting that the relation of the pattern of consciousness to the behavior of the brain is very much like the relation of a sound wave to the wooden door in this example. The pattern of the wave in this case arises partly from the relation of the organism to its environment, from the structure of language communicated to us by others, and from the structure of intelligible reality. There are also some disanalogies, in that the sound wave originates entirely, and in its final pattern, outside the door, while the pattern of consciousness is influenced not only by the environment but also by the motivational activities of the midbrain as it interacts with other brain areas. Nonetheless, there is an important sense in which the order and rhythm constituting the larger *patterns* of interaction among particles cannot be reduced to a simple summation of the movements of the particles themselves: most importantly, the pattern may be realizable in a variety of possible material instantiations (Putnam 1994), and in the case of consciousness the pattern may even seek out, appropriate and reproduce the substratum elements needed to instantiate the pattern.

In some respects, the brain also acts as an amplifier and equalizer of this 'wave-patterning' process. I. e., the brain 'amplifies' a consciousness which at first is only very faint (and appropriates only a small amount of material as its substratum) by allowing it to grow so that many elements of the brain now become substrata for an expanded version of that same process. This is confirmed by Edelman (1989) and Posner and Rothbart (1992), who see the function of the focusing of attention *via* anterior activation (observed with PET scans) as in part serving the function of enhancement of signals (for example, Posner and Rothbart 1992: 103). And the brain 'equalizes' the pattern (i.e., refines the pattern, eliminating irrelevant 'static') in the sense that an initial 'desire' cannot seek out that which it desires until a more and more refined image or concept of the desired state of affairs can be produced. The more exactly the image or concept corresponds to the desire (i.e., can serve to provide it with an appropriate substratum), the more conscious the organism is of that particular desire (Ellis 1986). The more closely the 'representation' produced by a 'desire' matches the desire in this sense, the more *conscious* the organism is of both the representation and the corresponding desire (Ellis 1990). I shall suggest that this ontology of consciousness is more consistent with some version of connectionism (perhaps a 'nonlinear processing' version) than with other cognitive architectures which have been proposed. According to connectionism, as Bechtel (1987) explains,

> The behavior of the system results more from the interaction of components than the behavior of the components themselves . . . [and] does not rely on internal representations as its processing units. It produces internal representations as *responses* to its inputs and it is possible to develop systems that adjust the weights of their connections in such a way as to develop their own system for categorizing inputs (19-21). . . When a pattern is not present in the system, it is not stored, as in traditional cognitive models. Such patterns are not retrieved from memory, but are reconstructed on appropriate occasions (Bechtel 1987: 22).

Poggio and Kotch (1985) believe that many cognitive processes — most obviously mental imagery — can be understood only if we adopt this viewpoint by preference over the digital computer-inspired models of the past two decades:

> Neurons are complex devices, very different from the single digital switches as portrayed by McCulloch and Pitts (1943) type of threshold neurons. It is especially difficult to imagine how networks of neurons may solve the equations involved in visual algorithms in a way similar

to digital computers. We suggest an analogue model of computation in electrical or chemical networks for a large class of visual problems, that maps more easily with biologically plausible mechanisms (Poggio and Kotch 1985: 303).

However, it is also very true, as Tienson (1987) and Butler (1993) both astutely point out, that no version of connectionism as yet devised is really consistent with what we know about the actual connections between neurons in the human brain. Part of the purpose of this book is to point in the direction of a better neurophysiological substrate for the contents we actually phenomenologically experience, and thus also toward a more workable version of connectionism.

6. Finally, we can deduce from these considerations, combined with some further neurological information, that *symbolic* behavior utilizes this same process. A symbol for a state of consciousness is a representation which works especially well to help provide the substratum for that state of consciousness. Saying the word 'tree' helps me to enact the corresponding consciousness in myself (Ellis 1986). But I would not have said the word 'tree' in the first place had I not already desired to enact that pattern of consciousness or at least some similar or related pattern of consciousness (Gendlin 1962). The use of symbols is a way for consciousness to grow to include more and more substratum elements, thus expanding the process that appropriates that substratum. The symbolic behavior serves both to 'amplify' and to 'equalize' the pattern which is the state of consciousness.

In the same process, the symbolization also serves to change the state of consciousness into a next one which is 'called for' by it (Gendlin 1973, 1981, 1992). Since consciousness has the ontological status of a higher-order process or pattern of change in its substratum, it wants not only to reproduce elements of its substratum in order that the process may remain the same in certain respects, but also that the process may change in certain respects (Gendlin 1971; Rogers 1959). Every process contains within itself a tendency to evolve over time into a somewhat differently patterned process. I shall explain why more fully in the appropriate part of the text.

These and many other consequences of the ontological status of conscious processes will be explored as we proceed. But first, some groundwork must be laid on the basis of which the theses I have been preliminarily summarizing here can be established. The first part of this groundwork involves reassessing the legacy of behaviorism in contemporary cognitive science.

## 1. The Legacy of Behaviorism

When John Watson made the original case for behaviorism in the social sciences at the turn of the twentieth century, the state of neuroscience and the development of phenomenology were very different from what they are today. Almost nothing was known about the physiology of the brain. Husserl had not even published his first important book, *Logical Investigations*, which would initiate the process of working out a careful and systematic way to observe the subjective experiencing process 'from within.' Certainly, the sophisticated phenomenological methodologies of Giorgi (1971), Gendlin (1961, 1971, 1973, 1992), Gurwitsch (1964), and Merleau-Ponty (1942-1963, 1962) were completely unheard of. Self reports of internal experiencing were therefore inaccurate, unreliable, ambiguous, difficult to quantify, impossible to control, and often tended not to be repeatable in a precise way. Moreover, subjects often tended (as we still do) to substitute explanatory interpretations for what we experience in place of naive, direct and unprejudiced descriptions of the raw data of experience as it actually presents itself. And although they could describe (in vague terms) what it felt like to find the solution to a cognitive problem, they could not say how they did it (Hunt 1985).

Given the undeveloped nature of both neurology and phenomenology, it was no wonder that scientists would opt for something that could be unambiguously and objectively observed and measured. (It remained for Thomas Kuhn to point out sixty years later that this kind of objectivity does not lead to as unbiased a theoretical outcome as one might suppose, but that is a different matter.) Thus it was natural that scientists would want to rely on what is physical, and therefore measurable. Since it was impossible to look inside peoples' heads, and subjective reports could not be relied on, what this left was behavior. Moreover, behaviorism could leave open the possibility that those few neurophysiological facts that *could* be directly observed (and did not result from speculative *theories* about the brain) could be incorporated into behavioral studies. From this viewpoint, the behavior of the brain is just another form of behavior. Thus it was believed that behaviorism allowed the study of all and only those phenomena that *could* be studied scientifically. As a result, cognitive psychologists were allowed to correlate brain states with behavior, but they were not allowed to correlate either brain states or behavior with the subject's consciousness. (The problems in trying to do so were dramatically illustrated by the failure of the experimental Gestalt introspectionism of Wundt and Tichener, which will be discussed in a moment.) As a result, behaviorism became a veritable Kuhnian 'paradigm' — a set of assumptions that could be easily thrown in to complete any neurophysiological explanation that did not quite work without the help of such assumptions. For example, consider the following explanation in Young (1988):

> The relations between these areas and other parts of the brain are no doubt greatly influenced by learning, especially during childhood. Unfortunately little is known in detail about this relationship, but many traits of character and personality presumably depend upon the particular connections established by these 'reward centers', especially in relation to parents and siblings. One cannot emphasize too strongly that human 'needs' are for emotional and social satisfaction as much as for food and sex (Young 1988: 182).

It is striking that we must presume that there are 'reward centers' which are somehow structured by postulated 'needs for emotional and social satisfaction' in order to explain the physical workings of the brain. But the need to substitute theories of learning in place of direct observation was essentially built into the epistemology of behaviorism from the very beginning, because it placed such severe limits on what was deemed 'directly observable.'

Today, however, the epistemological situation is very different from what it was in Watson's day. First of all, neurology is in an explosive period of development. Secondly, neurology is an outgrowth of medicine, which is at least as much a practical as a theoretical discipline. A practicing physician's first priority is usually to pay attention to the subject's subjective self reports. If the subject says 'I feel pain when you do that,' or 'I suddenly remembered my grandmother's face when you delivered that electrical stimulation,' or 'I've been more lucid and less depressed since you increased my medication,' a physician is not likely to completely ignore such potentially useful information just because of some abstract epistemological theory. And, although a good research physician does try to devise objective ways to measure subjective processes, there is little pretense that the purpose of the operation is not in fact to measure a subjective process; thus the importance of understanding what the subjective process is and how it interrelates with other events in the subject's stream of consciousness remains a paramount concern.

The more reliable information accumulates about the functioning of the brain, the easier it becomes to formulate coherent and testable theories about the ways in which this functioning can be correlated with careful phenomenological accounts of the corresponding subjective events in consciousness. For example, ways to map patterns of electrical activity in specific areas of the brain are becoming increasingly sophisticated. EEG patterns, CT scans and other measures of neural activity in various parts of the brain have now been extensively correlated with conscious acts such as remembering (Damasio 1989; Damasio et al 1985); attention (Hernandez-Peon et al 1963; Posner and Rothbart 1992; Cohen et al 1988); the integration of sensory and memory mechanisms via frontal lobe activity (Nauta 1971); obsessional thought patterns (Gibson and Kennedy 1960); hysterical conditions (Flor-Henry 1979); feelings of elation and depression (Ahern and Schwartz 1985; Damasio and Van Hoesen 1983; Gainotti 1973); the activity of listening to music (Miller 1990: 79) — which apparently involves very different brain areas for trained musicians (more left-lateralized); word recognition (Petersen et al 1989); language acquisition (Dore et al 1976); and many other such consciousness/brain-electrical correlations, some of which will be discussed later in this book.

In some instances, this information combined with phenomenological analysis facilitates reasonable inferences about the ways the physical and conscious processes are related. For instance, we know that, when a novel stimulus is presented, about a third of a second is required for increased electrical activity to be transferred from the primary projection area of the relevant sensory modality in the cortex (which receives direct sensory information from the outer nervous system but does not yet result in conscious awareness of a visual object) to the parietal and prefrontal areas whose activation does result in a conscious visual, auditory or tactile image of the object (Aurell 1983, 1984, 1989; Srebro 1985: 233-246; Runeson 1974: 14). Yet the primary sensory area and the relevant parietal area are almost immediately contiguous with each other. Why should a nervous impulse, which normally travels in the neighborhood of several hundred miles an hour (Restak 1984: 40), take a third of a second to travel a few millimeters? Obviously, it must be that much more complex processes are involved in activating conscious awareness of some perceptual content than a simple passive reception of a signal or stimulus in some particular part of the brain. More global processes must be involved before even the simplest possible conscious state, the having of a visual image, can be produced. But to understand what these more extended processes are requires putting together many bits of phenomenological and neurological information. This book will try to make a beginning in this direction.

One of the most important pieces of information relevant here is a phenomenological one: The selection of perceptual elements for conscious attention is partly a motivational process involving judgments about what is important for the organism's purposes. And the transmission of emotional purposes (which involve midbrain activity), into questions that conscious beings formulate for themselves in order to seek out relevant information in the environment, is a process which involves extensive prefrontal activity (Luria 1980, 1973; Damasio *et al* 1985, 1989; Eslinger and Damasio 1985; Nauta 1971). Thus we shall see that what goes on during that third of a second between primary projection area activation and parietal-prefrontal activation is a complex process involving emotion, motivation, and value judgments about what it is important to 'look for,' resulting in an efferent image formation which becomes a visual perception only when a match is finally found between the pattern of this efferent activity and the corresponding afferent input from the outer nervous system and the primary projection area. This means that the midbrain, the prefrontal cortex, and the parietal association areas are all involved in the production of the simplest possible conscious content. Besides the studies by Aurell, Runeson and Srebro just cited which show that passive stimulation of the 'visual cortex' does not result in perceptual consciousness unless there is frontal and parietal activity, there are similar findings with regard to the role of the reticular activating system in perception and the role of the frontal-limbic connection in recognizing the meaning of a remembered image (Ludwig 1977; Thompson 1975; Miller 1984, 1990; Gainotti *et al* 1993). According to Miller,

Conscious appreciation of a particular sensory impression . . . depends not just on the sensory pathways conveying that sensation, but also on the participation of a separate collateral system, the reticular activating system . . . responsible for literally 'directing attention' to incoming sensory information at different levels of processing.

Damage to this system produces a curious dissociative condition where the sensory areas of the brain process the information normally (as shown, for example, by the EEG), but the person remains subjectively unaware of the stimulus; it simply doesn't 'register' (Miller 1990: 173).

And, according to Damasio *et al* (1985: 252-259), unless the network of frontal-limbic connections is intact, images may produce a vague 'feeling of familiarity,' but their meaning and context cannot be recalled. It is also well known that Luria (1980) finds that physical disruption of almost any part of the brain (midbrain, frontal, parietal, temporal, etc.) interferes with memory function.

The need for all this interrelated frontal, limbic and parietal activity even for the simple perception of an object certainly dispels any notion that a given bit of cognitive information (say, the image of a horse, or the concept 'horse' occurring as the subject of a proposition) could correspond to a particular neuron or neural pathway, as some hypothesized cognitive architectures would require. It thus becomes increasingly obvious that for a cognitive theorist to posit models of information processing without considering what now can be known about neurophysiology and phenomenology is as though an architect were to design a bridge without attention to the tensile strength of the materials of which the bridge will be constructed, or as though a composer were to ignore the range limitations of the various instruments of the orchestra. Moreover, knowledge of the nature of an instrument not only *limits* what can be composed for the instrument; it also suggests musical possibilities *for* the instrument which one would not have thought of without some general understanding of the nature of the instrument on which the music is to be played. In the case of cognitive theory, we are looking for music which can be played on a *conscious* and *organismic* instrument.

Behaviorism in principle does not allow us to distinguish between an instance of conscious information processing and an instance of non-conscious information processing. Both *look* the same in measurable terms, especially if prior phenomenological research has not pointed us toward observable patterns we would not otherwise have looked for. But non-conscious information processing is the simpler kind, and is much easier to spell out in operationally intelligible terms. As a result, what the legacy of behaviorism has done to cognitive theory has been to systematically select for hypotheses that can explain only non-conscious forms of information processing.

According to Irwin Goldstein (1994), this behaviorist bias is still very much alive in contemporary cognitive theory. "Functionalism," he says, "is a descendent of the behavioristic approaches to the mind-body problem Ludwig Wittgenstein and Gilbert Ryle advanced (60)." The reason is that most functionalists, like behaviorists, hold that a mental event can be exhaustively described by citing its 'inputs' and 'outputs.' According to Goldstein, the essential problem with both behaviorism and functionalism is that "Statements connecting 'pain' to dispositions to withdraw, moan, wince, or behave in other particular ways are not analytic (60)." For example, consider Fodor's definition of a headache as

[That which] causes a disposition for taking aspirin in people who believe aspirin relieves a headache, causes a desire to rid oneself of the pain one is feeling, often causes someone who speaks English to say such things as 'I have a headache,' and is brought on by overwork, eye-strain and tension (Fodor 1981b: 118).

Against this view, Goldstein argues that

What does not attend every headache is not necessary for a headache. None of the causes and effects Fodor mentions attends every headache. . . . Nor is there some determinate *disjunction* of causes and effects an event must satisfy to be a headache. Suppose I have a sensation with a headache's location, duration, and unpleasant quality. I realize the sensation has none of the causes and effects on Fodor's list. I need not conclude this sensation is not a 'headache.' Other disjunctions of causes and effects people might propose would fail as Fodor's does. . . . *Every* headache has *all* of a headache's defining properties — its felt location, minimum duration, [and] unpleasant quality. . . . Refinement of these necessary conditions will yield conditions that are jointly sufficient for a headache. . . . When [behaviorists] define 'pain,' . . . they miss that property that unites different pains and makes them instances of a single kind of experience (Goldstein 1994: 57-61).

Note that this 'introspectable interior' includes more than mere *qualia*.

There are properties other than qualitative complexion in an experience's introspectable interior (duration, location, and others). An experience's qualia — unpleasant or otherwise — present only one dimension of an experience's introspectable interior. A sensation's duration and felt location are distinguishable from its quale. A two second itch need not differ qualitatively from a one second itch (Goldstein 1994: 55-56).

Of course, the notion of an 'introspectable interior' raises one of the major problems that still prompt many researchers to prefer a behaviorist approach: Introspection seems to be inevitably connected with 'conscious' processes. But there are apparently many mental events and activities which do not have the character of being 'conscious.' Many mental processes are 'unconscious.' Before tracing further the implications of the behaviorist bias in cognitive science, it is important to clarify this problem.

Talk about the relationship between 'conscious' and 'unconscious' processes is often ambiguous, because 'unconscious' can mean such widely different things. There are unconscious processes which are essentially *derivative* from earlier conscious ones, and therefore bear many of the structural earmarks of conscious processing; by contrast, there are 'originally' or 'primitively' unconscious processes which are not derivative from conscious ones, are not structured like conscious ones, and do not interrelate functionally with conscious ones in the same way as 'derivatively' unconscious processes. Also, between 'conscious' and 'unconscious' there may be a whole range of different *degrees* of consciousness or semi-consciousness. These distinctions need to be emphasized before we can proceed much further.

**2.  'Derivatively'** *versus* **'Primitively' Unconscious Processes and the Various Levels of Semi-consciousness**

By emphasizing the contrast between conscious and non-conscious information processing, I do not by any means intend to deny that unconscious processes can have a mental character in the same way as conscious ones.  For example, I may sense (without consciously realizing it) that a drunk man in a bar is angry (although he is smiling and showing other supposedly friendly mannerisms) because I notice (again without consciously realizing it) that he is standing too close to me (under a guise of friendliness which does not deceive me), repeatedly clenching his fists as if getting ready for a fight (though I am not conscious of seeing this), and making inappropriate jokes about his wife from which I infer (due to his generally irresponsible demeanor) that he is angry at her, and I fear that the anger could be easily displaced.  I then tell the bartender that I do not want another drink so that I can prepare to leave, although I am not conscious of the reason.  There is plenty of evidence for such unconscious interrelations between thinking, feeling and perception in everyday life as well as in psychotherapeutic literature.

But the reason we call these unconscious processes thinking, feeling, and perceiving in the same sense that we would in the case of conscious processes — rather than merely 'thinking,' 'feeling' and 'perceiving' of the metaphorical kind that thermostats and thermos bottles do — is that, in the first place, they occur in ways that are structurally analogous to the ways they would occur if they did occur on a conscious basis; secondly, they could not occur in this particular structurally-analogous way unless they were to occur in beings which as a whole do have consciousness, because they result from the habituation and sedimentation of past conscious processes; and third, they do not occur on a *completely* unconscious level, but there is some minimal level of awareness of them even while they are occurring — as exemplified by the typical psychotherapeutic remark, 'I realize now that I was conscious of his clenching his fists, although I didn't pay much attention to it at the time.' Posner and Rothbart (1992), who will be discussed more fully in Chapter 1, frame this relationship between completely conscious processes and the very analogous yet unconscious or semi-conscious processes in this way:

> The degree of activation of [the anterior attentional network associated with conscious awareness] increases as indexed by PET with the number

of targets presented in a semantic monitoring task and decreases with the amount of practice in the task. . . . Anterior cingulate activation was related to number of targets presented. The increase in activation with number of targets and reduction in such activation with practice corresponds to the common finding in cognitive studies that conscious attention is involved in target detection and is required to a greater degree early in practice (Fitts and Posner 1967). As practice proceeds, feelings of effort and continuous attention diminish, and details of performance drop out of subjective experience (Posner and Rothbart 1992: 98).

From the completely conscious processes of which we are fully aware, to the semi-conscious thinking we do as we 'feel' our way through a heated argument or navigate while driving a car, to the completely non-conscious processes which are not even capable in principle of becoming conscious, there is no sharp dividing line, but a gradual continuum. For example, when we learn to read music, there is no definite point in time when we no longer need to 'figure out' each note. The 'figuring out' gradually gives way to a habitual response, and in this way becomes 'sedimented' (Merleau-Ponty 1962). But, as sedimented, it retains the earmarks of earlier conscious processing — for example, that bass clef notes are processed less readily than treble clef, sharps and flats less readily than natural notes, and infrequently-occurring sharps or flats less readily than more frequent ones.

In this sense, unconscious processes which are structurally analogous to conscious ones are ultimately derivative from conscious ones, and would not occur in the way they do in beings that lack consciousness altogether. These derivatively unconscious processes (such as the unconscious processes discussed in psychotherapy, and the habituated processes discussed by Posner and Rothbart above) should be distinguished from those which are primitively or originally unconscious (such as the regulation of heartbeat, or a thermostat's computation of the desired temperature). Derivatively unconscious processes, which may be conscious to greater or lesser degrees, function very much like conscious ones, but in an increasingly truncated way as they become habituated and no longer require conscious attention. It would be exactly backwards, then, to try to explain consciousness as merely a superadded 'appendage' to an underlying non-conscious processing system. This argument will be developed more and more fully as we proceed.

The explanation of even 'originally' or 'primitively' non-conscious information processing is not a complete waste of time, for two reasons. First, such theories lead to the design of more effective computers and computer systems. And secondly, not all information processing in humans is of the conscious variety. Humans (and probably many other animals) use both conscious *and* non-conscious kinds of information processing, and we need to understand the architecture of both kinds if we want to understand how people think and process information. Programs of research in artificial intelligence can contribute a great deal to the development of concepts needed to understand the non-conscious type of processing, which not only is important in humans, but also interrelates with conscious information processing in complex ways.

But, in order to understand how conscious information processing is different from non-conscious processing, we must understand at least some aspects of the conscious type of processing in its own right. And to carry out this kind of investigation inevitably requires some phenomenological reflection. This objective cannot be achieved, however, unless we eschew the rigid rejection of phenomenological data still all too prominent among neuroscientists (for example, see U.T. Place 1993).

One of the main habits of thought which must be questioned if we are to move beyond a strict behaviorism in this regard is an increasingly prevalent tendency to speak as if there were no difference between the meanings of terms like 'knowing,' 'seeing,' 'remembering,' etc. as they are used in the context of conscious information processing, and their meaning as used in the context of non-conscious information processing (i.e., in thermostats, thermos bottles and the like). If we cannot distinguish between these meanings, then it seems unlikely that we can move beyond behaviorism's bias in favor of non-conscious information processing. Let's consider this problem next.

**3. The Danger of Equivocating the Language of Consciousness: The Crucial Distinction Between 'Knowing' and *Knowing***

Artificial intelligence theorists often speak of 'states of consciousness' in a metaphorical sense. Electric eye devices are said to 'see' things. Robots 'recognize' complex objects by comparing them with 'concepts' or 'mental images' which they 'introspect,' having 'remembered' them from previous 'learning.' Robots thus 'know' when a familiar object is presented. Thermostats are said to 'want' to keep the temperature constant, and one might suppose that, in the same metaphorical uses of language, thermos bottles 'remember' what temperature they 'want' to keep the coffee at and 'try' to keep the coffee from cooling off.

These metaphorical usages serve a useful purpose, provided that we guard against equivocating them in an attempt to equate 'seeing,' 'knowing,' etc. in the metaphorical sense with *seeing, knowing,* etc. as states of conscious awareness. Such usages are useful because they designate real phenomena that need to be discussed. A great deal of non-conscious information processing goes on, not only in computers and other machines, but also in human beings. For example, as I was writing this passage, I thought of a book I wanted to use as an example, but could not remember the author. I pulled the book out of my bag, but did not pay attention to the author's name on the front, because I was also eating lunch at the time. Before I had a chance to read the name, I remembered it — Jeff Coulter. The reason I remembered it was that the image of the name had impinged on my retina but without conscious awareness, and my brain had non-consciously processed the information to enough of an extent to jog my memory of the name. I had 'seen' the name in the non-conscious, metaphorical sense, just as a robot would (as in the 'blindsight' experiments by Weiskrantz and others mentioned earlier). Similarly, when I throw a baseball, my brain 'figures out' just when to release the ball given the distance and angle of the target; and when I play a piece of music in b-flat minor, my brain 'infers' that the note I can't quite remember must be a d-flat because that note fits into the b-flat minor chord that my 'knowledge' of music tells me would 'make sense' as the next chord. All this non-conscious information processing does indeed take place, and results achieved by it are analogous in certain ways with the results that would have been achieved by the corresponding *conscious* processing of the same information. The robot 'recognizes' a face, with results very similar in many ways to those of a conscious being's recognition of the face. The computer adds a column of numbers and ends up with the same conclusion a human being would end up with.

Historically, in fact, this was the essential reason why the Wurzburg controversy led to the widespread rejection of introspectionist and Gestalt methods in cognitive psychology (Hunt 1985). The question at stake was what kinds of phenomenal states or mental images subjects use when solving cognitive tasks. Subjects in these experiments seemed to be aware of having a sudden 'insight' in which the solution to a problem suddenly 'came to them,' but they could not describe their conscious experiencing of the cognitive process through which they attained the solution. The solution seemed to come to them involuntarily, the result of a process which they were either unaware of, could not reflect on, or could not describe in any intelligible way. Thus psychology moved to the view that, when it comes to the 'how' of cognitive operations, as Dennett (1991: 97) puts it, "We simply do not know how we do it." Or, as Miller (1990: 80) says, "There are very few people who think what they think they think." Cognition thus came to be regarded as a fundamentally unconscious process. In folk-psychological terms, we are obviously 'aware' of having solved the problem, but this awareness seems useless in understanding *how* the problem was solved. It was thus assumed that consciousness is an epiphenomenon which contributes nothing to the understanding of how cognition functions.

But this is the point at which a behaviorist bias in the philosophy of the human sciences exacerbates our tendency to equate 'knowing' in the non-conscious sense with *knowing* in the conscious sense. If the only thing that can be studied scientifically is what can be observed and measured, i.e., the behavior which *results* from information processing, then one tends to assume that there is no way to tell the difference between conscious and non-conscious processing. Once we have described the way a stimulus input is structurally transformed into a behavioral output, we have said all there is to know about the processing of information. Thus there is no need for any distinction between non-consciously 'knowing,' 'seeing,' etc., and consciously *knowing, seeing,* etc. The temptation, then, is to simply equate them in order to avoid a needless proliferation of theories and hypotheses. It is therefore very common to find passages in contemporary cognitive theory in which an author starts out by putting words like 'knowing,' 'seeing,' etc. between single quotation marks to indicate that the words are being used in a metaphorical sense, but as the passage develops the quotation marks gradually begin to be dropped, and the author begins to speak as though there were no difference between 'thinking' and *thinking*, and as though any adequate explanation for the one should also suffice as an adequate explanation for the other.

The reason for this, of course, is that behaviorism was formulated at a time when it was reasonable to assume that little could be known about what goes on between 'stimulus' and 'response.' But we have reached the point now in both neurophysiology and phenomenology that a great deal can be known about these processes — certainly enough to tell us that both conscious and non-conscious information processing occur in the organism, that the two types of information processing are very different, and that they utilize very different patterns of brain function and emphasize different regions and different processes in the brain.

But, at the point when behaviorism inspires us to ignore the differences between conscious and non-conscious processing (resulting in non-reductive materialism), why are people then so inclined as their natural next step to outright deny that there *is* any difference, and to argue that the description of *conscious* processes (or 'folk psychology') is merely a confused and distorted attempt to describe a non-conscious process? The Wurtzburg controversy well illustrates the significance of this jump. Although subjects were unable to explain *how* they had solved cognitive problems, it was clear that their conscious processes of thinking were at least a necessary (if not sufficient) condition for the solution. Why then did psychology write off conscious awareness as an irrelevant epiphenomenon?

Ultimately, the reason for this step is the same reason that, throughout its long tradition, the philosophy of mind had led the advocates of mechanistic explanations to reject explanations framed in intentional terms. The reason is that, for any given occurrence, there can be *only one* necessary and sufficient explanation. If we have succeeded in showing that certain physical antecedents are *sufficient* to explain a certain behavioral outcome, then no other explanation is *necessary*. And if we have shown that these same physical antecedents are *necessary* to explain the behavioral outcome, then no other explanation can be *sufficient* to explain it. Thus, if a set of physical antecedents are both necessary *and* sufficient to explain the behavior, then no other explanation (for example, an intentional explanation) can be either necessary *or* sufficient to explain it.   As the epiphenomenalist Jackendoff (1987) explicitly puts it, if consciousness has no causal efficacy, then the study of it "is not good for anything (26)." But if the intentional explanation is neither necessary nor sufficient to explain an outcome, then it is causally irrelevant to the outcome.   So any description of a conscious or intentional process which holds that this process is causally relevant must be false.   But our subjective explanation of our own mental processes (i.e., 'folk psychology') leads us to believe that these mental processes *are* causally relevant to our behavior and to the output of our information processing.   Thus our subjective explanation of our own mental processes (or 'folk psychology') is false — as Fodor, Stich, the Churchlands, and to a great extent also Dennett, have insisted.   It is thus a short step to conclude that the notions of consciousness and intentionality are only confused and misguided attempts to explain what could be explained much more adequately in purely mechanistic terms if we had enough empirical scientific information (and of course we eventually will).

Cognitive theorists also tend to assume, again like traditional philosophers of mind, that the only way to avoid actually denying the *existence* of consciousness is to postulate that it is 'identical with' its underlying neurophysiological processes.    If M (a mental process) and N (a neurophysiological process) are identical with each other, then there is no problem with saying that, on the one hand, N is both necessary and sufficient for some outcome, and on the other hand that M is necessary and sufficient for that same outcome.   Of course if M and N are the same thing then they can both be necessary and sufficient for the same outcome; thus they can both cause or bring about the same outcome.

But if this is true, then nothing that can be said about consciousness or intentional processes can possibly add anything to what has already been said when we explained the same outcome in purely mechanistic terms.   It follows that every description of a conscious process must be equivalent in meaning (or at least in extensional reference) to the description of some corresponding physical process.   But, here again, our experience of our own consciousness presents this consciousness as something that cannot be known or understood through any amount of knowledge of objectively observable physical events.   For example, no amount of knowledge of the physiological correlates of a headache can ever lead a neurologist to know what a headache feels like unless the neurologist personally has at some point felt something that feels like a headache. Since our experience of our own consciousness obviously does make the claim that knowledge of subjective events can never be exhausted by any amount of knowledge of objectively observable physical events, and since the mechanistic cognitive theorist is committed to the claim that the objectively observable physical events do constitute an exhaustive explanation, then here again the mechanistic cognitive theorist must conclude that our experience of our own consciousness is false. Even theories of psychophysical identity do not succeed in avoiding this conclusion. 'Folk psychology' (which includes all forms of phenomenology) must be rejected as false by the very nature of what it is. This point has been made very well with regard to functionalism and eliminative materialism by William Lyons (1983, 1984, 1986); see also Donald MacKay (1984).

Yet there is obviously something that rings true in the notion that we cannot know what a headache feels like unless we have actually felt something like a headache before. So we need a better solution to the mind-body problem than simply to ignore the phenomenological data of consciousness. Moreover, we *cannot* ignore these immediate data. We need them in order to delineate the difference between conscious and non-conscious information processing, which I am arguing here correspond to two completely different physiological processes in the brain. And we shall see that the conscious form of information processing is the kind that most typifies the human brain as compared with computers and the brains of lower animals. Without understanding the differences between conscious and non-conscious processing, we would end up completely misconstruing many aspects of brain functioning — notably, the functioning of the prefrontal cortex, the relationship between the parietal and secondary sensory areas (as I hinted briefly above and will discuss more extensively later), the ways in which neural activity and mental processes correspond to each other, and the ways in which the different parts of the brain are coordinated with each other in different forms of consciousness.

Luckily, there is a better solution to the mind-body problem than the eliminative materialism just discussed. A full explanation of it must await Chapter 4, where we can give it the analytic attention it requires. A brief caricature of it can be intuited by pursuing our comparison of the relation between consciousness and neurophysiology to the relation between a sound wave and the medium through which the wave is propagated. The medium is not the ultimate cause of the wave, which may have originated elsewhere. Similarly, the pattern of consciousness may have originated elsewhere than in the medium through which it is propagated in the brain (for example, in the structure of intelligible reality, or in the structure of human languages which convey ideas to individuals in a culture, or even partly in the structure of emotional demands of the organism as a whole). So the brain by itself does not simply 'cause' consciousness any more than a wooden door 'causes' a sound wave to have the pattern of Tchaikovsky's Sixth Symphony as the wave passes through the door. Also, just as there is a sense in which the pattern of the wave is 'equivalent' to the pattern of the movement of wood particles in the door, there is an analogous sense in which consciousness is 'equivalent' to some combination of patterns of change in its physical substrata (the brain, language, etc.). But there is another sense — a more important sense, in many respects — in which it is absurd to equate Tchaikovsky's Sixth Symphony with a particular wooden door. The door is incidental to the existence of the symphony. Though *some* medium for the propagation of the wave is needed, many other media would have done as well as this particular wooden door. In the same way, it is absurd to say that consciousness is 'equivalent' with certain patterns of change in its physical substrata. But to spell out the sense in which consciousness is not precisely identical with its neurophysiological substratum — the sense in which the relation must be more complex than this — we must await the appropriate point in the development of our argument.

We see, then, how an epistemological confusion can lead to an ontological one. By assuming that anything which can be explainable must be explainable in objectively observable and measurable ways, we must also relegate intentional explanations not only to the epistemologically useless, but to the ontologically non-existent. The reason for this is not merely a matter of Ockham's razor. The reason is that two different explanations cannot *both* be both necessary and sufficient for the same explanans. And to solve this problem, correlatively, requires more than a mere rejection of the epistemology of behaviorism. It requires that we re-open the traditional mind-body problem and give it a more careful solution than either dualist interactionism or epiphenomenalism or psychophysical identity theories have given.

4. **The Distinction Between 'Desire' and** *Desire* **and Its Importance for Cognitive Theory; The Primacy of the Subjunctive Imagination in Conscious Processing**

Just as cognitive theorists are prone to equate 'knowing' in a metaphorical sense with *knowing* in the conscious sense, so some other scientists are prone to run together 'desiring' and 'feeling' in a metaphorical sense with *desiring* and *feeling* in the sense of a conscious state of which one is aware and upon which attention can be focused. For example, biologists speak as though organisms engage in sexual activity 'for the purpose' of procreating, or as though RNA molecules 'wanted' to reproduce themselves, or as though the body 'wanted' to achieve a better salt balance by eliminating potassium or sodium. Chemists even speak as if negatively charged ions 'wanted' to interact with positive ones 'in order to' achieve electrical neutrality, or as if atoms 'wanted' to fill or empty their outer energy shells.

These metaphorical senses of 'emotional' terms serve just as useful a purpose as the metaphorical usage of 'representational' terminology like 'knowing' and 'seeing' — provided again that we avoid equivocation. There seem to be 'purposeful' phenomena in the realm of non-conscious nature, and these phenomena need to be described and discussed. And they have a good deal in common with conscious desires and emotions.

Perhaps I should clarify my usage of the term 'representational' here. Throughout this book, I shall use 'representation' not in the sense of 'representational epistemology' — as if what is in the mind were a 'copy' of external reality — but in a broader sense. By a 'representation' in the mind, I mean any kind of intentional object whatever, in the sense that phenomenologists give to this term. I 'represent' something not only when I form the image of something which I think is real, but also when I imagine a completely fanciful object — an impressionistic rendering of a unicorn, a musical melody which I have never heard before, or even an abstract concept which I do *not* believe corresponds to reality (such as the idea of 'God' in the mind of an atheist). Is there any consciousness which is *not* 'representational' in this sense? That is the same as asking whether there is consciousness which is non-intentional in the phenomenological sense — as suggested by Husserl (1913-1969), Carr (1986: 26) and Globus and Franklin (1982). Globus and Franklin particularly emphasize the importance of non-intentional consciousness in even grasping the essence of what consciousness is, aside from its ability to refer and compute. Perhaps meditative trance states are examples. A pure pain without reference to any picture or image either of the painful limb or the pain-inflicting object might be another example (the pure *hylé* in Husserl's sense). Or perhaps there are desires with no awareness of any object of desire — such as a vague feeling of restlessness or dissatisfaction. This issue will be further discussed in a later context.

I have suggested that 'representation' in the realm of non-conscious information processing becomes *representation* in a *conscious* sense when *motivational* feelings lead us to 'look for' that which is considered *important* for the organism. We shall see that many 'desires' in the non-conscious sense interact with each other and become more and more characterizable as *desires* in the conscious sense the more they can find substratum elements which allow representations relevant to desired further unfoldings of the life of the organism. This 'focusing' process (the term used by Gendlin 1981, 1992, who will be discussed extensively later) begins in the limbic region, leads to generalized arousal in the reticular activation system, sets up selective neuronal gating in the hippocampus, and activates the prefrontal region to *formulate questions* about what we need to experience or think about to meet the emotional need of the moment; the prefrontal area of the frontal lobe then leads us to 'look for' certain images and concepts, which then become conscious notions through the activity of the parietal region and the secondary sensory areas; these in turn then become a conscious perception when the patterns of consciousness thus set up in the parietal and secondary areas find a match in the patterns of sensory stimulation affecting the primary sensory or 'primary projection' area. The stimulation of the primary projection area by perceptual data is not yet the perceptual consciousness of anything until this entire process has transpired. This is why the parietal and secondary sensory areas are not simply stimulated by the primary projection area which is in such close proximity to them, but must await a complex process which requires about a third of a second to transpire before conscious awareness of the object occurs, and before the secondary area and the other brain areas just mentioned become active.

The way this complex interrelation develops between 'representation' in the metaphorical sense and 'desires' at the preconscious level, finally resulting in a *consciousness* in the proper sense, can teach us a great deal not only about neurophysiological processes, but about what consciousness *is* and how it is produced by the natural world. Consciousness results when *representation* and *desire* become copresent in the same pattern of activity in such a way as to interrelate intentionally and purposefully. I.e., a representation intentionally and purposefully becomes the object of a desire, or a desire intentionally and purposefully becomes the object of a representation; there is a desire to represent something or an attempt to represent the meaning of a desire or emotion.

We shall see that the main way in which desire meets representation is in the process of *formulating a question* (in humans, primarily a function of the prefrontal cortex). The desire to fulfill some motivation prompts us to ask ourselves about the meaning of the emotion that gives rise to it, and what kind of circumstances might meet the emotion's desires. When we formulate a question to ourselves, we must in the process envision the possibility that things could be different from the way they in fact are. We use subjunctives. We ask, 'What *if* things were this way, or that way, or if they *had been* this way or that way?'

The hallmark of conscious information processing, then, is that (I shall argue) it uses thought processes built up from elements that are essentially *imaginative* in nature. Rather than simply reacting to what is, to a stimulus input, it questions what is by comparing it to an image or concept of what might be, or might have been. A causal concept, for example, is a judgment that if the causal antecedent had occurred differently, given a certain context, then the consequent would have occurred differently — a subjunctive judgment. Similarly, a moral statement in its most important and primary meaning is a judgment that if someone had acted differently in some way, then things would have been better — and often that if someone were to force the person to act differently, the results would be worth the effort. In one way or another, even a moral judgment is a judgment about what might be or what might have been — a subjunctive.

According to Piaget (1928, 1969), Streri *et al* (1993) and Becker and Ward (1991), infants even learn to perceive elementary physical realities by using subjunctives. The object is one that if pulled would bounce back, or if grabbed would lend itself to being sucked, or if thrown would knock something else aside. And, of course, every object is one which, if turned around, would turn out to have another side, and thus would have thickness. These are all subjunctive thought processes.

The process of questioning is where desire overlaps with representation, and it is just in this overlap that 'desire' becomes *conscious* desire and 'representation' becomes *conscious* representation. I shall explain more completely what I mean by this in the body of the text.

Before we can discuss why it is that consciousness occurs only when desire meets representation in a certain way, and render really intelligible what this 'certain way' is, some other more elementary propositions must first be established as the groundwork for such a difficult discussion. That is what the first four chapters will attempt to do. Chapter 1 will examine the relationship between the imaginative and the perceptual consciousness of the same content element from a physiological and phenomenological perspective, ending with the conclusion that the efferent and imaginative production of an image or concept always precedes the afferent and perceptual consciousness of the same or a related content. In this way we can begin to understand how emotion, motivation, the formulation of questions, negations, mental images, and finally perceptual input interrelate with each other to form perceptual consciousness.

Chapters 2 and 3 will then consider how it is that mental images are refined, reorganized and elaborated so that they can be transformed into the abstract concepts that make up the building blocks of the more sophisticated adult cognitive processes. Adult logic is built up from concepts rather than just mental images. In the view that will be developed here, one must understand what is involved in the transition from the formation of a mental image to the formation of a mental concept before one can begin to describe the neurophysiological correlates of logical thought.

Chapter 4 will show that the process-substratum approach to the mind-body relation is the only one that does not become logically impossible given certain very elementary observable facts about the interrelations of conscious and neurophysiological processes. We can then lay the groundwork for the more difficult questions that must be considered in the remainder of the book. In what sense can one say that a process can determine the activities of its substratum elements rather than (only) the other way around? What is consciousness? How and why is it that 'desire' meets 'representation' to form conscious desire and conscious representation? And how do the various processes of the brain contribute to this outcome? These questions will be addressed in Chapters 5 and 6.

We shall see that the most elementary building block in this whole problematic is a phenomenological one. We must begin by carefully reflecting on what it means to imagine something.

# CHAPTER ONE

# The Relation between Imaginary and Perceptual Contents

## 1. Different Conscious Modalities with Similar 'Content': A Puzzle for Neuroscientists

The problem posed by the fact that imaginary and perceptual consciousnesses can have virtually identical 'content' shows very quickly some of the ways in which phenomenology can contribute to the solution of problems in contemporary cognitive theory and *vice versa*. Husserl's discussion of this problem (1913-1969, esp. Chapter 10), as further clarified in Merleau-Ponty's *Phenomenology of Perception* (1962-70, esp. Part Two, section 1), provides a clue and a method for the solution of a problem posed by Dennett (1969, esp. Chapter IV), which has troubled many subsequent cognitive theorists: Is there any hope of correlating each efferent event-type in the brain with some afferent input, and at the same time with an intended meaning in consciousness? Dennett poses the problem this way:

> The problem of tracing the link between stimulus conditions and internal events far from the periphery should not be underestimated. . . . It is not to be expected that central events can be easily individuated in such a way that they have unique or practically unique sources in external stimulation. Suppose we tentatively identify a certain central event-type in a higher animal (or human being) as a perceptual report with the content 'danger to the left'. . . . We would expect the *idea* of 'danger to the left' to be capable of occurring in many contexts: not only in a

perceptual report, but also as part of a dream, in hypothetical reasoning ('what if there were danger to the left'), as a premonition, in making up a story, and of course in negative form: 'there is no danger to the left'. What is to be the relationship between these different ways in which this content and its variations can occur? . . . Certainly for any event or state to be ascribed a content having anything to do with danger to the left, it must be related in some mediated way to a relevant stimulus source, but the hope of deciphering this relation is surely as dim as can be (Dennett 1969: 80-81).

A very similar problem arises for Husserl in his analysis of the 'neutrality-modifications' of intentional experiences — i.e., the fact that essentially the same intentional object can be experienced sometimes as existing, sometimes as merely imagined, sometimes as remembered, believed to exist, actually perceived, etc. This possibility of experiencing the same intentional object in different 'modalities' must be understood in order to make sense out of Husserl's 'noetic-noematic' structure (his version of the correlating subjective and objective aspects of experiencing). In this context Husserl describes the situation in which the consciousness of an object is occurring, but not the consciousness of the object *as really present in perception* (1931: 292-293). The question arises as to whether our consciousness of an imaginary object is exactly the same as the corresponding perceptual consciousness, except that the imaginary consciousness does not posit the actual existence of the object. This question, of course, complicates the project which is frequently attributed to Husserl (though, as I have argued elsewhere, with misleading oversimplicity — see Ellis, 1986) of elaborating a theory of intentionality in which every consciousness is a 'consciousness *of something*'. (Dennett, in fact, betrays an oversimplified interpretation of the phenomenological concept of intentionality in his premature dismissal of this approach — see his 1969, Chapter II.) Ultimately, the problem of distinguishing and relating the intentionality of imagination and the intentionality of perception leads to the charge of solipsism against Husserl because, as Georg Lukacs (1966) eloquently put it, once we have completed our phenomenological description of the Devil, the question remains completely unanswered as to whether any such Devil actually exists. The problem is that it is well known among phenomenologists that the phenomenological description of an act of *imagination* will look very different from a phenomenological description of the analogous *perceptual* act (Husserl 1913; Merleau-Ponty 1962; Sartre 1966). For example, as Sartre (1966: 50) points out, an imaginary mental picture of the facade of the Pantheon, for most of us, does not have a definite number of columns, whereas a perception of it does. The image of an object is not simply the same as the perception absent the positing of the existence of the object. Thus the problem of relating different conscious modalities with similar 'content' is a puzzle within phenomenology as well as a neuroscientific one.

For Husserl, every act of perception is accompanied by a latent or implicit act of imagination, the physical reality of whose object is not necessarily posited in the imaginative act *per se,* though it is posited in the parallel perceptual act.

> The relation of the parallel 'acts' consists in this, that one of the two is a 'real *(wirklicher)* act,' the cogito a 'real,' 'really positing,' cogito, whereas the other is the 'shadow' of an act, an act improperly so-called, a cogito that does not 'really' posit. (Husserl 1913-1969: 294)

Against this point, Sartre (1957) and others object that, if phenomenology is supposed to be a description of what occurs *in consciousness,* then we must admit to ourselves that, when we look at an object, we are not really *aware* of two states of consciousness, but only of one. The 'parallel' state of consciousness which Husserl posits, the non-positional 'fancy-consciousness' of the idea or essence of the same object, appears to be absent from our real experience of perception — at least as Sartre experiences it. But Sartre's analysis of imagination does little to help explain the phenomenon of neutrality-modification — the fact that the 'content' of a mere mental image can seem so similar to the 'content' of the corresponding perception, yet the two forms of consciousness are so unmistakably and utterly different. He insists simply that every imaginative consciousness is a negating of the really-existing, actual, physical world, and that this physical world is therefore the true intentional object of the imaginative experience — that each state of consciousness is simply a different manner of relating to this actual, physical world. This point is most clear in his *Sketch for a Theory of Emotions* (1971), and in his *Psychology of the Imagination* (1966). The idea that imaginative consciousness 'negates' the physical world, in fact, is the basis of Sartre's often over-romanticized notion of the 'nothingness' that is supposed to constitute the essence of consciousness.  Our question here, however, is where the idea of 'danger to the left' comes from when I am conscious of my environment as *not containing* such a danger:   When my consciousness 'negates' physical reality (as Sartre would have it), why then do I not 'negate' it, for example, by imagining 'no danger to the *right*' instead, or 'no *algebraic functions* to the left'?

A foundation for a correct understanding of the nature of imagination requires that it be capable of resolving Husserl's and Dennett's problems, which really center around the same problem:  If there is a similarity between what is happening in my consciousness (and in my brain) when I *see* an object, and on the other hand what is happening when I merely *imagine* or *remember* the same object, how do we account for this similarity?  At the level of brain functioning, we want to know why utterly different afferent inputs (for example, the image of a tree impinging on my retina, and the memory of having read the word 'tree' last week) can produce such presumably similar efferent brain events, yet events which in no way can be confused with each other in our consciousness.  At the level of phenomenology, we want to know why the intentional consciousness of a physical object before us seems so similar to that of a merely imagined or remembered object, while at the same time we are so certain of being able to distinguish between the two.

## 2.  The Crucial Relation between 'Looking-for' and 'Looking-at'

Suppose I look at a pink wall.  Certain afferent inputs originating with the patterns of light from the pink wall are, we may reasonably suppose, evoking certain efferent events in the brain, and these efferent events correspond to the consciousness of the pink wall.  (This assumption is based on the studies by Srebro, Aurell and others mentioned in the Introduction.)  Now suppose that, while I am looking at the pink wall, I say to myself, 'What if the wall were blue?' or 'How would this wall look if it were blue?'  At this point, the intentional notion 'if the wall were blue' flashes into my consciousness.  To what does this intentional notion correspond at the physiological level?  Careful phenomenological description can help us to answer this question.  What actually happens in my consciousness (which still includes the perception of the pink wall) in the instant that I think the concept 'if the wall were blue'?

It is *almost* as if, for a brief fraction of a second, I can 'see' the pink wall as being blue.  But, of course, this is not an accurate description, because I know all the while that the wall is pink, and there is no possibility of my confusing this experience with one in which the wall *really does* become blue for a fraction of a second.  A closer description of what is happening would be that, in the instant when I think 'if the wall were blue', I focus on the wall as if trying to become intensely aware of any amount of blue that *is* or *might be* mixed in with the pink, almost as if I were to hypothesize to myself that perhaps there is more blue in the pink than I had originally thought, and then quickly reject the hypothesis as soon as I see that there is  not.  There is a sense in which I *look for* blueness in the wall and *do not find it*.  (I.e., I look for blueness and find pink instead).

The sense in which forming a mental image involves 'looking for' the imagined object is clearly experienced by subjects in perceptual experiments who are instructed to imagine an object before it appears on a screen, or to continue looking for the object while other objects are being flashed intermittently; the object being imagined or looked for is in fact perceived more readily (Corbetta 1990; Pardo *et al* 1990; Logan 1980; Hanze and Hesse 1993; Legrenzi *et al* 1993; Rhodes and Tremewan 1993; Lavy and van den Hout 1994).  Posner and Rothbart (1992) report that "During vigilant states the posterior attention network can interact more efficiently with the object recognition system of the ventral occipital lobe (96)." This attentional process "increases the probability of being able to detect the relevant signal (97)." To imagine the object is to be on the lookout for it, and *vice versa*.  This is the sense in which to form a mental image of a wall as blue means to 'look for' blue in the wall.  The 'looking for blue' that occurs when I imagine a pink wall as blue, then, does not mean that I literally expect to find more blue than is really there, but rather that I prepare myself in such a way that, if blue were to appear in the wall, I would see it more quickly and more easily.  I put myself 'on the lookout' for blue.

Some people's first reaction, when asked to imagine a pink wall as blue, is to look away from the pink wall in order more easily to imagine another wall just like this one, except that it is blue rather than pink.  The reason for this is that the perception of pink interferes with the imagining of blue, as will be discussed below.  But the important point for now is that, if we do succeed in imagining *this* pink wall at which we are actually looking as blue, then we are putting ourselves into a state of readiness or vigilance to see blue if it should occur. If this were not true, then subjects asked to imagine an object would not see it more readily than those who are not already actively imagining it at the point when it is presented.

There may be some people who, in order to imagine a pink wall as blue, must first look away from the wall or pull their attention away from it in order to imagine or remember *the color blue in general,* and then look back at the wall in order to 'fill in' the outline of the wall with the blue color they have imagined or remembered. For many people, these kinds of maneuvers may be necessary precursors for the act of putting ourselves on the lookout for blue to occur in the actual wall we are looking at. But once we *do* put ourselves into this condition of readiness, then by imagining the wall as blue we are doing the same thing we would be doing if we were to look for blue in the wall but fail to find it.

Someone may object that not everyone goes through such an elaborate process of envisioning mental images of these colors. Some people merely make rational inferences from abstract definitions — for example, by thinking 'Colors with different names are not the same; the name "blue" is different from the name "pink"; therefore, a blue wall would look correspondingly different from this wall.' But the person who raises this objection is simply using the word 'imagination' in a different sense from the one intended here. I am speaking of 'imagining' in the sense of *forming a mental image.* It is very true that there are many instances of 'imagining' which do not involve visual 'imagery'; this other kind of 'imagining' is a more complex process and will be discussed in Chapter 2. (We might also note, however, that even thinking the *word* 'blue' involves visual and/or auditory imagery because it involves envisioning the appearance of the printed word, or imagining the sound of the word. I shall also argue later that the forming of mental images is a more basic process — developmentally, phylogenetically, and neurophysiologically — than abstract, conceptual thinking, which must be built up step by step from the more primitive, 'imagistic' thinking of infants and lower animals.) Further description of the imaginative experience, as we shall see in a moment, reveals that this *looking-for-blue* which facilitates imagining the wall before me as blue is both a phenomenological and a physiological response which has a definite effect, for a fraction of a second, on the way I see the pink that is actually before me.

But first we must further clarify what is happening at the phenomenological level when I look-*for* something. It is not really necessary to look into studies of after-images, and Gestalt studies in which what appears to be there is affected by the subject's expectations, etc., all of which Merleau-Ponty (1942, 1962) explores in great detail to make essentially the same point with which we must begin. The point is that, when I look for something, I *prepare myself* to see what I am looking for. As Merleau-Ponty says, "I give ear, or look, in the expectation of a sensation, and suddenly the sensible takes possession of my ear or my gaze, and I surrender a part of my body, even my whole body, to this particular manner of vibrating and filling space known as blue or red" (1962: 212). And again, "It is necessary to 'look' in order to see" (1962: 232). And "The warmth which I feel when I read the word 'warm' is not an actual warmth. It is simply my body which prepares itself for heat and which, so to speak, roughs out its outline" (1962: 236). Helmholtz (1962) makes a similar point which is now widely accepted among neurologists: "We let our eyes traverse all the noteworthy points of the object one after another." I.e., the organism must actively search for information in the environment before that information is consciously seen. Vision is active, not passive. Thus, as Yarbus (1967) emphasizes, there must be some plan in the brain that instructs the eyes where to go. If I am looking for an image to appear on a blank screen, and am told what the image will be, I then focus my eyes in such a way as to maximize the ease with which what I am expecting can be seen, when and if it occurs. In a sense, I also 'focus' my brain in this same way. If I am told, for example, that I should expect to see the number '3' flash briefly, interspersed with a variety of different numbers or images, and if I am told to pay attention especially to the '3's (for example, I am told to count the number of '3's), then I do not really *see* the other images which occur between the '3's, because I am looking only for '3's. What is happening here, clearly, can only be that I am preparing myself — not only my eyes, but my brain as well — in such a way that the 3, when it occurs, will readily make its impression. I am *looking for* '3's.

What does this mean at the physiological level? First of all, it does not mean that I think that I see a 3 before it actually occurs; thus I am not causing my *afferent* nerves to fire in the way that they would if the 3 were really there. Nor, for the same reason, am I doing in my nervous system as a whole that which would correspond to thinking that I see a 3. Any adequate neurophysiological interpretation, then, must include the following point: Thinking that I see a 3 is, as Dennett rightly concludes, an activity which includes both afferent and efferent components. When I *look for* a 3, I cause my efferent nervous system to be in such a condition or alignment that, if certain signals *were* received from the afferent system, I *would* be conscious of seeing a 3. Both the activity of the afferent system and of the efferent system are components of the state of consciousness 'I see a 3'. When I merely align the efferent system in the right way — which corresponds phenomenologically to 'looking for' a 3 — I do not *see* a 3, but I do arrange certain nerve activities in the pattern which I know from experience they *would be* arranged in if I *were* to see a 3. This enables me to see the 3 more readily when and if it does occur. And what this means for physiology, above all, is that there is something happening in the efferent nervous system when I actually see a 3. For the efferent system to align itself in the expectation of the afferent input from a 3 *which is not yet on the screen* is to imagine the mere *concept* or *fuzzy mental image* of '3'. (Neurologically, this is related to measurable 'expectancy waves' — for example, see Libet *et al,* 1983; Granit, 1977. I shall discuss this more extensively later.) For the efferent system to align itself in this way *and then be actually fulfilled* by such afferent input is to see an actual 3 in perception.

To pursue the implications of this point further, let's return to the example of the pink wall. Suppose, while I am looking at the pink wall, someone says to me 'Now imagine the blue wall at your office.' In the instant when I imagine the blue wall, my perception of the pink wall becomes less sharp. I may even momentarily lose it altogether; I may de-focus my eyes from the wall for a second in order more easily to imagine the blue wall. This conflict between imagining one object and simultaneously perceiving another is demonstrated empirically by Segal (1971). On this same point, Merleau-Ponty (1962: 214) quotes Werner (158): "If a subject tries to experience a specific color, blue for example, while trying to take up the bodily attitude appropriate to red, an inner conflict results, a sort of spasm which stops as soon as he adopts the bodily attitude corresponding to blue." In less subjective terms, we know empirically that subjects are more likely to see an image flashed on a screen while holding in mind the mental image of that type of object (Logan 1980, Posner and Rothbart 1992, and the other studies listed earlier confirm this fact). Correlatively, it is difficult to hold in mind one image while seeing another object which conflicts with the image. Why is there this *conflict* between what I see before me and what I simultaneously attempt to merely imagine? If we grant the point that was made above, i.e., that to imagine something is to arrange my efferent nerves in such a way as to look for the imagined object, and that looking for something makes it easier to see that particular thing or quality, then it is easy to explain why the conflict occurs. In order to imagine the blue wall at my office, I must arrange my efferent nerves, at least to a certain extent, in such a way as to look *for* that blue wall. When I do not find it, I also have the conscious concept 'the blue wall is not here' in my consciousness, even as I continue to imagine the blue wall by continuing to look for it. To a certain extent, this manipulation of my efferent nerves in such a way as to look for a *blue* wall *interferes* with my manipulating my efferent nerves in such a way as to look for a *pink* wall. Since this means I am no longer as vigorously looking *for* the pink wall, I no longer see it as sharply, no longer notice as much of the detail of it. Looking-for is needed to facilitate looking-at. The most obvious instance of this connection is in the eye: If my eye does not focus in a certain way, I do not see the wall.

Imagining something, then, consists of arranging certain aspects of my efferent system (probably primarily in the prefrontal, parietal, and secondary sensory areas of the brain — we shall explore this in more detail later) in such a way as to look for that thing or thing-type. To know that something is not present is to imagine it — i.e., look for it — without finding it in my afferent input. Normally, therefore, the act of imagining something in the absence of corresponding perceptual input is inseparable from the act of knowing that what one imagines is not really present.

### 3. Consciousness of Images and of Negations; Consciousness of *A Priori* Negations of Contradictory Images

It is also possible to merely *imagine* what it *would* be like to look for something without being able to find it if circumstances were different from what they in fact are — i.e., to imagine something as *hypothetically* not-being-the-case, or to imagine something as not-being-the-case when in fact one knows that it is the case. Here consciousness must achieve a higher level of abstraction: I prepare my efferent system for the experience of being-frustrated-in-the-expectation-of-the-afferent-input, but then rearrange other aspects of the efferent system in the brain so as not to be surprised when the preparations of the efferent nerves do not meet with fruition in terms of any afferent input.

In order to think 'The wall is not blue' *one time only,* it is necessary only to align my efferent system so as to look for blue one time; once this is done (which takes only a fraction of a second), the looking-for-blue efferent constellation quickly disintegrates. On the other hand, in order to *imagine* a blue wall, I must *maintain* the efferent looking-for constellation *throughout* the entire time during which I am imagining the blue wall. And this constant maintaining of the looking-for-blue necessary to imagining the blue wall is very difficult to maintain *while at the same time* I am looking *at* an actual pink wall. To try not to let the image of the blue wall momentarily slip from my imagination under such circumstances is somewhat like trying not to blink.

Let's go a step further. It may be that all the various intentional modalities can be framed in the same way. Suppose I am looking at the pink wall, and someone asks me, 'Would it be possible that the wall be both pink and blue all over at the same time?' What happens in this case (if I confront the question seriously and do not fall back on past learning or formulas told to me by others) is that, in order to answer the question, I try to imagine a wall which is both pink and blue all over. But I find that I *cannot* arrange my efferent nerves in such a way as to look for a blue wall, and at the same time arrange them so as to look for a pink wall. For I know from experience that, if the afferent input were that which corresponds to pink, the efferent nerves would behave in one way, and if the afferent input were blue, the efferent nerves would behave in a completely different way. To know that the efferent nerves cannot behave in both these ways at the same time is to believe that a wall cannot be both pink and blue all over.

(Many *philosophers'* first response to this question would be to attempt a deductive proof: 'Something cannot be two different colors all over at the same time. "Blue" and "pink" are the names of two different colors. Therefore this wall, which is something, cannot be both blue and pink all over at the same time.' But such a proof assumes prior knowledge of precisely what is being asked: How do we know that something cannot be two different colors all over at the same time? In any event, the philosopher's abstract thinking is at a higher level, architecturally speaking, than the elementary process of concept formation that must precede it, as Piaget shows and as we shall discuss in the next chapter.)

Someone may object at this point that the knowledge that something cannot be both pink and blue all over is too general and too certain to be explained in terms of a mere empirical generalization about the ways in which the nervous system can or has functioned in the past. But that depends on how sophisticated a nervous system one is talking about. Obviously, a color-blind animal would have no such belief that 'nothing can be both pink and blue all over.' In the same way, a person whose logical ability has not developed very far may believe that it is impossible for a person to be both opposed to censorship and a non-communist at the same time. This is because the person has not yet developed his or her nervous system in a complex and well-differentiated enough way to learn *how* to arrange the efferent nerves in such a way as to look for a non-communist *and at the same time* (like patting one's head and rubbing one's stomach) to arrange the efferent nervous system in such a way as to look for a censorship opponent. Not having yet learned this cognitive trick, the person may assume that the trick by its very nature is impossible. The problem is simply that this assumption is wrong. It *is* possible to perform this trick. After trying it in a determined enough way, with suitable lessons from someone who is initiated in the trick, most people could learn to do it — unless their system is not well enough wired to begin with.

The rudimentary concept of 'impossibility' in the mind of a logically sophisticated person is therefore a subtle one. It is not merely the phenomenological correlate of the contingent fact that I have *not yet* learned to arrange my efferent system in such a way as to look for both phenomena at the same time. To say this would be to commit the error of psychologism against which Husserl vigorously warns in his *Logical Investigations* (1900-1970). Rather, we form the concept of impossibility by first trying to imagine what it would be like *not to be able to arrange the efferent system in the two conflicting ways no matter what we do.* What we are imagining when we imagine what this would be like is not so much comparable to imagining what it would be like to be unable to run 440 yards in 45 seconds given that we have not yet done it, but is more comparable to imagining what it would be like to be unable to run the 440 on a track on which impenetrable steel walls are placed at ten-yard intervals. I.e., we are imagining what it would be like to be unable to do something, not because of limitations in ourselves, but because of the limitations inherent in the task set. It is true, of course, that it is often difficult or even impossible to distinguish whether a particular real-life case is a case of one or the other of these states of affairs. But, in principle, we can imagine what it would be like to fail because of the limitations inherent in the task itself rather than in our own inadequate training; i.e., we can form the concept or, if you will, we can imagine a scenario in which we are unable to do something for this kind of reason. And it is when we imagine that we would be unable to coordinate two imaginations at the same time for reasons inherent in the types of objects we are trying to look for, that we believe that to do so would be impossible in the strongest possible way, i.e., would be logically impossible. Because we believe that the inability to imagine a logical impossibility is inherent in the nature of the task rather than in our own limitations, it is possible to avoid the error of psychologism against which Husserl warns. The consciousness of a logical impossibility corresponds at the physiological level to a condition in which we try to arrange our efferent nerves in such a way as to look for two states of affairs simultaneously, the looking for which would require us to try to arrange our efferent nerves in two different and incompatible ways. But to understand how more complex logical computations take place requires that we move beyond mere mental images to abstract concepts, which will be the subject of the next chapter.

In immediate phenomenal terms, when I think 'the wall cannot be both blue and pink all over', I do not by any means imagine a wall which is both blue and pink all over at the same time, and then cancel this image as not being instantiated by my afferent inputs. Rather, I imagine the wall as pink all over and then as blue all over, then pink again, then blue, in very rapid succession, trying to get myself to imagine the impossible juxtaposition, which I quickly determine cannot be done (because I know from past experience how to make quick work of the task). Or I imagine a translucent blue wall standing in front of a pink one and then try to imagine myself as an observer looking through the translucent blue wall at the pink one, and then collapse the two walls in my imagination — which again is impossible to imagine.

A very interesting point in all of this is that we have here a rudiment for the way the physiological correlates of logical thinking occur. Logic, after all, is a system for determining what is possible and what is impossible. When I try to imagine a contradiction — for example, 'The wall is there' and 'The wall is not there' — I find myself confronted with the most impossible of all neurophysiological tasks: To prepare my efferent nerves in such a way as to receive the afferent input of the wall, and at the same time *not* to prepare the efferent system in this way. I experience my inability to do this not as an inability resulting from my own constitution, but rather as an inability inherent in the task itself. What are my reasons for believing that the inability is inherent in the task itself rather than in my own constitution? We are not yet ready to answer this question at this point in our inquiry. The next two chapters will try to build a foundation for understanding logical thinking by showing how the mind evolves the abstract concepts needed for this purpose. One might well imagine that past experience has taught us a great deal about how to distinguish between logically impossible kinds of mental tasks on the one hand, and on the other hand merely difficult ones. When students learn deductive logic, perhaps they are convinced to accept the principle of *hypothetical syllogism* or *modus tollens,* for example, because they cannot find an example of an argument that follows this form and has true premises but a false conclusion. At a certain point in their attempts to do so, they become convinced, not merely that *they personally* cannot do so, but rather that *it cannot be done.* Does this mean that the belief in the universal inviolability of *modus tollens* is based on a mere empirical generalization? The outcome of this question is not directly relevant to our present inquiry. The fact is that there is a difference between the consciousness 'I cannot do so-and-so' and 'So-and-so cannot be done,' although both states of consciousness may result from the attempt to do so-and-so.

What I have tried to do so far is to account for the 'neutrality modifications' of a given mental content — i.e., for the fact that the same content can be thought as present or not present, possible or impossible, a remembered event or a perceived presence or merely a fantasy image. We can clearly see at this point that it is possible to give a simple physiological description of the relationship between perceptual and imaginative consciousness of the same object or of similar objects, and therefore also of the relationships between physiological and phenomenological states of affairs themselves. This explanation is facilitated by the purely phenomenological description of what is happening in consciousness when these relationships occur, combined with very minimal assumptions about the way the nervous system works. In this way, we can account for the phenomenological and physiological correlates of the categories of 'possibility', 'existence', 'necessity', and 'negation'. In a later context, we shall also develop similar descriptions which can help us to understand the relationship between phenomenal states and physiological processes in the cases of recognition and recall memory. A recognition memory occurs when the imagination of an object is accompanied by another physiological process whose meaning corresponds to a 'feeling of recognition' — a feeling that 'this efferent condition occurred earlier, in such-and-such circumstances.' Recall memory occurs when some afferent input triggers only a part of the relevant efferent reaction (for example, 'the person that gave the phenomenology talk in Memphis'), whereupon the brain voluntarily completes the reaction ('Ah, yes, John Smith, whose paper dealt with Sartre') — accompanied again by a 'feeling of recognition.' This will be discussed in detail in Chapter 6.

The kind of phenomenological-physiological correlation advanced here tends to be congruent with Dennett's insistence that states of consciousness correlate not with specific, highly localized neural events, but with global patternings of complex constellations of events — a view for which I argued extensively in *An Ontology of Consciousness* (1986). Perhaps the most obvious illustration of this global nature of consciousness is the fact that the cortex and hypothalamus function very similarly in most respects during sleep to the way they do during waking consciousness, except that the coordination or synchronization of the two parts of the brain is different (Asimov 1965: 193ff). Given one global coordination, consciousness exists; given another global patterning of essentially the same elements and activities (or the absence of a coherent pattern but with the same elements and activities existing alongside each other), consciousness is absent (at least, waking consciousness is absent). The reason what has been said here tends to support this holistic interpretation of the ontological status of consciousness in relation to brain events is that the efferent patterning which corresponds to 'looking for a blue wall' must surely be at least somewhat global in nature; the pattern which then corresponds to 'a blue wall is there' does not then exist in the brain *alongside* 'looking for a blue wall'. Rather, it places the 'blue-wall' patterning of the efferent system in the brain into a larger *context,* corresponding to the fact that the pattern which the efferent system was looking *for* is now fulfilled by the pattern of afferent inputs being received into this same efferent pattern. Obviously, this analysis of states of consciousness as corresponding to relatively global patternings of efferent functioning is congruent with Baars' (1988) notion of the 'global workspace.' Many afferent signals might compete with each other for conscious awareness, but only those afferent patterns that are attuned to the efferent pattern, or to what the efferent system is aroused to look for by the motivational system, can occupy the center of conscious attention. This conceptualization in turn fits nicely with the findings of Aurell, Posner and Rothbart, and Luria about the function of conscious attention.

Christina Schües (1994) describes the phenomenology of this process as follows:

> The continual course of experiences takes place as a process of actual anticipations followed by subsequent assurances in which the same object of perception, remembering, etc., is held in awareness and is determined more closely. If an anticipation is not assured, but dissapointed, then I might be surprised and a modalization of my experience takes place. . . We find here the possibility of a meaning which may even retroactively *inhibit* the already constituted meaning and overlie it with a new one, and hence, transform the experience accordingly. . . . When an object of experiences affects me, it seems to have an affective power which motivates me to perceive it. . . a movement of interest aiming at the object. . . . If the anticipation is disappointed and its motivational power diminishes, then the original mode of the experience is transformed into negation (Schües 1994: 12-14).

The relationship between looking-for and looking-at is similar to the one Husserl, in the Fifth Logical Investigation, describes as obtaining between the meaning-intention (e.g., 'chair') and the meaning-*fulfilling* intention ('a chair is there'). The description we have given of what actually goes on in consciousness also establishes the existence of Husserl's 'parallel' acts of imagination which are supposed to accompany each act of perception. When we see an object, we both 'look for' and 'look at' the object, and one of these two acts is capable of occurring in isolation from the other. The looking-for aspect of perception, corresponding to the ordering of the efferent system in the expectation of certain afferent inputs, does frequently occur in isolation, in the form of the imagination of the object in question. To look for X is to imamgine X. To look for X while receiving the input from X is to perceive X.

## 4. Early and Late Selection for 'Attention': A Synthesis

The theory we have begun to develop here can enable us to resolve the controversy regarding early selection (Broadbent 1958) *versus* late selection (Treisman 1964) of objects of attention. Moray (1970) demonstrated a serious problem for the early selection theory by presenting subjects in dichotic listening tasks with a sentence like 'Swan caught the ball, but her selection of music is strange' in one ear, simultaneously with 'Ronstadt sings marvelously, and he ran for a touchdown' in the other ear. The subjects could not continue to maintain the focus of attention on the message to one ear, but switched the focus to the other ear according to the meaning of the sentence. The fact that *meaning* rather than *sensory input* determined the direction of attention was supposed to undermine the early selection hypothesis, since it was assumed that the meaning of information cannot be 'processed' until the information is first perceived. Since we obviously *do* filter information, however, and are not conscious of the information which is filtered out, the *late* selection theory had to posit that the information must get processed on a non-conscious basis before we decide which (already-processed) information to attend to. But the price to be paid for this hypothesis is the difficulty of coming to terms with the fact that processing is tremendously more successful for information to which we do attend.

In the model proposed here, none of this is problematic because we have dropped the assumption that information must be perceived before it is organized. The organization of our predisposition as to what kinds of information we are 'looking for' occurs prior to perception, and the efferent system is already geared up to enact patterns corresponding to the chosen type of information before it is presented. The Moray study just mentioned shows that subjects are already predisposed toward the selection of meaningful sentences and toward concept-relationships that are consistent with past experience, prior to the presentation of those sentences and relationships. That which the afferent system presents has already been screened before it is presented.  At the same time, the efferent system stands ready to revise its preference as to what it should 'look for' if certain cues alert the midbrain *arousal* system (not the forebrain *attentional* system) that a different kind of object in the environment is emotionally and motivationally more important than what was initially 'looked for.'  At this point, attention shifts so as to look for and thus focus on different afferent input.  The priority of the efferent over the afferent in determining conscious awareness is what makes this kind of perceptual selection possible.

There are two interrelated objections to this notion of efferent pre-selection.  First, the efferent system cannot just arbitrarily decide what to 'look for,' but must *already* have received some sort of input in order to know what to look for; otherwise, the 'looking for' would only occasionally find a matching afferent input, and the perceptual system would be hopelessly inefficient — much more inefficient than it in fact is.  The other related objection is that attention and conscious awareness are not the same thing.  There are studies in which subjects non-consciously learn to execute tasks requiring attention, in the sense that an item must be distinguished from surrounding items and thus becomes an intense focus point for sensory and cognitive processing, while the surrounding items are not focused on in this way (Cohen *et al* 1990; Bullemer and Nissen 1987, 1990).  All of this occurs without any conscious awareness of the item on which 'attention' has been focused in this way.

Posner (1990) and Posner and Rothbart (1992) answer both these questions in a very neat and thorough way.  There is a posterior 'attentional' mechanism which involves no conscious awareness, whose purpose is simply to orient perceptual and cognitive processes toward a certain location in the phenomenal field, and to intensify processing of stimuli from that location.  The posterior system is aroused to focus non-conscious 'attention' in this way by means of signals from the thalamus, as noted earlier, prior to any frontal activation, and prior to any conscious awareness of the object.  The thalamus has a very primitive ability to discriminate what kinds of incoming information are emotionally important (Posner 1990; Posner and Petersen 1990), and the thalamus alerts the efferent anterior attentional mechanism to begin formulating questions or hypotheses about the more precise nature of the important stimulus, while *simultaneously* the thalamus also relays the sensory information to the primary sensory areas for further afferent processing (Aurell 1989, 1984). This posterior focusing function, which sometimes can facilitate 'learning without awareness' as in the studies just mentioned, is dissociable from the *anterior* focusing function orchestrated by the frontal-limbic system, which results in *conscious* attention to some intentional object (whether perceptual, imaginary or conceptual; the conceptual ones will be considered in Chapter 2). The studies described by Posner and Rothbart (1992) show with great detail, and in a variety of learning contexts, that the limitations to what can be computed in the absence of this *conscious* attention are quite drastic. For example, "While simple linear sequences seem to be learned without [conscious] attention, when hierarchical structures or new associations are involved, this becomes impossible (99)."

The main problem, then, is that there is a serious ambiguity in the word 'attention.' As Posner and Rothbart emphasize, the word can mean three entirely different mental processes, associated with different brain systems. Posner and Rothbart clearly distinguish (1) a posterior 'attentional' mechanism which works to orient the subject toward a certain location in the phenomenal field; (2) an anterior function which brings items to the center of our *conscious* attention; and (3) a general cortical arousal system governed by the reticular activating system, which by itself does not lead to focusing on a particular object of attention until one or both of the other 'attentional' systems become involved; the reticular activating system does, however, screen in a very rough way for the kinds of input that seem emotionally important. It has been conditioned to preconsciously screen in this way because of past learning.

We can avoid confusion by using different terms to describe these three different functions. 'Arousal' is usually used to refer to the third of Posner and Rothbart's three functions (as executed by the reticular activating system). 'Orienting' has often been used for the second function (the posterior selection of a certain point or area to focus on, as initiated by the thalamus which receives early signals and vaguely estimates their possible emotional importance prior to frontal activation or conscious awareness). 'Conscious attention' would seem to be the clearest way to refer to the conscious direction of attention (the anterior or frontal function associated with 'conscious awareness').

Much of what has been said here hinges on the distinction between efferent and afferent processes. The efferent processes dominate the direction of attention prior to consciousness of afferent input from the posterior sensory areas, and this efferent functioning corresponds to our consciousness of mental images, whether the latter are perceptual (as when corresponding afferent input is found) or only imaginative (as when the corresponding afferent input is not found). But the distinction between efferent and afferent itself needs to be clarified, since very central processes are hard to designate as 'incoming' or 'outflowing' signals. Making this distinction more clear will also help toward a better understanding of the relationships between efferent and afferent functions.

## 5. The Primacy of the Efferent over the Afferent in Conscious Processing

What is the meaning of 'efferent' and 'afferent' activity where the most central processes in the brain are concerned? Is it possible to clearly distinguish and apply these notions? Traditionally, afferent signals are supposed to be those which move from the peripheral to the central area of the nervous system. Efferent signals are those which move 'outward' from the central to the peripheral parts of the system. But the movement of signals within the cerebral cortex is so complex that it seems difficult if not meaningless to designate activities as afferent ('moving inward') or efferent ('moving outward'). We know that signals are 'received' and 'sent' by the cerebral cortex, but how do we classify the activity *within* the cortex? Are we to assume some absolute central receiving station (perhaps Descartes' pineal gland) which is the terminus of all afferent impulses and the initiator of all efferent ones?

Recent neurological research has been somewhat helpful in this regard. It has been known for some time that the posterior portion of the brain receives incoming input from the senses (Hubel and Wiesel 1959; Posner and Petersen 1990; Warrington 1985). Obviously, these are afferent. And we know that many signals from the midbrain move upward into the prefrontal cortex in humans (Posner and Rothbart 1992; Gray 1990; Luria 1980; Olds 1977), and from there 'outward' to less 'central' areas of the brain (if we take the midbrain as 'central'). So signals from the midbrain and prefrontal cortex (as well as those from the midbrain *to* the prefrontal cortex) can be regarded as 'efferent' in the traditional sense.

As far as the rest of the brain is concerned — the part 'between' the prefrontal cortex and the posterior area — much research has been done recently with regard to the extreme differences between what happens in the 'primary projection areas' of the various sensory modalities and the 'secondary' sensory areas and 'association' areas of the parietal and temporal lobes (Aurell 1983, 1984, 1989; Luria 1973; Sperry 1966). We know now, thanks to EEG studies, PET scans, etc., that incoming sensory signals first activate the primary sensory area which is at the surface of the cortex, and then activate the 'secondary sensory area' in Luria's (1973) and Hubel and Wiesel's (1959) terminology. This secondary layer of cells adjacent to the primary projection area contains 'feature detectors' which have been arranged through long-term learning and development to react only to specific features of environmental images — some cells reacting to right angles, some to vertical lines, some to horizontal, etc. We also know that *consciousness* of an object does *not* occur at the point when only the primary and secondary projection areas of the relevant sensory modality are activated (Aurell 1983, 1989; Posner and Rothbart 1992; Posner and Petersen 1990). Consciousness is associated with activation of the prefrontal and parietal areas, and this activation is not a direct causal result of primary or secondary projection area stimulation. The nerve impulse as it travels from the sensory organs (eyes, ears, etc.) to the primary projection area first passes through the thalamus, which alerts the reticular activating system that something important might be going on; this in turn stimulates the prefrontal cortex to begin formulating *questions* about what kind of information might be coming in from the environment (Luria 1973), and this in turn — as we have seen in this chapter — prompts more and more definite images to form in the parietal and secondary sensory areas (depending on sensory modality). When these imaging activities of the parietal and secondary sensory areas succeed in finding synchronized or matching patterns of activity in the primary projection area, *then* perceptual consciousness occurs. With respect to the frontal function of formulating questions, Luria sees the frontal lobe as "formulating the problem" to be solved by the brain (1973: 188). "This increase in cortical tone resulting from formulation of the problem is disturbed in patients with a pathological lesion of the frontal cortex (188)." Lesions of the frontal lobe "disturb . . . activity which is controlled by motives formulated with the aid of speech (199)" and "The patient can no longer direct and control his behavior with the aid of speech, either his own or that of another person (211)." Perhaps most revealing is the observation, "Having read the conditions of the problem, the patient [when asked to repeat them] . . . usually omits the most important part of the problem, namely its final question, or replaces the question by inert reproduction of one of the conditions (219)." Thus, in Luria's view, the frontal lobe is active when we pose a problem or question to ourselves that requires that we do some thinking. (This function of the frontal lobe will be discussed much further in the next two chapters, and in Chapter 6.)

This conceptualization of active, motivated efferent patterns as dominant over the selection and enactment of the perceptual consciousness corresponding to afferent patterns in the primary sensory areas would also be consistent with Tucker's empirically based 'frontal-activation' theory. Tucker (1981, 1986) hypothesizes that the function of 'activating' the organism toward emotionally motivated motoric behavior is facilitated by a left-anterior-ventral brain system. I.e., the midbrain activates the left frontal area to prepare for action. Meanwhile, the right-posterior-dorsal system is geared toward passively 'taking in' information, which does not become *conscious* until the left-anterior-ventral system *motivates* this consciousness. In a sense, the frontal-limbic system 'proposes,' and the primary and secondary sensory areas merely 'dispose' of what the frontal-limbic system has already proposed. There is also the often implicit assumption in Tucker's view that efferent activity is oriented toward activating *motoric* behavior, and that consciousness is largely a truncated, imaginary motoric behavior. For example, we may be conscious of the memory of a piece of music by imagining ourselves playing the piece. This interpretation is consistent with PET scans by Petersen *et al* (1989) showing that both the anterior cingulate and the supplementary motor area are involved in attention to language. (This will be discussed more extensively in Chapter 6.) It is also consistent with Olds' finding (1977) that there can be no consciousness unless the basal ganglia interact in certain specific patterns with the cortex. We shall also see as we proceed that there are many instances in which the *synchronization* of diverse brain activities is necessary for consciousness, not just the activity of those brain areas *per se*. Tucker's idea that imagination is truncated motor behavior is also consistent with the fact that motor neurons mature earliest in ontogenesis (Restak, 1984: 46-47), and the finding of Kimura and Archibald (1974), Studdert-Kennedy and Shankweiler (1970), and Liberman *et al* (1967) that speech evolves neurophysiologically as a truncated form of motoric behavior. I.e., to think a word is to imagine ourselves saying the word. Consider also the way motoric (and obviously efferent) action is crucial to the development of perception in kittens (Held and Hein 1958). These findings are summarized by Varela *et al* (1991):

> Held and Hein raised kittens in the dark and exposed them to light only under controlled conditions. A first group of animals was allowed to move around normally, but each of them was harnessed to a simple carriage and basket that contained a member of the second group of animals. The two groups therefore shared the same visual experience, but the second group was entirely passive. When the animals were released after a few weeks of this treatment, the first group of kittens behaved normally, but those who had been carried around behaved as if they were blind; they bumped into objects and fell over edges. This beautiful study supports the enactive view that objects are not seen by the visual extraction of features but rather by the visual guidance of action (Varela *et al* 1991: 174-175).

This complex process of motoric-imaging (and interrelated symbolic) development will be explored further as we proceed.

The most important point for our immediate purposes here is that the parietal and secondary areas do not simply receive input directly and passively from the primary projection area. We know this because PET scans and other imaging techniques which show the distribution of electrical activity in the brain reveal that, from the time when the primary projection area becomes activated to the time when a subject becomes conscious of a perceptual object, there is a time delay of about a third of a second. As I have already emphasized, this is much longer than it would take for nerve impulses to travel the distance from the primary projection area to the parietal areas associated with consciousness of visual images (Srebro 1985; Aurell 1989; Restak 1984).

To avoid a possible oversimplification, we should note that some recent studies (summarized by Richardson 1991) seem to suggest that there is a certain amount of occipital activity when we form imaginary visual images. This seems to occur especially with 'vivid imagers,' and in some subjects the occipital activity seems to occur only some of the time. These findings are currently being refined and clarified; Martha Farah (1989), for example, seems to find efferent but not afferent occipital involvement in imagery. Also, the verbal instructions in some of these studies might require extensive neural activity to assimilate, aside from the activity that corresponds to the actual production of the image. In any case, if we assume that there is indeed some occipital activity involved in imagery — especially in particularly vivid imagery — it is important to realize that from a phenomenological point of view there is no indication that even 'vivid imagers' are unaware of the difference between a 'vivid image' and an actual perception. The vivid imager is better able than others to get the brain to act in ways similar to the way it would act in an actual perception. Since this activity results from directions from the frontal lobe (and ultimately from the limbic system) rather than from perceptual input, it is efferent rather than afferent, even though it may extend somewhat into the occipital area (thus rendering visual images more 'realistic' and more 'sharp'). We should not speak as though there were some sharp boundary between a completely efferent area and a completely afferent area. Instead, the brain uses functional 'modules' (Gazzaniga 1986) — i.e., overlapping systems which are widely distributed; yet the efferent activity is decidedly more pronounced in the anterior areas, and the afferent activity is more posterior, reflecting the fact that the posterior region is more concerned with receiving input from the senses, whereas the anterior is more directly connected to the emotional-motivational system which guides the direction of attention.

It follows from the overall analysis here that consciousness, which always involves efferent activity, never results passively from stimulation by incoming sensory signals. Consciousness is the result of a motivated searching operation in which a complex efferent system of activity takes place, whose effect is to *select* certain incoming data as worthy of attention. Only *after* the organism purposely chooses to focus attention in a certain way can the 'looking-for' consciousness occur in the form of the consciousness of an image or possibility. And only after this imaginal consciousness develops (which is associated with parietal activation) does perceptual consciousness occur corresponding to the perceptual object whose input is activating the primary projection area. Activation of the parietal area, which results from a motivational and attentional process originating in the midbrain and guided by the prefrontal cortex, is always a *prerequisite* for perceptual consciousness.

When the pattern of activity in the parietal and secondary areas (corresponding to the mental image of the object) finds a matching afferent pattern in the primary sensory area, perceptual consciousness results. The secondary sensory area, then, can be viewed as the terminus of a series of efferent activities. The borderline area between the primary projection area and its proximate secondary area seems to be the dividing line (roughly speaking) between afferent and efferent activity in the brain. But this borderline area is also integrally connected to the 'motor cortex,' a comparatively small area which is located just between the frontal and parietal lobes. We shall see as we progress that this motor area is tied up completely with all forms of consciousness — imaginative, perceptual, or logical. Consciousness always involves subjunctives — imagining what would happen *if* we were to do something (rotate the object, squeeze it, drop it, etc.) This is where the findings of Piaget, Streri *et al* (1993), and Becker and Ward (1991) regarding the development of perception in neonates and of logical thinking in older children becomes extremely valuable. If the subjunctive imagination of a possible sensorimotor activity is presupposed even by the perceptual consciousness of an object, then imagination is the most basic building block of perceptual consciousness, and the efferent always has primacy over the afferent. We shall see that this is one of the most consistent differences between conscious and non-conscious information processing.

## 6. Afferent-Efferent Relations in Dreaming and Waking Consciousness

Another interesting research area in which the relationship between afferent and efferent functioning is beginning to become clear is the physiology of dreaming. It has now been established that anterior or efferent activity occurs throughout sleep, even when the subject is not dreaming (Winson 1986: 46ff; Restak 1984: 315-333). Jouvet's (1967) classic studies show continual neocortical activity throughout sleep, including non-modally-specific parietal activity. But this active neocortex is isolated from the environment as well as from the muscular control of the body — the condition Jouvet termed 'paradoxical sleep.' In addition to this extensive neocortical activity during non-REM sleep, something else happens during REM sleep, when dreams occur: More afferent, secondary sensory and secondary association activity

can be detected than during non-REM sleep (Winson 1986; Restak 1984) —
at least as much as in the waking 'vivid' imagery reported by Richardson
(1991), and consequently more than in 'non-vivid' imagery. Clearly what is
happening here is that, in the absence of much input from the senses during
sleep, the looking-for activities of the efferent anterior system are able to cause
the posterior system to behave in the patterns associated with them, so that one
has the impression that one is really looking at the merely imagined object.
This finding is highly consistent with our phenomenological account of the
conscious correlates of the afferent-efferent relationship.

Dreams, in fact, can be regarded as another indication of the priority
of imaginative over perceptual consciousness, for the following reason: When
auditory stimuli compete for our attention while we are asleep, we often dream
about things associated with those stimuli. But the interesting point is that,
when we reflect on the content of the dream, we often realize that the sounds
that caused the dream are not present *as sounds* in the dream.    This is
consistent with neurological findings by Symons (1993) and Dement (1958)
that, during dreams, it is primarily the *non-modally-specific* imaging areas of
the parietal and secondary sensory areas that are most activated, and that by
casting mental representations in visual rather than auditory imagery we allow
the 'vigilance mechanism' to function only for the most important auditory
stimuli that might impinge from the real environment.

For example, I once dreamed of being in an enclosed area with some
red birds of various sizes, which I tried to let out by opening windows.
However, it turned out that each window I opened had a screen on it, so that
the birds could not escape. On awakening, I wondered why I had had such a
dream. I then noticed the sound of periodic small flocks of birds flying very
close to my window. But the remarkable thing was that the birds in the dream
*made no sound.* The sound of the birds outside the window did not cause me
to consciously *hear* these sounds, but it did lead to the *idea* of a bird in my
consciousness, which took the form of a visual rather than an auditory image.
Most people can probably think of many similar examples from their own
experience. It is not that we cannot have auditory images in dreams (music,
people's voices, etc.); it must therefore be that the process through which
sensory input affects consciousness is a somewhat circuitous one in which the
general *idea* of the type of thing involved (in this case, birds) occurs *before* the

actual sensory information (in this case, the *sound* of the birds) becomes an element in conscious awareness.

Neurophysiologically, what these examples suggest is that the stimulation of the primary sensory area for sounds in the temporal lobe does not directly produce a stimulation of the very nearby secondary sensory areas and parietal imaging areas. If it did, then one would expect the image in the secondary and parietal areas to be an *auditory* one. Instead, the stimulation of the primary sensory area leads first of all to an increase of general cortical arousal (involving the reticular activating system *via* neuronal 'gating' in the hippocampus). This arousal system is geared toward 'letting through' into awareness only those stimuli judged to be *important* for the organism. This role of hippocampal gating for censoring incoming data for awareness is consistently confirmed by empirical studies — for example, by Symons (1993), Winson and Absug (1977, 1978a, 1978b), Dahl *et al* (1983), and Aston-Jones and Bloom (1981). Since the judgment of importance is largely a motivational-emotional issue, it makes sense that it must involve the midbrain, crucially implicated in the production of all emotions. If there is some tendency to 'let through' a general type of stimulus (animal sounds, or the sound of one's own name, or a very loud noise, or a surprising stimulus such as an alarm clock, an important person's voice, etc.), the next step is to form a *general idea* of the type of object or event the stimulus might represent. If the idea seems important enough to worry about, the prefrontal cortex will then be aroused to ask questions about the generic image used to form the general idea of the type of object in question: Is it really present, or only remembered? Is it near or far? Is it a threat, or does it call upon me to act in some way? If this process continues long enough for the 'looking for' process in the secondary sensory and parietal areas (as guided and motivated by frontal lobe questioning) to result in finding a match between this mental-imaging activity and the corresponding activities of the primary projection area, then not only is the sound actually *heard* in the form of the perceptual, conscious awareness of the sound in the environment, but also *waking consciousness results.* We shall see in a later chapter that full consciousness always results when a looking-for process finds its appropriate match with a corresponding pattern of sensory stimulation.

Of course, most dream images do not arise from external stimuli, but from internal motivational-emotional activity which gives rise to frontal and parietal activation which in turn may cause the primary sensory area to 'resonate' with it (if the contents involved are important enough), so that we experience ourselves phenomenologically as actually 'looking at' something rather than just imagining it. Whether imagery results from external stimuli which are processed from auditory to visual modality (as in the bird dream), or from internal emotional activity, what both mechanisms clearly confirm is that 'looking-for,' which is mainly anterior, precedes and is a necessary condition for the phenomenal experience of 'looking-at,' which involves both anterior and posterior activity.

Such an explanation of dreaming is consistent in many ways with Foulkes' (1985) approach, in that it reverses the direction of information processing: In waking life, we receive (afferent, posterior) sensory input, and the (efferent, anterior) pre-perceptual 'inner experience' (Aurell 1989) interprets and transforms the input. In dreams, we begin with 'inner experience' — emotion, motivations, feelings, etc., then transform them into images which are so vivid that they force the posterior system (especially the occipital lobe) — which would normally be a receiving system — to resonate with the images generated from our 'inner experience.' It therefore seems as though we were actually 'looking at' the object of the image.

But the approach I am advocating here avoids the problems Foulkes has in accounting for the way the 'inner life' *transforms* its general concepts back into specific images. As Globus (1987) points out, a computational approach like Foulkes' requires that the 'inner life' contains 'processing rules' which are more abstract than the incoming 'data' from the senses.

> The abstract representation is a universal that has indefinitely many instantiations; a particular instance cannot be recovered from it. We might go from a particular triangle to the concept of triangles, but then we cannot get back to that particular triangle or any particular triangle, except arbitrarily (Globus 1987: 122).

Thus, here again, in the computational approach the particulars of dreams must come from 'stored memories,' and a proposed mechanism of 'information processing' cannot become plausible until we know how and where the information is 'stored.'

In the holistic-connectionist model I am using, the information is not stored, but is re-created on each occasion. The brain actively generates imagery (and, as the next chapter will show, concepts) based on what it is 'looking for' to address the emotional-motivational interests of the organism. Because a state of consciousness is associated with a complex *pattern of change* in the elements of its substratum rather than as *contained in* the configuration of the elements themselves, conscious information processing is different from that of a computer. Rather than passively receiving input and then 'responding,' the organism first generates anticipations, and then seeks out input patterns which resonate with the anticipations. The state of consciousness so produced then becomes a basic term to be manipulated in more complex ways (as discussed in the next two chapters) to produce logical or rule-governed thinking. There is no need to explain how the input causes the response, because the input does not simply *cause* the response, but rather is selected according to the *needed* or *desired* response. We shall find more and more as we proceed that this element of *desire* is one of the key differences between the ways in which a conscious being and a computer process information.

This way of thematizing the situation is also capable of resolving a problem that has bothered Neisser (1967, 1976) over the years. On the one hand, Neisser wants to hold that dream images are 'constructions' of the visual imagination, but on the other hand he needs to accommodate the conflicting phenomenal experience in which we do not seem to be just 'imagining' the object, but rather 'seeing' it. Some way is needed to understand how, on the one hand, dreams can arise in the way thoughts and mere images do during waking life — constructed from within — yet, on the other hand, are phenomenally experienced as if they were real perceptions not constructed from within. The model of efferent-afferent relationships we are developing here solves this problem. Imagination can *cause* occipital activity in sleep.

There also seems to be an intermediate condition between waking and dreaming consciousness. It is the one that we often pass through for just a moment after awakening from a vivid dream. We know that the dream was only a dream, thus we are not simply still dreaming. Yet the ideas in the dream still seem more worthy of being taken seriously as representations of reality than they will be when we are more fully awake. For example, suppose we have dreamed that the solution to correctly interpreting any text is to translate it into Latin, and then back into its original language. In the first instant after awakening, we might still think, 'Yes, that's it! And perhaps it would also work for German texts, like Hegel's *Phenomenology!*' But then an instant later, when we are 'fully awake,' we easily see how ridiculous the idea is. Or again, we may dream that we are madly in love with some person we hardly know, and that this person reciprocates our affection. Immediately on awakening, we may think, 'Yes, I must call her right away and tell her how I feel, since I feel sure now that she reciprocates!' Or we may dream that a spouse or lover is unfaithful to us. An instant after awakening, we feel very angry, and are convinced that the person really has betrayed us simply because we dreamed it. In empirical studies of sleep and dreaming, this intermediate condition seems to resemble very closely the 'dream-like thoughts' reported by Dement and Kleitman (1957) during stage I of sleep.

The reason I emphasize this intermediate condition is that it can tell us a great deal about the difference between waking and sleeping consciousness. If we think of waking consciousness as a process in which the *desire* to represent some aspect of reality results in the actual representation of it (so that both elements of consciousness, desire and representation, are present), then dreaming consciousness can be conceived as a lesser degree of consciousness. It is one in which there is a desire to represent something, resulting in a generic image of the object or situation, but the 'looking for' consciousness that constitutes the image does not lead to a 'looking at' or perception, even though the perceptual data may actually be present in the primary projection area — as in the example of the bird dream mentioned above. Both the desire and the perceptual 'representation' (in the non-conscious sense) are present, but they are not *coordinated* with each other in one mental act. Usually, this is because the desire to represent that information is not strong enough to motivate the completion of the mental processes involved, which would lead not only to the conscious representation of the information, but also to wakefulness. Thus we observe that, before awakening, many of the same neurophysiological processes are occurring as in wakeful consciousness, but they are not *synchronized* with each other in the way needed to produce wakefulness (Azimov 1965; Ellis 1986). Similarly, Winson (1985: 190), Macrides *et al* (1982), and Komisaruk (1977) find that hippocampal theta rhythms are necessary to synchronize sensory information before we can be conscious of it. Still further evidence for the importance of synchronization shows up in studies where the disruption of circadian and ultradian rhythms leads to desynchronization of the hypothalamus and cerebral cortex, which in turn leads to severe mental conditions such as schizophrenia and psychotic depression (see Restak 1984: 101-145).

How does the intermediate condition just mentioned between dreaming and 'complete' wakefulness fit into this conceptualization?  It seems that, in fully wakeful consciousness, the desire to represent a situation leads to conscious awareness of some reality *as it actually is*.  Since attention is both motivated and selective, it is of course obvious that we may ignore things we prefer not to see.  But what we *do* want to see is seen pretty much *as it is*. In the intermediate condition just described, however, the desire to see things in a certain way leads directly to the conviction that things *are* that way.  I.e., a 'looking for' *is taken for a 'looking at.'*  The fact that an image in a dream presented a certain person as our enemy is taken as direct evidence that this person *is* our enemy.

In dreaming consciousness, as Sartre observed in his earlier work (before becoming involved in metaphysical speculations), there is seldom any distinction between a hypothetical and an actual situation.  As soon as the idea occurs to us that some object *might* be present, it usually *is* present in the dream.  The emotional evaluation of what is important to us thus completely and directly determines our assessment of what is the case.  As soon as we think 'What if there were snakes all over the floor!' we immediately see that there *are* snakes on the floor.  Or, if we think 'I wonder if such-and-such operation would make them disappear,' in that instant either the snakes *do* disappear, or the idea of that which was to disappear (the snakes) is so worrisome or important to us that we are unable to stop entertaining the idea, and as a result the snakes on the floor cannot disappear.  In either case, whether something is present or not depends on whether we are able to stop imagining the image of it.  In a dream there is never much distinction between the imaginary and the apparently perceived, and seldom *any* difference between them.  This is consistent with the above-mentioned empirical findings (Restak 1984: 315-333) that, during dreaming, efferent activity may simply *cause* corresponding afferent activity, whereas during wakefulness the afferent activity is constrained by reality.

In the context of dream research too, then, we find that when what our 'desires' are imaginatively 'looking for' come into synchronization with what our senses are delivering by way of 'representation,' that is when waking consciousness occurs — i.e., we wake up. (For example, in the dream about the birds, as soon as I actually *heard* the birds in the auditory modality in which they had really presented themselves — rather than only visualizing them — I was awake and simply listening to an actual sound.) This is entirely consistent with the fact mentioned earlier that waking consciousness occurs when the activity of the thalamus and the activity of the cerebrum (both of which may have been already ongoing) come into coordination and synchronization with each other.    Consciousness always involves the interrelation of a 'desire' and a 'representation' in which the 'desire' seeks out the 'representation.'  In Schopenhauer's terms, we might say it involves both a 'will' and an 'idea.'

## 7.  Transition to the Problem of Concepts

Our aim is to outline the parameters of a theory of human cognition which can unify observations available to phenomenological investigation and also facts that are now well established about neurophysiology.  Such a theory must show how various cognitive content-elements, such as perceived and imagined intentional objects, mental concepts, affirmative, negative and relational judgments, memories, etc., can be given a coherent accounting which accommodates both the phenomenological experiencing of the cognitive processes involved, and at the same time the neurophysiological basis of these processes.  I shall argue further in the next two chapters that such a phenomenologically-accurate account is crucially needed in contemporary cognitive theory as the question arises as to which of the proposed 'computational architectures' and 'models' (if any) resembles the structure of information processing used by *conscious* beings.  Should we opt for a connectionist model (Churchland 1989), even though such models have been criticized as neurophysiologically unrealizable (for example, by Butler 1993; Tienson 1987; Bechtel 1987), or a more traditional 'production system' model (Anderson 1983), even though these are at odds with *phenomenal* experience (Searle 1984; Dreyfus 1979)?

Our discussion so far of the phenomenology and neurophysiology of the mental image can provide a fruitful starting point if it can be developed in such a way as to ground an understanding of the more complex mental and neurophysiological operations just mentioned — especially conceptual and logical thinking (see also Ellis 1990, 1986, 1980). We have seen that, phenomenologically speaking, when I look at a pink wall and say to myself, 'What if the wall were blue,' the mental image of a 'blue wall' normally occurs as part of this thought. Yet it is also true that in some instances, and for some people more than others, the *abstract concept* 'blue' occurs in this context rather than a *mental image* of blue. For example, Bill Bechtel (1986) insists that he *never* forms visual images. We shall see in the next chapter that abstract concepts correspond to more complex neurophysiological operations which are *built up from* the simpler mental images — not just visual ones, but imagery in all modalities, including audition, kinaesthesia and proprioception. In essence, to think an abstract concept means to feel that I *could,* if needed, enact an interrelated series of mental images corresponding to the empirical observations that ultimately would be involved in an ostensive definition of the concept in question. I cannot stress too much that, as Newton (1982, 1993) also emphasizes, the imaginable observations relevant here need not be *visual* ones. We can kinaesthetically imagine what it would be like to make a physical measurement, or we can auditorily imagine obtaining ostensive reports from research subjects, or we can proprioceptively imagine what the rhythm of a certain form of logical inference would be. This approach to the phenomenological and neurophysiological basis of concepts will be developed in the next chapter.

We saw in this chapter that the consciousness of a physical object as an intentional object, regardless of doxic modality, must correspond to an efferent looking-for pattern of activity which is the same in certain neurophysiological parameters as it *would* be if the organism were to look *at* the same or a similar object. But to fit this theory into a coherent account of cognitive functioning, we must endeavor to see whether memory, language, learning, logical information processing, and, most of all, the consciousness of *abstract concepts* can be accounted for in these terms. The next chapter will concentrate primarily on the crucial phenomenological and physiological status of the consciousness of abstract concepts, without which the 'computations' discussed in cognitive theory could not take place. We have noted already that to form a mere mental image is not the same as to think with a precise logical concept. Those who have taken computational models to task because of their neglect of the role of mental images (such as Rosch, 1975, many proponents of Johnson-Laird's 'mental model' approach, 'prototype' theorists, and the connectionists generally) must also consider the implications of this problem for their own models.   It is an obvious phenomenological datum that human beings *do* often think in terms of abstract concepts and precise inferential rules, and not just with mental images.   That is what we must consider next.

# CHAPTER TWO

## From Images to Concepts

In describing phenomenologically the relationship between the mental image and the concept, it is natural to begin, as did the early Sartre (1966: 145 and *passim*) and more recently Rosch (1975), Keller and Lehman (1991), and Schyns (1991), with the generalized or generic image. In contrast to the 'prototype' theories of Sartre and Rosch, however, I shall end up with a cognitive role for concepts which is clearly and utterly divergent from the role of images, although it can also be shown that concepts ultimately are built up from images, which are the more elementary cognitive function. I make no objection to the prototype theorists' claim that concepts often (or usually) fail to include precise decision rules for category membership (see Margolis 1991; Barsalou 1987; Fodor and Pylyshyn 1988; Lakoff 1987). The important question for our purposes here is whether all concepts can be generated by means of blurring or leaving ambiguous some of the features of a mental image (such as 'horse') so that the concept would consist of a thus-genericized mental image which would work as a 'prototype' for that type of object or phenomenon. We shall see in this chapter and the following one that the relationship between mental images and concepts is a good deal more complicated than this, that concepts often are genuinely more abstract than mere fuzzy images, and that the neurophysiological and phenomenological correlates of these abstract concepts are correspondingly more complicated.

A 'generic image' (the phenomenal correlate of a 'prototype') is merely an image some of whose features have been left vague or indefinite enough that the image can be felt to match a variety of different approximations to the image. For example, suppose I form a generic mental image of 'horse' — i.e., not any particular horse, just 'horse,' a horse that stands for 'any horse.' What color is this horse? I have either purposely left the color indeterminate so that no particular horse will fail to match the image, or I have made the horse an indeterminate gray so that it serves as a 'prototype' which particular horses will resemble closely enough that this image adequately reminds me of them. Of course, this means the same as to say that if I 'look for' this image in my environment, it will feel itself closely matched by any horse I look at. Viewed as an object, the generic image is a fuzzy or prototypic pattern whose approximate instantiation I look for. From the subjective perspective, I sense an (efferent) activity which would become a perception should it meet with its associated (afferent) fulfillment.

Up to this point, the role of generic images fits nicely into the overall model of efferent-afferent patterns we have hypothesized. But how do logical concepts — true concepts in the *abstract* sense — fit this picture? That is a more difficult question which we must now address.

## 1. The Relation between Images and 'Imageless Concepts'

Natika Newton (1993), in her assessment of the role of images in consciousness, emphasizes a point which we should bear in mind throughout this discussion: The term 'image' may be used to refer to any instance of imagining something, and this includes much more than imaginings that involve mental pictures or sounds. I can imagine what it would be like to *move my body* in a certain way. Or I can imagine what it *felt* like when I went to bat in the last inning of a league championship baseball game with the game on the line. Any of these imaginings are 'images.' Many of them ground the rudimentary subjunctives used by an infant to interpret the visual field. For example, an item which reflects light uniformly is one which, if grasped, would not feel warm and fuzzy like a blanket, but would feel hard and slick. The infant knows how to imagine what it would feel like if she were to grasp the object, throw it, bite it, etc. When I speak of 'images,' then, I mean to include these 'proprioceptive' images — which Newton argues are the most fundamental data in our awareness (because knowing how to move our bodies is the most basic kind of knowledge) — as well as the visual and auditory ones that Wittgensteinians are usually thinking of when they deny that thinking involves forming images.

In Newton's (1993, 1992, 1991, 1982) formulation, 'mental images' include any conscious process in which we know (or think we know) what it would be like (or feel like) to do something which we are not presently doing — either with our whole bodies or only with our brains. To entertain in consciousness what it would feel like to reach down and grab my left foot, for example, is to form a proprioceptive mental image of this action. The images involved are not merely perceptual images (for example, the touch sensations being received by the hand), but also images of what it is like to move my own body, to be pulled by gravity, etc.

Notice that the 'feeling of recognition' associated with memories (i.e., the 'feeling of confidence' discussed in memory retrieval studies — see Chapter 3) can also sometimes function as a proprioceptive image in this sense. I.e., I can imagine what it would feel like (or 'be like') to have a feeling of recognition for a name, even if I do not presently have the feeling of recognition for the name. (This is the familiar sensation called the 'feeling of knowing' in memory studies — see Chapter 3.) I refer to my proprioceptive image of what the feeling of recognition would be like in order to reject or accept particular names which I pose to myself as candidates for the one I am trying to remember. Suppose we recall an example in which we tried to remember a name we had forgotten, and then suddenly the memory came. There was a specific 'feeling of recognition' or 'feeling of familiarity' that accompanied the name. We can imagine what that feeling of familiarity was like, so this too is a proprioceptive mental image in Newton's sense. This feeling of recognition or familiarity is in principle separable from the consciousness of the specific mental content remembered. Sometimes the feeling of recognition is present without any actual remembered content, as in *deja vu* experiences; conversely, sometimes the content is present without the feeling of recognition, as in cases of amnesia. If we can imagine what it is like to have a *deja vu* experience, then we are forming a proprioceptive mental image of the feeling of recognition without entertaining any specific content. A remembered image, then, is really a juxtaposition of the image of the content we remember (which may be either sensory or proprioceptive), and the feeling of recognition (which is always proprioceptive). The implications of this point for memory functioning will be explored further in Chapter 6.

Newton (1993) also stresses that imagining, in this broadened sense, often may occur at a very low level of conscious awareness. I may imagine that the rug in a room would feel soft to the touch, and therefore see it as soft, without consciously rehearsing the action of putting my hand or foot on the rug. Somehow this image is implicit in my immediate interpretation of the meaning of the way the rug looks, without my having to consciously think about it.

Given these qualifications, then, is it possible to understand how concepts are built up from images? The most formidable obstacle to such an explanation is that, when we think in terms of abstract conceptualizations, we may indeed 'imagine' whether certain conceptual relations are possible, impossible, unlikely, etc., but this kind of 'imagining' does not seem to involve the presence of *'images'* or *'imagery'* — as Wittgenstein (1953) and White (1987) have emphasized. In the same way, let us suppose for the sake of argument that Johnson-Laird (1994) is correct in that, when we make logical inferences, we 'imagine a scenario' in which the pattern of logic in question does not work and that, if we can 'imagine' such a scenario, we judge that pattern of logic to be invalid. The problem still remains that we normally do not seem to form spatial or visual *images* in our consciousness of many of the concepts we are 'imagining.'

In fact, it seems obvious that not all instances of imagining can be reduced to instances of entertaining images. To imagine what it would be like to be president (to use the example discussed in Newton's 1989 article) does not necessarily entail having visual (or auditory or olfactory) images of the White House, or myself sitting in the president's office, or any other specific intentional object that could be used as the content of a 'mental picture.' And to think the concept 'president' is correspondingly different from forming the mental picture of any particular president's face, the White House, the president's office, etc. To suggest, then, that entertaining the concept 'president' can be explained as the result of some combination or pattern of images (even in the expanded sense in which imagining a stomach ache or a feeling of being in love or a roller coaster ride would be 'sensorimotor and proprioceptive images') therefore requires extensively more justification than we have yet given. It requires that we show in detail just what kind of imagery is at work when we think a given concept (for example, 'president') without forming an image of the content of that particular concept (for example, a particular president's face, the White House, etc.). And the objection against an imagistic theory of concepts posed by this problem is that we do not usually seem to form the various images which are involved in defining the concept 'president' when we actually use the concept in context. So when we 'imagine a scenario' as a possible counterexample to a proposed pattern of inferential reasoning (as for example in Johnson-Laird's 'mental model' approach to reasoning), we are not really forming 'images' of the concepts in the examples we are considering. (This is probably why Johnson-Laird always stops short of equating 'mental models' literally with mental *images.*)

The answer to this question, which I again infer from Newton's 'Sensorimotor Theory' (1993), is that to form an 'imageless' concept (such as 'president') is to put ourselves into a condition of neurophysiological preparedness to call up the various combinations of (visualizable, audibilizable, feelable, etc.) ostensive conditions needed to define the concept 'president.' Normally, we do not enact such an ostensive explication of a concept unless we are asked 'What do you mean by "president"?' But what we feel is that we *could* provide such an explication if needed. By an 'ostensive' definition, I mean a definition in terms of elements which in principle are empirically observable (and thus imageable in some modality). I shall speak of an 'indirectly ostensive' definition as one which can be defined with reference to other concepts which in turn can be defined in terms of elements which are empirically observable (and thus imageable in some modality). This assumes, of course, that the *relationships between* the imageable elements can also be grasped as patterns which themselves are imageable in some modality, or combination of modalities — i.e., that the relationships between the elements of an ostensive definition can themselves be ostensively defined. When we use concepts, we usually do not think their definitions, but we feel 'confident' that we could do so.

We should note here that feeling 'confident' that we could explicate a concept is different from the 'feeling of confidence' in memory retrieval, where we feel confident that we *have correctly retrieved* the information (as I shall discuss in Chapter 3 and Chapter 6). In feeling confident that we *could* explicate a concept, we do not believe that we have actually 'retrieved' all the images that would be needed just because we feel confident that we *could* do so. The feeling of confidence in the context of concept usage also differs from the 'feeling of knowing' in memory studies.  To feel that we know what a concept means is not necessarily to feel that we can retrieve some item full-blown from memory, as if the explication of the concept were a unitary mental act which would occur in a flash, as in memory retrieval.  The explication of a concept like 'president' may be a lengthy process in which we string together a long series of imageable stipulations, the order of which is also important. Of course, it is also possible to feel confident of being able to *remember* what 'president' means, without actually remembering it at the moment; but, as explained earlier, this is not necessarily the same as feeling confident that, at the present moment, we *do* know what it means.

For example, suppose that 'to be president,' in someone's usage, means to have sworn an oath after having been elected, which in turn means that the person said certain words in front of certain witnesses after certain individuals marked certain cardboard computer cards in voting booths behind curtains, following in turn an older occurrence in which a group of men designated by their constituents (*via* certain symbolic movements such as voting) wrote on a piece of paper that the person so sworn in would be obeyed by certain individuals whom he or she told to perform certain actions — i.e., that if these persons did not do what the president said, they would stop receiving paychecks from the president, would be barred from certain government offices, thrown in jail, etc.  This would be an indirectly ostensive definition of what it means to be president — i.e., in terms of relationships between component concepts which in turn can be reduced to something which is empirically observable, and which we can therefore visualize (or hear, smell, feel, etc.).  But, paradoxically, we do not visualize any of these referents when we think the word 'president.'  The problem, then, is that it is very hard to separate what we do mentally when we *use* the concept 'president' from what we would do if we were asked to *define* what we mean by it.  But the definition — unlike the mental act we perform when we think the meaning — can ultimately be articulated in empirical and thus visualizable (or 'audibilizable,' or 'olfactoralizable,' or 'emotionally feelable,' etc.) terms. Thus, when we ask ourselves what we mean by a concept, there is always much more that was 'implicitly' in our consciousness of the meaning than we were 'explicitly' conscious of at the time when we used it, and the real meaning of the concept seems to be embedded in these implicit elements rather than in what we were explicitly conscious of at the time (Gendlin 1992).  The 'feeling of knowing' can be present with a content not presently being entertained in consciousness, as Metcalfe (1994: ixff) and other researchers cited earlier emphasize.

But now compare this explication of 'president' to the explication of a fuzzier concept — for example, 'in love.' When we begin to say what we mean by 'in love,' most of us find ourselves struggling, questioning and revising what we think we mean by it. For most people, this is also true of moral terms ('fairness,' 'moral desert,' etc.), aesthetic terms ('great,' 'romantic,' etc.), and many everyday concepts. If we reflect on our consciousness just after having used the concepts 'president' and 'in love,' we find that the term 'president' gave us a feeling of confidence that, if necessary, we *could* explicate what we meant in intelligible terms. But with a concept like 'in love,' we notice that there was less of a feeling of confidence in this respect. There was an unsureness, a hesitance, a fear of saying what we did not mean, or not being able to say what we did mean. We anticipated not being able to clarify what we meant. So to know what a concept means is to be able, if necessary, to show what it means by tracing this meaning ultimately to ostensive and thus imageable terms. It is to feel confident that we *could* call up certain images, but normally without actually calling them up in order to prove to ourselves that we can do it. The stronger this feeling of confidence that we could ultimately explicate the relevant ostensive (i.e., imageable) conditions, the more clearly we think we understand the concept.

This difference between a strong feeling of confidence that we could explicate a meaning (for example, 'president') and the weaker feeling of confidence when we doubt that we could do so (for example, 'in love') is exactly the same as a musician's feeling of confidence (or lack thereof) of being able to execute a given piece of music. If I am asked, 'Do you know Chopin's B Minor Sonata?' I feel confident that I do know it, because I could remember how to start playing it, and once having started, I feel confident that I could execute the entire piece. In the same way, if asked whether I know what 'Tchaikovsky's Sixth Symphony' refers to even though I cannot play it, I feel confident that I could mentally rehearse what the piece sounds like, or at least segments of it, or at least could identify it if heard. And this same feeling of confidence that I could ultimately execute a combination of imageable conditions is also felt when I am asked what 'president' means.

To explain completely what it is that I do neurophysiologically when I know what 'president' or 'Tchaikovsky's Sixth Symphony' means would be beyond our scope here. I shall try to outline later in this chapter the broad contours of the neurophysiological correlates of this kind of process. The important point for now is that there is a feeling in each case that certain patterns of images *could* be entertained, although we are not entertaining them at the moment.

## 2. The Role of Inhibition

It is apparent from these kinds of phenomenological considerations that in forming a concept we *inhibit* the execution of the consciousness of any of the various images that would be involved in explicating the concept, but feel confident that we *could* execute them if needed. In thinking the concept 'president,' for example, we do not entertain the images of the observable facts which would constitute an ostensive definition of 'president,' such as the counting of ballots, the Founding Fathers' writing of the election provision in a document called the Constitution, the swearing of the oath, etc. We feel ready to cite these ostensive conditions if necessary, so they are closer to the surface of our awareness than if we were not thinking the concept 'president' at all, but we still do not consciously entertain them. Thus there is something that we are doing when we use the concept 'president' in ordinary contexts that puts us into a state of 'readiness' to execute the series of images which would explicate the concept if needed. This 'something,' of course, is not itself just another image or act of imagination, but it is an activity whose purpose is to put us into a state of preparedness to execute the relevant images for the (usually indirectly) ostensive definition of the concept in question.

If the goal is to understand concepts that are more abstract than mere fuzzy or generic images (for example, the generic image of 'horse,' which is merely a vague enough image to fit a variety of instantiations), the simplest example of such a concept is probably the disjunctive concept. In this case, we have a simple instance of a concept whose explication would involve citing just a few imaginable representations rather than a complex combination of interrelated imaginable representations; to feel that we know what the concept means is to feel confident that we could cite any or all of these imaginable representations if needed (although in normal usage we refrain from actually citing them). For example, in the mind of a liberal, the concept 'conservative' could be instantiated by the image of a man in a business suit preoccupied with his own self-interest, or it could take the form of an ignorant farmer being taken in by traditional-moralizing rhetoric such as religious intolerance, gay-bashing and blaming-the-victim, or it could be represented by a military or police officer angry at the increasing amount of crime which he thinks is attributable to a lack of discipline in the way laws are written and executed. These three sets of images are very different, yet in thinking 'conservative,' the liberal stands ready to execute any or all of them if needed. Because the person feels ready for all of them at once, it is felt that they all have something in common with each other. There is a similarity in the *beginning phase* of executing them, and only this beginning phase is enacted; at the point where the enactment of the three images would diverge, that is where the person *inhibits* any further enactment. What remains uninhibited is the 'truncated response' — i.e., some part of the response that would be common to the way any of these alternative images would be responded to if they should occur. For example, if I am a liberal, my reaction to any of these images might include a subtle combination of disdain for stupidity, fear of moral perversity, and at the same time an empathic imagining of what frame of mind *I* would be in if I were to fit any of those images — obsession with my own self-interest, mistrust of human nature, condemnatory attitudes toward the weak and disadvantaged who fail to pull themselves up by their bootstraps, fear of rapid change, hatred and fear of homosexuals, etc. The empirical finding that attention to one meaning of a word literally neurophysiologically inhibits the activation of other meanings (Burgess and Simpson 1988) supports this role for inhibition in entertaining the meanings of concepts.

It is crucial to bear in mind that it makes no difference at all *which ones* of these efferent responses or which combinations of them *actually occur* when I think the idea; this could vary considerably from one individual to another or from one time to another. The important point is that there is some exemplary chunk of imaging activity which *could*, if I were to so desire, lead to the entire sequence of interconnecting images that *would* be needed if I were to explicate the concept. For example, the word 'Beethoven' might sometimes call up images of the rugged stoic who wrote the *Eroica,* or it might call up the dreamy unrequited lover who wrote the 'Moonlight' Sonata. It makes no difference which image or images occur — or even if no image other than the auditory image of the *word* 'Beethoven' occurs. What is crucial is that I have a feeling of confidence that whichever small chunk of efferent activity *does* occur *would* serve, if I wanted it to, as the beginning point of a complicated sequence of empirically specifiable (and thus imageable) conditions that would be more or less adequate to define what the word 'Beethoven' means to me. I know that I could explicate this entire set of images if I wanted to in the same way that I feel confident that, as soon as I have thought the first five notes of Chopin's B Minor Sonata, I could execute the whole piece if needed (though on most occasions I would graciously refrain from actually doing so). There is nothing special about the *first five notes* that makes me choose *them* as the truncated response to give me the feeling of confidence that I could execute the piece: I could use the beautiful melody in D Major that occurs several pages into the piece just as well; the first few notes of *that* melody could also provide me with a truncated response from which, if I wanted to, I could unfold an execution of the entire piece. But there is some chunk of the total set of imagery that is chosen as the chunk that I depend on to serve as a starting point to execute the concept 'Chopin's B Minor Sonata,' and which I normally use without fully explicating it, i.e., without thinking through the total constellation of images. And executing this small chunk of the efferent response (i.e., this 'truncated response') is enough to provide me with a feeling of confidence that I could explicate it if I wanted to — hence the feeling that I know what it means.

Of course, it is true that a 'feeling of confidence' to this effect may be completely erroneous, just as it may be in memory retrieval studies (Koriat, Lichtenstein and Fischhoff 1980). I may feel confident that I can execute Chopin's B Minor Sonata in my imagination, yet when I try to do so I fail. What this means is that the 'feeling of confidence' is only *part* of the act of knowing that I know what the concept means. I.e., I may *think* that I know that I know, but in fact do not know, and therefore do not really 'know that I know.' Another part of knowing that I know is that I am actually in a condition of readiness to execute the entire sequence of images, and do not erroneously *feel* that I am.

Our previous discussions of how mental images are enacted would imply that, in enacting an abstract concept like 'conservative,' we enact at least some of the efferent processes that the various elements of the fully-explicated ostensive definition would have in common with each other (perhaps including the look or sound of the *word* 'conservative'), and inhibit the rest. This must be the case because, if we were to enact any one of the images, we would be enacting an efferent pattern, but in thinking the abstract concept we do not enact any of these efferent processes to enough of an extent to make most of the images actually occur in consciousness. Yet in being in a state of preparedness or readiness to execute any of these images, we stand ready to 'look for' them, and in fact are at least partially geared up toward 'looking for' them in the same way that we would be if the images were to occur. This implies that an efferent process is occurring which has something in common with the efferent processes that would occur if any of these images were to occur, but is truncated so that none of them do occur. The neurophysiological correlate of an abstract concept, then, must be some sort of truncated efferent response.   Note, however, that a 'truncated efferent response' is a *physiological* process, not necessarily a conscious one, and it need not duplicate some earlier conscious process, or even a part of such a process. It may be accompanied by its own unique conscious correlate, but this conscious correlate need not be equivalent with any state of consciousness that occurred at some earlier time as part of a larger conscious process which (some might suppose) has now become truncated.

We know that the frontal lobe is much more developed in brains that are able to use sophisticated abstract concepts, such as the brains of humans, and we know that inhibitory neurotransmitters are more richly distributed in the frontal lobe than elsewhere, and are more plentiful in humans than in other animals (Cohen *et al* 1988; Kahneman 1973; Posner and Rothbart 1992: 98-99; Luria 1973, 1980).   Furthermore, our previous discussions of the efferent 'looking for' process that grounds mental images showed that this process is controlled with the participation of the frontal lobe, which guides the activity of 'looking for' in directions important for the emotional purposes of the organism, for example by controlling the selective inattention process (Mele 1993; Rhodes *et al* 1993; Lavy *et al* 1994; Sedikedes 1992).   The frontal lobe is elaborately connected with the midbrain (see Luria, for example), and the activation of the frontal lobe (as when we formulate a challenging question and try to answer it) in turn activates other areas of the cerebrum such as the parietal and temporal lobes; if answering the question involves observation, the frontal lobe activity also activates the primary sensory areas such as in the occipital lobe (as we saw in Chapter 1). It is therefore very probable that the way the frontal lobe accomplishes the truncating of image formations needed to shape a combination of related images into a concept operates at least in part by the chemical inhibition of the efferent responses corresponding to those images. This would be consistent with the observation that, when subjects think about abstractions, their occipital lobes are not very active (Posner and Rothbart 1992; Farah 1989).

In using the concept of inhibition in this context, it is important to notice that to inhibit a response is not merely to stop it midway. When an efferent response is inhibited, there is something more specific going on than merely stopping the response from occurring. What I mean can easily be made obvious by an example. Consider a 'checked swing' in baseball. A batter must always be ready to stop his swing at the latest possible moment if the ball curves, or if the pitch turns out to be different from what was expected. But a batter who 'checks' his swing is not merely stopping it. There are many different ways of stopping a swing that a batter would not want to use because they would constrain his choice too soon and ruin the form of his normal swing. To *check* a swing, on the contrary, is to stop it *in just such a way* that we *could* have continued it if we had wanted to. One of the main causes of 'batting slumps' among baseball players, in fact, is the temptation to rely on ways of checking the swing that, if they become habitual, interfere with the normal swing when it is not checked. For example, it is easier to stop a swing midway if the batter plants the front foot in such a way that it pushes back against the momentum of the swing. But if he plants it too firmly, he will develop the habit of readying himself to plant it in this way, so that his normal swing loses much of its power due to the opposition this creates to the normal momentum of the swing. On the other hand, the front foot must always be in a condition of readiness to plant if the pitch turns out to be unhittable. Thus the swing must be stopped in just such a particular way that the hitter feels that, up to the instant when it was stopped, he *could have* allowed it to continue in its normal, uninhibited way.

Inhibition means to 'check' a response in this sense rather than merely to stop it in the easiest or most convenient way. This is why the continual inhibition of a response does not necessarily lead to the eventual extinction of the response (Miller 1981: 139). To inhibit the response is to stop it in such a way that we could have allowed it to continue if we had wanted to.

One aspect of what it means to think a concept which is not equivalent with a simple, conscious image, then, is that we perform an efferent response that puts us in the condition of standing ready to execute any of several interrelated images, but inhibits the possible continuations of this response which would occur if we were to actually entertain the images in consciousness. The fact that we are in a condition of readiness to continue with the execution of the images, even though we do not do so, means that this execution is inhibited, not just that it does not occur. The condition of readiness consists in the fact that the entire sequence of images needed to define the concept *would* occur if not inhibited.

Furthermore, if someone says 'conservative forces in Russia oppose privatization,' the context of the use of 'conservative' is enough to make me feel that, if I were to explicate 'conservative' in this context, the explication would be in the direction of the set of images needed to ostensively clarify the notion 'fear of rapid change' rather than 'condemnatory attitudes toward the weak and disadvantaged who refuse to pull themselves up by their bootstraps' or 'hatred and fear of homosexuals.' When I execute the truncated efferent response in this context, it is done in a way whose momentum is carrying it more in the direction of this explication than the others. To say that I understand the concept in this context is, again, to say that I feel confident that I could explicate the sequence of images that ultimately would be needed to explicate it in this context.

## 3. Future Anticipations and Subjunctive Conditionals

Still another aspect of abstract concepts that must be integrated into this account is that concepts are subjunctive in nature. The most sophisticated concepts, in fact (and the ones that most involve frontal lobe activity), are *subjunctive conditionals*. (We know this because of the comparative performance of humans and other animals on complex discrimination studies — for example, see Premack 1988). This fact can help us further to understand how the frontal lobe is involved in producing concepts that are not merely equivalent with the mental image of the moment. The subjunctive conditional is a modification of a closely related mental activity — the expectation as to what will happen in the future given certain conditions (as suggested by Legrenzi, Girotto and Johnson-Laird 1993). I.e., the difference between 'If I throw this object at that one, this one will knock that one over' on the one hand, and on the other hand 'If I *were* to throw this object at that one, it *would* knock that one over' is very slight. What is the difference? It is only that the subjunctive conditional is an attempt to generalize the conditional future expectation to a slightly broader context, and this context is made broader in two ways. First, it is broadened in that, given my total past experience with physical objects, I would be willing to bet that this object would knock that one over, not just if I throw it right now, but also if some of the contextual circumstances were to be changed. For example, even if I and the two objects were in some different place or if some of the surrounding objects were not present, I would still feel confident that this one would knock that one over. I know this because I can *imagine* throwing it under those different circumstances, and I can proprioceptively imagine myself feeling confident, under those circumstances, that this one would knock that one over. (Newton 1994 has developed this point further still toward a theory of understanding based on the proprioceptive imagining of oneself performing a goal-directed action.)

The second way in which the context of a conditional future expectation can be broadened to yield a subjunctive conditional is to broaden its *chronological* context. The conditional expectation applies only in the narrow context of here and now. But I can remember from past experience that, whenever I said that I *could* do something, but then chose *not* to do it, I did not lose my feeling of confidence, after the fact, that I had told the truth when I said that I could do it. So I know from experience that, if I tell the truth now, it will still be the case later that I told the truth when I did tell it. Thus I feel confident that anything that *will* be true a moment from now, *will have been* true at any point in the future. I therefore feel confident that, if this will knock that over here and now, it would also knock it over in a variety of other times and places, even including past times, provided that certain key ingredients of the situation are (or were) present — for example, that I do not have a sore arm, that the object is not glued or nailed to its resting place, etc.

We see, then, that it is possible to provide a neurophysiological accounting of the way in which a condition of readiness or preparedness to execute a series of images can occur at a specific point in a series of mental events during logical reasoning, even though the images that we stand ready to execute do not actually occur at that particular point in time. The accounting of the 'imageless concept' is thus imagistic in two senses: First, it is facilitated only because of readiness to re-enact previous interrelated images whose explication would constitute the definition of the concept if we were called upon to define it. And secondly, in the context of ongoing thought processes such as logical reasoning, the 'imageless concept' occurs as part of a larger pattern — often recognized as a rhythm pattern — which in turn constitutes a pattern of which we can form an image (though not necessarily a visual one). This manipulation of concepts within larger patterns will be discussed further in the next chapter.

If the subjunctive conditional is this similar in cognitive content to a conditional expectation for future events, then it would be very surprising indeed if it did not involve similar neurophysiological substrates as well. These neurophysiological substrates will thus hinge on the inhibition of a series of related imaginings which we feel ready to execute, but do not actually execute unless we feel a need to explicate the concept in question by giving a (directly or indirectly) ostensive definition of it. This truncated efferent act always involves subjunctive conditional anticipations. And it takes place primarily through frontal activity. In believing that one thing will or would lead to another, we are imagining a future or possible occurrence which we feel confident will or would occur, given certain actual or imaginable conditions (in agreement with Johnson-Laird 1994). There is no need to imagine *all* the conditions for the expected event — just the ones which are crucial for our feeling of confidence that we can predict what would happen. By leaving out of account the irrelevant surrounding objects, we in effect say that *where* the event occurs is irrelevant. And by feeling confident that whatever is true now *will have been* true in the future, we say that *when* the event occurs is irrelevant. Thus it would seem that we focus on the relevant aspects of a conditional (i.e., those aspects that make us feel confident of our prediction as to what will happen) by *inhibiting* the irrelevant aspects in our imagination of the scenario in question. The reason we feel that we know which aspects are irrelevant is that the feeling of confidence in our predictions is not associated with them, but rather with the relevant aspects. All of this is also consistent with the findings of Legrenzi, Girotto, and Johnson-Laird (1993) that subjects 'focus' only on aspects of situations that are relevant to planning and hypothesis-testing (and this is certainly true whether or not one agrees with these authors' theory that all of this planning and hypothesis testing is done by means of 'mental models').

In order to feel confident that something would occur in a certain way under a variety of circumstances, we imagine the scene, but inhibit our imagination of the irrelevant elements in it. For example, whether the object we throw is round, square, or some other shape is irrelevant to our feeling of confidence that we can predict what would happen, so we inhibit those aspects of the imaginative act that would show the object as having a certain shape. We *begin* the imaginative act in a way that would apply to any physical object (for example, the feeling that 'it would resist me,' that 'it would be more or less heavy,' etc.), but as soon as the image is about to become more specific than necessary (for example, the feeling that 'it would resist me more sharply at the corners than on the surfaces, and thus is a several-sided or squared-off object rather than a sphere' or 'it would be so heavy as to strain me in lifting it'), at that point any further continuation of the imaginative act is inhibited, because we have learned that this kind of inhibition helps us to focus on the aspects of events that are the relevant ones for predicting what will happen now or what would happen at any time under those relevant circumstances. The reason is that failure to inhibit irrelevant aspects of the context would result in less reliable predictions. This is consistent with Ahn and Medin's (1992) findings that, in sorting tasks designed to test what kinds of categories people use, they "impose more structure than the examples support in the first stage and that the second stage adjusts for this difference between preferred and perceived structure (81)." Ahn and Medin in essence are observing the effects of neural inhibition on concept formation.

When we say that we have 'understood' a situation, we therefore mean that we have succeeded in imagining the essential conditions which would allow us to feel confident of being able to predict what will or would happen, while inhibiting our imagination of the irrelevant aspects. This involves truncating efferent neurophysiological responses so that only the ones corresponding to more general characteristics of objects are allowed to occur. And this is true whether the concept is a causal one or merely the concept of a unitary entity or relation. Even when we imagine a unitary entity, such as a physical object, we are imagining what would happen if we were to manipulate it in various ways.

A simple experiment by Becker and Ward (1991) sheds interesting light on this point. It is found that preschoolers can ignore postural variation in identifying animate objects, while small but essential differences crucial to the classification of the animal are taken into account. "Preschoolers distinguish shape differences that are related to category membership from those that indicate temporary postural changes (3)." This shows that children identify types of objects despite postural variation by imagining that the object could be 'bent' here and there without changing its identity. In identifying objects, then, we imagine what could and could not be *done* if we were to perform some manipulation of the object.

This implies that abstract concepts ultimately must include some idea of what could be done if the object were manipulated in some way, and this in turn means the prediction as to what will or would happen if we were to do something — a conditional future anticipation which, in the case of truly abstract conceptualization, becomes a subjunctive conditional. In this sense, abstract concepts — concepts which are more than mere images — involve the partial inhibition of images of possible conditional futures, which is the same as saying that they involve subjunctive conditionals. A cube is an object which, if held in the hand, would resist me in certain ways and not others. A soft, fluffy surface is one which, if crawled on, would not hurt my knees as much as a hard surface that reflects light more uniformly.

We saw earlier that, during the feedback loop which occurs between efferent and afferent systems during the approximately one-third of a second needed to consciously register an unexpected stimulus (subsequent to primary sensory area activation), when we move from the 'looking for' to the 'looking at' mode of consciousness, we are moving from the more general to the more specific features of the object. For example, when a baseball is thrown toward a batter, he checks first to see whether the object is moving directly toward him (and, if so, he gets out of the way before even noticing any of the object's other features); then he notices whether it is moving fast or slow; then whether it is spinning or not; then whether it is moving toward the strike zone; then whether it is moving in a straight line or curving. None of these more specific observations are made if he truncates the process (for example, in order to get out of the way). We thus may sometimes say only that 'something was going to hit us' (for example, while running through dense woods) without knowing what it was or even what color it was — i.e., without having specified any detailed features of the object.

This would imply that the human brain is organized in such a way that we look first for the more general features of objects and then, as we receive more and more feedback, we focus on more and more specific features. And it is consistent with Gelman's (1993) findings that, in early childhood, 'first principles' (i.e., very general categories such as animate vs. inanimate) "organize attention to and learning about relevant data (79)." Because we look first for very general features, then for more detailed descriptions, we are able to use cybernetic feedback loops to quickly make our efferent 'looking for' activity match the afferent activity of the primary and secondary projection areas in the various sensory modalities. Rather than 'feedback loops,' it might be more appropriate to use Pribram's (1974) term 'feed*forward* loops' — meaning that we first look for something, and what we receive is largely selected in accordance with what we are looking for (Mele 1993; Rhodes *et. al.* 1993; Lavy *et al* 1994; Sedikedes 1992). I.e., we select what is important to focus our attention on for the emotional-motivational purposes of the organism, rather than passively receiving information to which we react — as Chapter 1 emphasized.


## 4. Conclusion

To pull together these various points about inhibition, subjunctive conditionals and efferent activity in the frontal lobe, then: we can say that to entertain an abstract concept is to be in a condition of preparedness which makes us feel confident that we can predict what will or would happen given certain conditions. The more abstract the concept, the more the specific elements in the context become irrelevant to this feeling of confidence. For example, when I think the physical proposition 'F = MA', the size, shape and color of imaginary objects that would be used to explicate this interconnection of concepts are all irrelevant, and are not allowed to influence the feeling of confidence in our predictions. (We learned in early childhood to inhibit this influence.) The mechanism by which the act of imagination is truncated is likely to be by using inhibitory neural transmitters, since that is the way perceptual events are inhibited, and since according to Farah (1989: 395) "mental imagery involves the efferent activation of visual areas in prestriate occipital cortex, parietal and temporal cortex, and . . . these areas represent the same kinds of specialized visual information in imagery as they do in perception." These inhibitory transmitters must be closely related to and controlled by frontal lobe activity in order to allow abstract, conceptual predictive ability, because the frontal lobe is where the 'looking for' process is first orchestrated (Posner and Rothbart 1992; Ellis 1990). The 'looking for' must be truncated before it becomes too specific an image (for example, if the posterior parietal area or the secondary area of the occipital lobe were to become too involved) — otherwise the features of the situation that are irrelevant for accurate prediction cannot be ignored, and predictions become correspondingly unreliable. In effect, we then end up with false subjunctives such as 'If I wear a certain necklace, I will be more likely to hit the ball' or 'If John had not played the trombone, he would not have died of lung cancer.' What is happening in the false subjunctives is that irrelevant aspects of scenarios are not being inhibited in the conditional future anticipations and subjunctive conditionals that are formed. The same thing happens when monkeys fail to solve complex multiple-discrimination tasks, and when scientists fail to use adequate experimental controls for possible intervening variables in explaining a correlational finding. The same point can be made for concepts that merely define entities. Someone who has heard only frivolous, showy performances of Chopin's music may think of the music itself as frivolous and showy. What is happening here is a failure to inhibit the association of the *way in which the music has been played* from the content of the music being played.

The frontal lobe thus facilitates the focusing of attention and both conceptual and hypothetical thinking by partially inhibiting imaginative acts which may involve non-present objects or events. We know that lobotomized patients and animals with less extensive frontal cortex are less able to handle any of the skills just mentioned (for example, see Posner and Rothbart 1992; Luria 1980; Pribram 1974). They are less able to focus attention, and to control *how* they focus it. They are not good with abstract concepts or with solving complex multiple-discrimination tasks. They are unable to voluntarily reconstruct images from memory (which involves imagining a non-present object in an active rather than passive way). And they do not plan well in light of possible future contingencies. All these functions of the frontal lobe are consistent with the theory that imagination involves motivated efferent activity which anticipates possible perceptual input; that this emotional motivation at first involves primarily midbrain activity, which then activates the cerebral cortex, and especially the frontal lobe, to instigate an efferent process of 'looking for' which would result in perception if it were to find a match with corresponding activity in the primary sensory areas; that the motivation to predict what will or would happen in certain circumstances leads to an inhibitory truncating of imaginative efferent response patterns to focus attention away from irrelevant circumstances so as to increase predictive power; that this inhibitory process is largely carried out by the frontal lobe, which is rich in inhibitory neurotransmitters; and that the control of attention is motivated when the emotional reticular system activates the frontal lobe (richly interconnected with the reticular system) to 'look for' (via an efferent pattern of activity) objects and events that are emotionally important for the organism, prior to the point where afferent input would be perceived and responded to.

The kind of 'questioning' the frontal lobe is responsible for, then, is essentially *hypothesis*-questioning — i.e., questioning what would happen if certain imaginable conditions were present or absent, and which conditions are the relevant ones. It is an essentially hypothetical and subjunctive kind of questioning which asks, 'What would happen if things were different — if aspects of what is present were absent or if aspects of what is absent were present?' This is what I mean by the subjunctive imaginative and questioning process which I am claiming is at the heart of consciousness.

To ask a question is partly a motivational emotion and partly an act of imagination or conceptualization. It means to *desire* that a coordination be achieved between a 'looking for' and a 'looking at.' This could mean finding out whether an image is instantiated in perception (which is discovered through the coordination of efferent and afferent activity), or it could mean finding out whether a concept (i.e., a refinement of efferent 'looking for' activities) is coordinated with a feeling of confidence that if we were to explicate the concept it would yield images that would match *anticipated* perceptions, even though the actual explication of each of these anticipated perceptions is truncated through inhibition.

If this is the way conceptualization occurs in human consciousness, then we should be able to take another step and apply this analysis to the way the human brain executes *conceptual thinking*. In particular, it is often objected against such emphasis on manipulation of mental images that logical thought proceeds by means of the application of *inference rules* (Smith, Langston and Nisbett 1992; Jonathan Evans 1993) — not by means of imagistic manipulation of 'mental models' (Johnson-Laird and Byrn 1989, 1991, 1993, 1994). How can deductive-logical inferences be explained on the basis of the theory of selectively inhibited efferent functioning, given that the everyday use of inference rules does not always (or even usually) seem to involve mental images? Moreover, even if the thinking of an abstract concept can be explained in the way just indicated — as a readiness to execute a series of interrelated images — this does not account for how we are able to make logical inferences based on the meanings of these concepts *without taking the time to explicate them* in this way. As Bonatti (1994) reminds us, we usually execute formal inference rules without taking the time to call up images or to consciously explicate the meanings of terms. This problem will be considered next.

# CHAPTER THREE

# Images, Logic, and Mental Development

Now that we have seen how concepts are built up from the more elementary mental images, it will be possible to show how logical rule-governed thinking skills are developed. Not only is it possible, but it is also necessary to show this, since the use of inference rules is a kind of conceptual thinking for which we have not yet accounted. After describing in section 1 the way users of logic rely on imagery (not so much visual, but kinaesthetic and proprioceptive rhythm-pattern imagery), we can then explore, in section 2, the child-development issues relevant not only to the learning of logical skills, but also to the evolution of the kind of abstract concepts discussed in the previous chapter. Finally, section 3 will explore some general implications for cognitive theory of the approach being developed here.

## 1. How Logical Inference Rules Are Acquired and Executed

The recent shift in cognitive theory away from digital computer-like thought processes and toward parallel, widely distributed processing and more fuzzy, human-like thought patterns, exhibiting such features as holism, gradual decay voluntary search, and the 'pragmatic' use of 'mental models,' has raised renewed interest in the nature and cognitive role of mental images. Part of the fascination with imagery in recent cognitive theory is that the neural substrates of images seem to be holistic if anything is. If a visual image is first confined to activity of the parietal lobe, and then spreads to activate the secondary projection area of the occipital lobe and to increase the activation of the posterior parietal lobe, the image does not change its basic character or appearance due to this additional neural activity, but only becomes more 'vivid' (Paivio 1986: 25ff). Thus images are paradigm examples of mental processes which seem to lack any one-to-one correspondence between isolable elements in the image and isolable elements in the neurophysiological events that subserve the image. Of course, holistic *processing* does not necessarily entail a holism of *content,* but the fact that the substrates of imagery tend to be holistic lends them a special interest in the current climate of cognitive theory.

The complement of holism is gradual decay: As more and more brain matter is deactivated from the pattern of the image, the image becomes less sharp but retains its general contour. Images also if anything are motivated by voluntary search, often arising not from sensory input but from the organism's sense of what it needs to 'look for' prior to the corresponding sensory input (Aurell 1989: 747ff; Ellis 1990; Mele 1993: 19). Even the conscious registering of a perceptual input presupposes a motivated attentional process before perceptual consciousness (i.e., a perceptual image) can occur (Logan 1980; Ellis 1990; Posner and Rothbart 1992: 91ff).

Finally, the way in which humans *use* imagery in their thinking promises to be one of the factors that cause human problem solving processes to differ from those of computers. Many of the 'pragmatic' factors that can either facilitate or interfere with logical problem solving (Dascal 1987) involve our need to manipulate images in order to get the logical structures of ideas and thought patterns to register in our awareness (or in Johnson-Laird's 1983 terms, to allow us to form a 'mental model' of a situation).

Current thinking on the role of images in thinking can be divided into two main types, with some people taking a compromise position somewhere between them. At one end of the spectrum are what might be called thoroughgoing imagists like Eleanor Rosch (1975), Natika Newton (1993), Mark Johnson (1987), and Francisco Varela (1992), who emphasize a more fundamental role for images than for logical processes. They postulate that logical thinking necessarily makes use of mental images because it is built up by means of complex combinations of images in various modalities and in various patterns. The image corresponds to the more basic neurophysiological event, whereas logical inference is a derivative event which can occur only because images are combined and used in certain ways. Until very recently, this approach suffered from the major handicap that it focused almost exclusively on *visual* imagery and ignored the role of other modalities, including kinaesthesia, proprioception and audition, in inferential thought processes. Newton (1982, 1993) in particular has now begun to emphasize these other modalities. Following up on the work of Newton, Premack (1988), Dascal (1987), Cutler (1994), Boden (1982), Shaver, Pierson and Lang (1974-1975), and Kaufman (1980), I shall argue here that the execution of logical inferences occurs not only through visual imagery, but also through the imaging and recognition of rhythm patterns corresponding to logical syntax. Thus the thesis that imagery grounds logical inference cannot so easily be rejected simply because experimentors have failed to correlate all forms of logical inferences with *visual* imagery.

At the opposite extreme from this imagistic approach are the thoroughgoing 'computationalists' such as Dennett (1991), Pylyshyn (1973), P.M. Churchland (1979) and P.S. Churchland (1986), who maintain that the computer analogy remains the appropriate model for cognition because, even if processing is parallel, widely distributed or even holistic, such processing still occurs just as it would in a suitably complex computational machine designed along connectionist or something like connectionist lines. Even if information storage is only 'in the weights,' as the connectionists say (Bechtel 1987; Neisser, 1994), this is still just another way in which information is stored, just as music on old phonograph records was stored 'in the grooves' (McCauley 1994). Images are merely one of the types of output that information can exhibit once it has been processed using computational programs, just as certain robots are programmed to recognize faces, etc., by analyzing the patterns of features that enter their perceptual fields. According to this approach, images that occur during logical thought play the same role as illustrations in a physics textbook: They are neither necessary nor sufficient to move forward the thinking that is being done, but are only epiphenomena of the logical processing of information which is being illustrated by the imagery, and serve only to provide a quick and synoptic intuitive view of a situation; the important point here is that the illustration alone is inadequate to represent the situation being illustrated, and cannot even be understood *as* an illustration of that situation unless we first understand the situation itself in terms which remain independent of any illustration, and which are capable of standing alone. These latter terms, they hold — these purely inferential and computational terms — may sometimes *produce* mental images in the ways posited by Kosslyn (1983) or Paivio (1986), but are not themselves *produced by* imaging processes. If the angles, lines and contours received by the primary projection area are digitally analyzed to produce the image, it is argued, then a process of computational inference occurs *prior to* the image; therefore, the process of logical inference itself cannot presuppose images.

The term 'computational' has been used in a variety of senses, but essentially it involves the assumption that the nervous system enacts a 'program' (which could be written as if it were a computer program) that specifies certain 'operations' (which can be designated as logical or quasi-logical operations) to be performed on incoming 'information,' and that this incoming information can be analyzed into units capable of subserving the operations to be performed on it as specified in the program. Thus images occur as a *result* of information processing; the logical operations themselves cannot be dependent for their occurrence on some prior or more basic imagery.

Computationalists (for example, Dennett 1991: 459-460 and passim) also reject any foundational role for imagery in logical thinking for another reason: Using the definition of 'computational' given above, one could say that all events in nature are 'computational' in a way that does not require conscious states such as images. For example, when an electric eye door opens, it has 'computed' that something entered its visual field. In the same sense we could say that, when we run hot water onto a jar lid in order to expand the lid, the metal in the lid 'computes' the temperature of the water, thus calculating the appropriate amount of expansion and reacting accordingly. Obviously, if we want to call this a 'computational inference,' then every transfer of information would be a computational inference, and thus every cause-and-effect sequence in nature would be a computational inference. But imagists will argue that, if we disregard this trivial sense in which computational inferences are more basic than images (and more basic than anything else for that matter), and use terms like 'logical inference,' 'abstract thinking,' and 'computation' to refer to the thought processes which we actually undergo when we make a logical inference or which in principle would be accessible to consciousness if the inference were to occur on a conscious level — then we can meaningfully ask whether it is the images that are more primary than the logical inferences (or 'computations') or *vice versa,* and whether the logical inferences are built up *by means of* patterns of imaging — allowing, again, that by 'images' we mean to include auditory, kinaesthetic and proprioceptive images rather than just visual ones. This is one of the central questions that divide what I call 'imagists' and 'computationalists.'

Thoroughgoing imagists, such as Rosch (1975) and Newton (1993), reject models which attribute priority to computation over imagery because they hold that we do not first make inferences to analyze the logical implications of incoming information and then on the basis of these logical inferences construct images. Instead they argue that logical inference results from images, which are the more basic occurrence, rather than the other way around. Newton (1993) cites four important types of reasons for preferring this view. First, her 'expanded' version of the imagist view (expanded to include imagery in nonvisual, including sensorimotor, modalities) is consistent with the way humans, by conrast to computers, actually reason: "If deductive logic determines human reasoning, then we would be expected to draw certain types of inferences, but we rarely do so. . . . Deductive logic dictates that the logical implications of true beliefs are true. But no one believes all of the logical implications of his or her beliefs (Newton 1993: 276)." As another example of this point, "Even after success with realistic content, . . . [subjects] fail to transfer the reasoning pattern to absract problems. . . . This result is unexplained if people reason by logical inference rules, which apply in abstract as well as realistic situations (Newton 1993: 277)." A second argument is that the imagist view is consistent with the way the human brain is organized. For example, "the language system is closely associated . . . with certain motor processing systems, and . . . it does not independently determine the structure of higher cognitive abilities. . . . [One of these systems is] the supplementary motor area (SMA) [in the frontal cortex] . . . [which] has many reciprocal connections with the posterior parietal area, a region involved in somatosensory perception and bodily orientation. . . . Activity in the SMA is associated with the formation of a conscious intention . . . [and is] equally active whether the subject is actually carrying out the plans or merely imagining them (Newton 1993: 284-286)." A third type of argument for the imagist approach is that it is consistent with evolutionary evidence. For example, "Premack [1988] show[s] that apes can apply relations between physical objects analogically to relations themselves, and thus that they have the basic cognitive apparatus necessary for mental model use. . . . Cognitive differences between apes and humans do not depend on language; rather they turn on . . . attentional selection of abstract features or aspects of sensorimotor representations . . . rather than the existence of a separate conceptual system (Newton 1993: 291). A final argument for an imagist view (again, expanded to include nonvisual modalities) is that it is consistent with the way humans *consciously experience* themselves as reasoning, and thus can account for 'intrinsic intentionality' (see Newton 1993: 294-296).

Between these extremes is a possible intermediate position which holds that neither imagination nor inferential thinking is more basic or elementary than the other, but rather the two kinds of mental processes are simply different and independent, although often interrelated. Inference is not based on images, nor are images produced as the result of inferential processes. Given the contentious and reductionist bent of philosophers and scientists, it is not surprising that proponents of this moderate compromise position are more difficult to find than the other two, but Kosslyn (1983), Michel Denis (1991) and Johnson-Laird (1972, 1994) seem to be examples. According to Kosslyn, imagery is a useful tool for the performance of spatial and perceptual tasks, but is hardly a necessary ingredient of all thought processes, and definitely is not necessary for deductive logical inferences. According to Denis (1991: 104), "imagery is not the *core* of thought processes, but rather a potential *medium* for them." Denis also interprets the data of Shaver, Pierson and Lang (1974-1975) along the same lines:

> Their experiments on syllogistic reasoning provide evidence that imagery, without being a necessary component of processes involved in reasoning, has a significant facilitatory effect on reasoning. Their data suggest that some problems are more likely than others to benefit from strategies relying on *visualization* (Denis 1991: 106, italics added; note again the emphasis on *visual* imagery).

Johnson-Laird (1972; 1983; 1994) also remains neutral as to whether and to what extent reasoning relies on imagery. Although imagery might seem to be a likely possible way of realizing 'mental models,' the mental models themselves are not images, and Johnson-Laird leaves open the possibility that they could be realized in some other way. This chapter will extend Johnson-

Laird's reasoning and suggest that mental models are indeed realized by means of complex combinations of imagery — not only visual, but also the imaging of rhythm patterns and sensorimotor and proprioceptive conditions. The notion that we use imagery in other than visual modalities when learning and/or applying inference rules is highly consistent with Johnson-Laird's approach. That people construct mental models does not entail that the models are always (or even usually) *visualized*. In fact, Johnson-Laird explicitly acknowledges this point: For example, "[a model] may be experienced as a visual image, though what matters is not so much the subjective experience as the structure of the model (Johnson-Laird 1994: 192)." And "[visual images are] views of models (Johnson-Laird 1983: 157)." The visual images themselves are not the models. The extension of inference rule usage to situations that involve auditory and proprioceptive rather than visual imagery therefore does not contradict mental model theory, but does suggest that modalities other than visualization often ground the construction and use of our models of the way the world works.

I shall thus argue here for a version of the imagist view which in principle is consistent with the notion that 'computations' (in the sense defined above) are built up from images. The key to seeing how images are used to facilitate logical inference is to shift our attention away from the 'visualization' which Shaver, Pierson and Lang (1974-1975), Johnson-Laird (1972; 1994), Mark Johnson (1987), and most other researchers in this area have concentrated on. In making this shift away from visual images, I am making use of the suggestion continually emphasized by Newton, that we should broaden the field of image research to include these other modalities, which are just as important as the visual modality, and often (as in the present context) are *more* important. Of course, it is true that, when a problem especially lends itself to visual imagery (for example, 'Tom is taller than Sam and John is shorter than Sam'), it is not surprising that subjects visualize the situation, as Huttenlocher (1968) shows. But when inferences are made in contexts where the problem being reasoned about is not particularly visual by its very nature (for example, when subjects must use inference rules such as *modus tollens* or hypothetical syllogism with regard to concepts which themselves are not necessarily imaged), it becomes important to see how imagery in other modalities is involved, especially auditory and proprioceptive rhythm-pattern imagery.

The objection might be raised that this broadening of the term 'image' to include these other modalities merely ambiguates the term rather than clarifying it. Some would say that, by definition, this would construe any instance of memory retrieval as an 'image.' But, even if it were true that memory retrieval always involves an imagistic component (as some researchers, such as Luria 1968 and Restak 1984 think that it does), this would not make 'imagery' in our broadened sense *equivalent with* memory retrieval, but rather only a component part of it. The fact is that we *can* imagine what it would be like to hear, smell or emotionally feel something, and to do so is just as much to form an image as to imagine what something looks like. Similarly, we can imagine what it would be like to undergo a sensorimotor or proprioceptive state (for example, 'what it would feel like to ride a roller coaster'), and this too is a kind of imagery.

The idea that human subjects often rely just as crucially on non-visual as on visual imagery when doing everyday logical reasoning is consistent with the findings of Johnson-Laird (1972) and Kaufman (1980) that 'spatial' strategies are used to facilitate reasoning in unfamiliar contexts, but then as the reasoning task becomes more familiar the subjects switch to 'linguistic' strategies. But, again using the work of Premack (1988), Newton (1993), Dascal (1987) and Cutler (1994) as a starting point, I shall suggest that these 'linguistic' strategies can be explained in terms of rhythm-pattern recognition, which can be conceived as a kinaesthetic, proprioceptive, and in many instances auditory imaging process. These image patterns facilitate logical thought in a way very consistent with Newton's 'sensorimotor theory of cognition' (1993), in which all cognitive processes are viewed as derivative from patterns of sensorimotor (and not just visual) imagery. We shall see that Newton's theory is also correct in assigning a crucial role to the proprioceptive imaging of motivational conditions and the motivated guidance of action in logical thought processes.

*(a)  Learning and executing inference rules: Two sets of images or one?*

One way to explore the way subjects use imagery in their thinking is to examine the way logic students and other young people learn to use correct rules of logical inference in their normal thought processes.  At the age when students usually take logic courses, most of the important inference rules are already being used on a hit-or-miss basis, and the task of the logic teacher is to get them to hit more and miss less.  The most common strategy used to move students to a more sophisticated level of reasoning ability — and also the most effective one (Annis and Annis 1979) — is to get them to consciously reflect on the inference rules they rely on in their everyday deductive reasoning; to abstract the patterns they normally follow so as to formulate abstract rules such as *modus tollens* and transitivity; to make sure that invalid rules are not followed (by allowing students to see that these cannot be trusted to guarantee true conclusions from true premises); and then to consciously apply the rules to various kinds of examples in order to increase the students' skill at making reliably valid inferences.  David and Linda Annis (1979) have documented that a logic course structured in this way increased their students' IQ scores by an average of 10 points (after compensating for the normal test-retest increase, which is about 2 points).

Since the type of logic course described ay Annis and Annis apparently does improve students' ability to make logical inferences, let's consider more carefully the skills that students must master in order to learn logic in this setting.  The learning task facing a student entering a logic course structured in the way Annis and Annis (and most standard formal logic courses) have structured the course consists essentially of four components:  (1) Students must become convinced that one can tell whether an inference is valid by the *form* it takes.  We shall see that this component involves a very different cognitive process from components (2) - (4), so I shall discuss it separately after presenting the other three.  (2) The students must see that certain valid and invalid examples have certain recognizable patterns in common.  I shall argue that these similarities are grasped by means of similarities between patterns of images, not only visual but also auditory, proprioceptive, etc.  (3) They must learn to *identify* the form of a verbal argument when they see it (or hear it).  This is done by bearing in mind that, in any valid argument, *each key term must be used at least twice;* then one looks for the recurrences of 'essentially' the same term even though a synonym or synonymous phrase may be used. Semantically, the person must learn to experience synonyms as 'similar' rather than 'different'; and syntactically, certain interchangeabilities must be learned so that different-sounding syntax can be experienced as equivalent with, or transposed to, the learned pattern of the logical rule. (For example, 'John was hit by Bill' means 'Bill hit John.' In everyday logical reasoning, this becomes a matter of pattern recognition, similarly to the way a baseball player learns to recognize a fast ball, curve ball, screwball, etc.) (4) Once the students can recognize the patterns in a *visual* diagram, then they have to learn to recognize the same pattern in a *temporal rhythm* which they hear or imagine hearing when someone speaks an argument. For instance, using a notation similar to Premack's (1988: 63ff) method of designating image patterns, we could say that 'this implies that; this; therefore that' is *modus ponens,* whereas 'this implies that; that; therefore this' is the fallacy of affirming the consequent. 'This implies that; not that; therefore not this' is *modus tollens,* whereas 'this implies that; not this; therefore not that' is the fallacy of denying the antecedent. We can hear these temporal rhythms just as we would hear a recognizable pattern in music. For example, a drum beat that goes '**loud**, soft, soft, **loud, loud**, soft, soft . . .' in an even rhythm is a bossa nova. 'Boom boom **bap** boom boom boom **bap** boom . . .' is a rock beat. No one has to make a visual diagram of these relationships to recognize these temporal patterns. Logic presents a greater difficulty in hearing the pattern because the rhythms include more interruptions and requirements for transposition due to parenthetical phrases, synonymous phrases, passive voice, etc. As explained more fully below, these transpositions require past learning through experience that certain locutions are interchangeable.

Although syllogistic reasoning often may be accomplished through visualization of the relevant mental models, it is not necessary to use visualization in performing syllogistic reasoning. Such reasoning also may often be performed by means of rhythm-pattern recognition of the kind just mentioned. For example, 'Some thises are thats; all thats are such-and-suches; therefore some thises are such-and-suches,' is a rhythm pattern which can be recognized as essentially the same rhythm pattern regardless of the content of the 'thises,' 'thats,' or 'such-and-suches.' Of course, logical connectives, such as 'implies' or any of its many synonyms, obviously occupy a special place in such a rhythm pattern, analogous to a recurring dominant or tonic chord in a musical phrase. Thus 'this implies that' is heard as a very different pattern from 'this *and* that,' just as the pattern 'tonic-dominant-tonic' is distinguished from 'dominant-tonic-dominant' in music. But, if it is possible to recognize the pattern of a certain inference type in this kind of imagistic way (again, taking account of previously learned equivalences of interchangeable locutions), then it is entirely conceivable that a child can learn through experience that, anytime such-and-such a pattern is relied upon, the truth of the premises will guarantee the truth of the conclusion. I am not arguing that the recognition of rhythm patterns is *more often* important than visual imagery or *vice versa,* but simply that such rhythm pattern recognition is a possible way in which valid and invalid argument forms can be recognized even where *visual* imagery is not present; thus the lack of visual imagery in inferential thought processes does not show that such processes are not relying on imagery *per se.*

As far as the role of imagery is concerned, it is important to notice that steps (2) - (4) in the 4-step learning sequence require the acquisition of *how-to* skills, very much like performing a physical action like playing a musical instrument, and obviously they are amenable to a sensorimotor explanation. More precisely, they involve the sensorimotor imaging and recognition of rhythm patterns. Only step (1) is different. It involves becoming *convinced* that, if one were to do something a certain way, *it would work.* And what does it mean to be convinced of this? It means to have a *feeling of confidence* associated with doing it that way, accompanied with a proprioceptive image of oneself doing it that way. So the key here is to be aware that there is a very sharp distinction between *what one does when one executes a logical inference* on the one hand, and on the other hand *what one does when one initially becomes convinced that, if one were to execute it in that way, it would work.*

To make this point more convincing to experienced abstract thinkers, it might help to use a somewhat obscure type of inference as an example. Recently a friend of mine (who likes to base what he says on formal-logical rules) used the following inference in conversation: The negation of 'A implies B', he said, would be 'A and not-B' — and then he proceeded to make his point. But I had to say, 'Wait a minute — I'm not so sure of that. Let me see: If you caught the ball, I would be out. So someone who wanted to deny that would have to say you caught the ball *and* I was not out?' I had to *imagine a scenario* that followed the pattern he was talking about, and then I had to think whether it would be possible to imagine a scenario in which someone denies the original statement yet does not assert 'A and not-B' (i.e., the rhythm, 'this and not-that'). We finally realized that the problem was that we were speaking in a counterfactual context, where the rule he was using did not apply. I.e., it was imaginable that someone might deny that the rules of baseball require, under the given circumstances, that 'if he caught the ball, then I was out,' without anyone's actually having caught any ball; thus such a denial would not necessarily entail that 'he caught the ball and I was not out.' But the point is that, when I question the validity of a rule, I assign myself the task of imagining a scenario matching the rhythm of the propositions connected by the rule, in which the rule fails to work (the process described by Johnson Laird in 1994: 192ff; and also by Lewis 1973). When I see that this cannot be done, I develop the feeling of confidence that, anytime I use the rule, it will work.

As a simpler example of how confidence in such a rule might be acquired, suppose I try to imagine a scenario following the rhythm 'this implies that; not this; therefore, not that.' And suppose I choose as an example of a scenario following this rhythm, 'Voting implies being registered; this person didn't vote; therefore he wasn't registered.' I then ask myself whether it is possible to imagine the scenario corresponding to these premises, in which the conclusion is false. If so, then the rule cannot be relied on. On the other hand, suppose the rule I am considering is 'this implies that; not that; therefore, not this.' The more instances I have tried of statements matching the rhythm of the statements in the rule, in which it is *not* possible to imagine the premises true and the conclusion false, the more convinced I become that this rule *is* reliable. But there is no need to go through this whole process every time I use the rule; I only go through the process of *executing* the rule, which involves a completely *different* set of mental images (steps 2-4) from those which are involved in *becoming convinced of the validity* of the rule (step 1). Step 1 involves images, but it also involves more than images. It involves a self-questioning process (based on imagining and/or perceiving various scenarios in which a particular recognizable pattern does or does not work) as a result of which we develop a feeling of confidence associated with certain imaginable patterns, such that we feel confident that a given pattern is a reliable one. When we use the rule, of course, this feeling of confidence that the rule will work is there as well, but not the reasoning (i.e., self-questioning combined with imagining) that originally *convinced* us that we should have the feeling of confidence on this score.

The 'feeling of confidence' that a given inference pattern will work is analogous in some ways to the 'feeling of confidence' discussed in memory retrieval studies (for example, Miner and Reder 1994; Metcalfe 1993; Metcalfe 1994; Koriat, Lichtenstein and Fischhoff 1980; Reder and Ritter 1992), but the different context presented by the use of inference rules leads to a corresponding difference of function. In memory studies, the 'feeling of confidence' is distinguished from the 'feeling of knowing' in that the "feeling of knowing [is] . . . believing that a particular piece of information can be retrieved, [whereas] confidence [is] . . . believing that a particular piece of information has been correctly retrieved (Miner and Reder 1994: 49-50)." But, when we speak of a 'feeling of confidence' that, if we were to apply a certain inference pattern, it would work, the problematic nature of the notion of 'information' comes into question more than it does in mere memory retrieval. To use an inference pattern is not merely to retrieve some 'content' which is 'stored' in memory, but to feel confident of being able to *execute* a fairly complex combination of pattern-recognition *skills* which may involve numerous images which are not all in awareness when we have the feeling of confidence. It is true, of course, that the content retrieved in memory may be a complex 'how-to' skill — such as, for example, remembering how to tie a shoelace. But, in the usage intended in the present context, the 'feeling of confidence' that I can, say, tie my shoelace, does not necessarily entail remembering the specific skills involved in doing it, and thus does not entail imaging or visualizing any of these concrete steps. Similarly, to feel confident that I could execute Chopin's B Minor Sonata is not to have all the images in mind, but to feel confident that I *could* pull them up. In this respect, confidence of being able to execute an inference rule (and that this rule will work) is somewhat similar to the 'feeling of knowing' in memory studies. But, here again, the 'feeling of confidence' that an inference pattern would work is also different from the 'feeling of knowing': To feel confident that, if I were to use *modus tollens,* I would end up with a true conclusion given true premises is not at all to feel that there is some 'item of information' floating around in a storage system which I could 'retrieve' if I wanted to. The 'feeling of confidence' I mean to refer to in the present context is not confidence that I could remember how to execute the rule, but rather confidence that, if I were to use the rule, the rule would work. It is more like the feeling of confidence that a driver has, not merely of being able to remember how to turn the wheel to the left, but rather that, if the wheel *is* turned to the left, the car will indeed veer to the left. Thus the 'feeling of confidence' in the context of inference rule usage cannot be precisely equated with either the 'feeling of knowing' or the 'feeling of confidence' in memory studies, because the skill we feel confident of being able to execute is more complex in cognitive structure than either of these.

This feeling of confidence — as Metcalfe (1994: ix-xii), Koriat, Lichtenstein and Fischhoff (1980: 539-541), Reder and Ritter (1992: 55ff), and Miner and Reder (1994: 48ff) have suggested for the 'feeling of knowing' in memory studies — often occurs on an unconscious, minimally-conscious, or habituated level. For example, I may think to myself, using Metcalfe's (1994: xii) example, "I know many things about space travel, so I must know the code name for the first space module to land on the moon," without actually entertaining the name in awareness. This issue will be discussed further in a later section.

The fact that we do not feel dependent on the imagery we use in order to feel that the inference rule we are using is a valid one is one of the main reasons why non-imagists, such as Dennett (1991: 459-460) deny that thinking is reducible to the use of mental imagery. They mean that our knowledge that the rule will always work is not reducible to the imagery that we have when we *use* the rule. And this is true. But to say this does not work at all as an argument against imagism, because it does not block in the least the plausible imagist response that our knowledge that the rule will work *is* dependent on the imagery that we had (including temporal rhythms of the kind just mentioned) *when we initially became convinced that the rule would work.* As Kaufman (1980) and Shaver, Pierson and Lang (1974-1975) have shown, we often use *visual* imagery when we initially convince ourselves that a given inference pattern is correct (i.e., will work), but once we have become convinced of this, we tend to rely on linguistic patterns (or, in imagistic terms, rhythm-patterns) when applying the inference pattern in a habituated way. Thus the fact that we do not use a certain kind of imagery when executing a rule does not at all show that we did not use that type of imagery at the time when we initially underwent the process of becoming convinced that the rule would work.

There are several main objections against the 'expanded' version of imagism I have outlined here — i.e., an imagism expanded to extend the kind of imagery under consideration to other modalities besides merely the visual. By responding to these objections, not only can we see how such an 'expanded' imagism is more resistant to anti-imagist objections; by developing the thesis in light of these objections, we can also develop a more coherent form of imagist theory, capable of incorporating a much wider range of problem-solving activities than an imagism that confines itself only to visual images. Accordingly, the following three sections will suggest answers to three types of objections that are especially crucial.

## (b) How can images ground syntax?

It might be objected that word order does not necessarily correspond to the order of the concepts in the logical relation. The sentence might say 'A if B' rather than 'If A then B,' or it might say 'A is necessary for B' rather than 'B implies A.' But, as Newton (1989a), Dascal (1987), Wason and Johnson-Laird (1972) and many other researchers have shown, observing what people do when confronted with these kinds of situations only further supports the imagist view. When presented with the following example

> The number of police officers will increase if the pay and working conditions improve. The pay and working conditions have improved. Therefore, the number of police officers will increase.

logic students much more frequently say that the argument is invalid than with similar examples where the word order is closer to the logical order. Similarly, they do much better with examples involving sufficient conditions than those involving necessary conditions, because the word order matches the logical order, so there is no need to mentally reverse the order in their minds. In fact, they do much better with necessary conditions if they think of 'A is necessary for B' as meaning 'Not-A implies not-B' rather than 'B implies A.' It thus seems that, when we learn the various ways of saying the same thing in a verbal language, we go through a process in which we convince ourselves that certain locutions are interchangeable, and then we interchange them as needed in our imaginations when we need to make logical inferences. The process of convincing ourselves of these interchangeabilities would be the same process of image-pattern recognition combined with the 'feeling of confidence' (in this case, that equating them will work) as when we convince ourselves that a form of inference will work. And when our feeling of confidence about this flags for a second, we go through the process over again just to refresh it. Also, to a great extent we actually learn to associate the 'feeling of confidence' with *redundant* inference rules. For example, we might learn, as children, that 'All As are Bs; X is an A; therefore X is a B' is valid, and also learn that 'X is an A; All As are Bs; therefore X is a B,' without realizing at first that these two patterns are interchangeable. This would explain why we can often use one of two equivalent rules more easily than the other. Here again, we should remember that it is possible to entertain the image of a word order as a visual or auditory pattern, and to have learned to feel confident that this word order is interchangeable with other word orders which we can image in the same way.

In principle, the fact that we re-enact a previously learned rhythm by forming an image of that pattern could be used to explain many instances in which humans perform differently in different kinds of problem solving tasks which would be considered logically equivalent to each other by a computer. As Dascal (1987: 183-188 and passim) emphasizes, enacting inference rules is a 'pragmatic' process in which performing logically equivalent inferences in different kinds of contexts may be more or less difficult, depending on the form in which we learned the rule, contextual aspects of the problem-solving situation, the difficulty of rendering the current problem 'analogous' to the rule we learned, the need to transpose expressions in our minds to make them match a previously learned pattern, and the need to accommodate negative information to its positive implications (Wason and Jonson-Laird 1972: 25ff; Newton 1993: 276-278 and passim) — all situations presenting especially difficult transposition problems for humans. I am suggesting here that these findings can be accounted for if we view the learning and execution of inference rules as a 'pragmatic' imaging operation in which we compare the rhythm pattern of a given problem to the learned rhythms of inference rules, often requiring transposition steps and choice between redundant versions of a rule.

*(c)  How are semantic differences bridged in working with image patterns?*

Someone might also raise the following objection.  Consider the argument:

> The delusions which mislead men arise from their tendency to believe that to be true which corresponds to their wishes.  One of the strong desires which affect human beliefs is the desire to live eternally in some ideal haven of bliss.  Therefore, no one who has any understanding of the origin of delusional belief systems can fail to realize that this belief in immortality is a delusion.

In this argument, the word 'immortality' *sounds* nothing like the phrase 'live eternally in some ideal haven of bliss.'  Yet it might be argued that, if 'temporal rhythm-pattern imaging' is the crucial ingredient in making logical inferences, then the analysis of the above argument would require that we 'hear' the two locutions 'immortality' and 'live eternally in some ideal haven of bliss' as essentially 'same' rather than 'different' with regard to the pattern the argument follows.  So it could be objected that we must be doing something more abstract or 'computational' than merely recognizing a pattern of images.

But, here again, the fact that students have a great deal of trouble analyzing this argument as an instance of the fallacy of affirming the consequent supports the imagist explanation.  The fact that the 'similar' terms sound so different interferes with the imaging of the temporal rhythm, and the irrelevant phrases that have to be ignored (for example, "no one who has any understanding of the origin of delusional belief systems") also get in the way of hearing the rhythm.  But what is actually involved is a complex and pragmatic process of retrieving associations between words like 'immortality' and 'live eternally,' and hearing them as 'similar' in the same way that in music **'boom** chick' is heard as **'boom** chick' whether it is a bass drum followed by a snare drum, or a snare drum followed by a choked symbol, or a choked symbol followed by a triangle.  An accented note followed by an unaccented one is recognized as such regardless of the instruments involved. Similarly, we hear an 'A' as an 'A' whether it is played on an oboe or a trombone. Or an 'interval of a fourth' is an 'interval of a fourth' whether the first note is played on a trombone and the second on a flute, or vice versa, whether the absolute pitches of the two notes forming the interval are high or low, and regardless of what key the two notes are played in. But in order to hear them as 'similar' in the appropriate respects, we must accomplish the pragmatic task of turning our attention away from the respects in which the two patterns present themselves as 'different,' and to overcome the various transposition problems that must be contended with. Of course, these examples illustrate only the *phonological* equivalence of different *tokens,* rather than the *semantic* equivalence of *types.* But if the expanded imagist view is correct, then the way we have previously acquired understanding of a type is by recognizing similarities between the patterns of different tokens in various contexts. Moreover, I shall argue in the next section that even the entertaining of a 'type' in the context of a thought pattern is to entertain a cognitive state which in principle is recognizable as a state which includes a feeling of confidence that, if this state were 'explicated,' then the apparently 'imageless' concept (the 'type') could ultimately be defined ostensively, i.e., in terms of empirically perceivable and imaginable phenomena (i.e., 'tokens').

*(d)  How users of logic recognize rhythm patterns*

To show how the pattern-recognition process just described might work out in practice, let me give an informal example from my own experience in teaching introductory logic courses over the past 10 years. In each of these courses, I have posed to beginning students certain questions about the way they executed logical skills. At the beginning of each course, I asked students to describe their thought process when deciding, prior to any instruction, whether a simple verbal argument is valid or invalid. This question was raised during the first full class period with reference always to the same six examples — three valid and three invalid — examples such as "Jane is a citizen over 18. All citizens over 18 can vote. Therefore, Jane can vote." The six arguments were simple enough that all students correctly identified which ones were valid.

Only in about half the sections did even a single student spontaneously describe a process of forming a visual image resembling a Venn diagram, and (as I shall describe more fully below) few students visualized the actual items in the sentences, such as 'Jane,' 'vote,' etc.

But when asked whether, in one way or another, it was their "mind's ability to recognize the pattern of the argument" that enabled them to identify the correct answer, all students unanimously affirmed this description. They were simply at a loss to describe how they recognized the pattern. I also asked students whether they formed mental images of the terms in the argument — a woman named Jane, a person voting, a person over 18, some sort of citizenship document, etc. Almost none visualized any of the terms in this argument.

It was not until I read Newton's 'Sensorimotor Theory of Cognition' (1993) that it occurred to me to check to see whether *non-visual* imagery was being used by these untutored students. In the Spring of 1994, I asked the above questions, with similar results. I then asked the additional questions: "How many students pay very little attention to the *meaning* of the terms 'Jane,' 'citizen over 18,' 'vote,' etc., and instead just notice that the term 'citizen over 18' is the *same* term in both places?" *All* students raised their hands. I then asked, "How many of you recognize the pattern of the reasoning by recognizing the *rhythm pattern,* just as you would when listening to a piece of music — in this case, the rhythm pattern 'This implies that, that implies the other, therefore this implies the other'?" Again, all students raised their hands. I then asked whether they literally formed an *auditory image,* or simply imagined the 'feel' of the rhythm pattern, as if in executing a bodily skill like riding a bicycle or dancing. Students expressed a great deal of uncertainty on this point. Some thought they relied mostly on the auditory image, but also had the 'feel' of the rhythm; others emphasized the 'bodily feel' of the rhythm pattern more than the auditory image. When asked how many had both auditory images and the bodily feel of the pattern, almost all students answered affirmatively. Interestingly, the one student who had initially reported visualizing Venn diagrams now said that sometimes she visualized Venn diagrams, but that more often she just 'felt the rhythm of the argument.' Another student said that she could feel the rhythm of her eye movements as she looked over the argument. This shows that we may be kinaesthetically imagining a rhythm pattern even when we are not imagining auditory images.

In initially *learning* and *becoming convinced of the validity* of an inference rule (by contrast to executing one already learned), students in the typical logic course (of the type used by Annis and Annis, for example) must try to imagine a scenario following the pattern of the rule while asking themselves whether they feel confident that the rule in question will work. For example, when becoming convinced of *modus tollens*, they must ask themselves whether they can imagine a scenario following the pattern 'this implies that; not that; therefore, not this' in which the first two statements are true, yet the last one is false. This involves a process of forming and comparing mental images of rhythm patterns, just as *executing* a rule does. But in this case the more difficult question arises: Is the 'imagining' involved in 'imagining a scenario' of this kind really an instance of *imagery* in the sense we have been discussing?

The idea that thinking an abstract concept or 'imagining' a scenario may not necessarily involve entertaining any particular 'images' raises perhaps the most formidable of all objections against the imagist explanation of logical reasoning. The process which students must undergo when trying to imagine a scenario in which the rule in question does not work, in order to become convinced that a particular rhythm pattern will always work, is obviously a kind of imagining; but does it consist of entertaining some sort of imagery? If not, then there is still an aspect of logical thought which cannot be explained imagistically — as Wittgenstein (1953), and White (1987) emphasize. In fact, it seems obvious that not all instances of imagining can be reduced to instances of entertaining images. To imagine what it would be like to be president, as we saw in the previous chapter, does not necessarily entail having visual (or auditory or olfactory) images of the White House, or myself sitting in the president's office, or any other specific intentional object that could be used as the content of a 'mental picture.'

But the answer to this question can again be inferred from our discussion in the previous chapter of the way concepts are entertained in consciousness. Each time we entertain a concept, such as 'president,' we are putting ourselves into a 'condition of readiness' to execute a series of interrelated images if the need should arise. The condition of readiness to explicate the concept 'president' is different from the condition of readiness to execute the concept 'liberal.' We can sense proprioceptively that these two conditions of readiness are not the same, and when we use the 'proprioceptive sensings' of the two conditions of readiness in the context of a pattern of inference, we count them as 'different' rather than 'same.' If someone says 'To be president is to be a liberal, because President Smith is a liberal,' the natural response is to begin explicating the concepts 'liberal' and 'president' to show that some elements in one concept are not present in the other and *vice versa.* This would be one justification for counting them as 'different' rather than 'same' when they occur in a logical argument. But if we are not asked to justify this, then we simply refer to our felt senses of the two concepts, which we can already sense are different without bothering to explicate them.

It is possible to *imagine* what it would be like to have the kind of conscious state that we have when we know what something means, just as we can imagine what it would be like to ride a roller coaster or to ride a bicycle. What we are doing when we imagine this is to *form a proprioceptive image.* To be sure, this is not a visual, auditory or olfactory image. But it is an image in the sense that we are imagining what a certain state of consciousness would be like, without literally being *in* that state at the moment.

To imagine what it would be like to see the Parthenon is to have an image of the Parthenon. In the same way, to imagine what it would be like to feel confident of being able to explicate the meaning of 'president' is to form an image — in this case, a proprioceptive one — of the concept 'president,' just as a musician who feels confident of being able to execute Chopin's B Minor Sonata has a proprioceptive 'image' (in this expanded sense) of the B Minor Sonata.

If it is allowed that some account similar to the above of the role of images in 'imageless' concepts is possible, then the last of our three main objections against the imagist view of inferential thought processes can be laid to rest. The objection was that, in order to acquire an initial feeling of confidence that a certain inference pattern will work, I must try to 'imagine a scenario' in which the pattern fails to work. In 'imagining' such a scenario, I am often imagining abstract concepts rather than concretely visualizable images. Thus at least part of what we do in logical thinking — the part that involves our real 'understanding' of the inference rules — is not dependent on images.

The response to this objection is that, if knowing what the concept 'president' means is to *stand ready* to form a series of (visual, auditory, proprioceptive, sensorimotor, etc.) images (i.e., to feel confident of being able to explicate the concept if needed — a feeling of 'readiness' to entertain certain patterns of images), then to try to imagine a scenario in which, let us say, 'Everyone holds the president responsible for every problem' *is* to put ourselves into a recognizable mental state in which we feel able to entertain a pattern of images should we wish to, although we normally inhibit the full carrying out of the imaging activity involved. Moreover, we must have carried out such imaging activities in the past in order to feel confident of being able to do so now, should we wish to. And we must be able to recognize a proprioceptive condition which is our signal that we *could* do so if we wished. So, in Newton's expanded sense of 'images,' even the process of becoming convinced of the validity of an inference rule must have been dependent, at some point or points in time, to some combination of imaginings.

Furthermore, the mental act in which we stand ready to execute the ostensive (and thus imagistic) definition, but without actually doing so, can itself form one of the elements of a rhythm pattern which in turn is recognizable as matching or failing to match a certain imageable pattern which has been learned in the past. Thus the term 'president,' without actually being an image, can correspond to a mental act which itself is part of an imageable pattern. To think 'Being President implies being elected; I was not elected; therefore I am not President,' involves imagining an instance of the overall pattern 'This implies that; not-that; therefore, not-this' — just as much so as if the terms of the argument were simple, imageable physical objects.

This expanded role for images in inferential thinking would also be consistent with the finding of Kaufman (1980) and Shaver, Pierson and Lang (1974-1975) that subjects use 'visualization' when learning their way around an unfamiliar reasoning context, but then shift to 'linguistic' patterns when the type of problem becomes more familiar. 'Visualization' often occurs when we are becoming convinced that a certain pattern will work, and at this stage we are engaged in explicating the concepts that we choose as examples to try out different problem-solving strategies (or inference rules). Once we are convinced that a rule will work, then our use of the rule consists in imagining (usually in proprioceptive and auditory modalities, but occasionally in the visual modality) a certain pattern whose rhythm we can recognize as associated with a feeling of confidence that we have previously developed that this pattern will work. At this point, there is no need to explicate the meanings of concepts, but only to hear them as 'same' or 'different.'

In sum, there is a trivial sense in which computational inferences are more basic than images, but this is merely the sense in which all cause-and-effect sequences can be called 'computational inferences,' as for example when a jar lid 'computes' the temperature of the water we run onto it in order to 'respond' by expanding. But if we define 'inference' non-trivially, as the kind of process which we sometimes consciously experience when doing logical thinking (but also could in principle do on an unconscious basis, once the process has become habituated), then it becomes apparent, from the study of the way people learn to apply logical rules, that each step in the process is grounded in and built up from various kinds of mental images which are prior to and presupposed by the logical skill in question.

A further important consequence of this point is that it further shows that the 'appendage' theory of consciousness, as criticized by Natsoulas (1993), is really an inadequate model of the relation between conscious and non-conscious mental processes. In the 'appendage' model, logical inferences are 'computed' on a biochemical basis without any need for the participation of consciousness. Consciousness is only an additional level of functioning whose effect is to pay attention to, report, or somehow 'read off' inferences which have already been made at the non-conscious level. But what we have seen is that consciousness plays a key role in the actual execution of the inferences. Without a conscious effort to guide and control the entire process in which we both learn and execute logical inference rules, as well as to learn to appropriately inhibit the ostensive elements in the definition of a concept, the thinking ability of humans would be much worse even than it is for most of us on a 'bad day' — not to mention worse than for machines that really *are* programmed to process information on a non-conscious basis — i.e., computers.

## 2. How Do Concepts Evolve from Images?  A Developmental Perspective

If images and concepts are related in the ways discussed above, and if logical thought is developed in the ways just proposed, then it should also be possible to understand how children begin with only images which are either specific or generic, and which are either sensory or proprioceptive (or both), and then build up from these images the abstract concepts needed for logical thought.

We know from neurophysiological observation of people in various stages of learning languages that the meanings of words are at first registered primarily as images (showing extensive right brain activity) and then gradually are taken over by the left brain (Vaid and Genesee 1980; Genesee *et al* 1978). And we know from Piaget's work (1928-65) that children first operate predominantly with images, then the images become increasingly generic and refined until somehow they evolve into the relatively abstract, complex and precise concepts used by adults.  It is true, of course, as Jorgensen and Falmagne (1992) have shown, that children can do some hypothetical reasoning.  But this reasoning is extremely flawed in that children reason better with concrete images than abstract concepts, and are very prone to confuse a statement with its converse (as Jorgensen and Falmagne acknowledge), indicating that children vaguely associate images with each other much more than they understand the precise relationship between the corresponding concepts.  In this gradual transition from vague associations to precise concepts, then, a generic image of 'horse,' for example, seems to function in many respects just as the *concept* 'horse' would function, with a very important difference:  The concept, as Piaget emphasizes, results from a much more *reflective* process than the mere image (Piaget 1928: 137ff).  A similar analysis of the role of reflection in converting images to concepts is found in Luria (1973):

> The young child thinks in terms of visual forms of perception and memory or, in other words, he *thinks by recollecting*.  At later stages of adolescence or in adult life, abstract thinking with the aid of the functions of abstraction and generalization is so highly developed that even relatively simple processes such as perception and memory are converted into complex forms of logical analysis and synthesis, and the person actually begins to *perceive or recollect by reflection*.

> This change in the relationship between the fundamental psychological processes is bound to lead to changes in the relationship between the fundamental systems of the cortex, on the basis of which these processes are carried out (Luria 1973: 32-33).

But before entering into the details of the neurophysiology involved, let's try to phenomenologically describe the difference this 'reflectivity' makes. Suppose I reflect on my generic image of 'horse.' Concretely speaking, this entails asking myself such things as: Would it still be a horse if it had no hooves? If its neck were shorter? What, specifically, are the aspects or features of certain things whose presence prompts me to count some of those things as resembling this image? Of course, we cannot formulate these questions so clearly until we have *already* begun to think with concepts and not just images. We can, however, experience ourselves as being functionally confused by the *inadequacy* of our images and wonder in effect *why* they are inadequate. For, as we continue asking ourselves these kinds of questions, or even non-thetically worrying about them (usually beginning around age 8-10, according to Piaget 1928, Chapter III), we ultimately begin to realize that reliance on the merely associative resemblances of mental images (in the sense that they merely 'remind us' of each other) is an *inadequate* way to experience and adapt to reality. It is inadequate because it continually leads us into errors and confusions which we feel must somehow be avoidable. The image of an 'enemy,' for example, is for a young child the image of a bad, menacing, malicious person. This image includes not only *sensory* qualities (lowered eyebrows, frown, threatening posture, etc.), but also (as Newton stresses) *proprioceptive* ones (how the child imagines she would *feel* toward such a person). But Piaget shows that when questions arise — does the bad, malicious person *himself* have enemies? And may some of these enemies not be good people? May I myself not be someone's enemy? — then the child ends in confusion and antinomy (Piaget 1928: 131ff). At a certain stage, this confusion and antinomy motivate the child to question the image of the enemy, and to ask whether perhaps there are some 'enemies' that require radical revisions of the image, and that the enemy of an enemy is as much an 'enemy' as the original enemy that was imagined.

To consider another example, an 'animal' to a young child is anything that fairly well resembles an indeterminately colored, fuzzy creature with limbs (approximately four — there is no specific number, just as for most of us a mental image of the facade of the Pantheon has no definite number of columns), a creature which moves itself (fast or slow) and eats things (plants or other animals). (See Gelman 1990; Becker and Ward 1991.) But when the child is told that some microscopic organisms, even though they do not *look* like the earlier prototype image of 'animal,' are animals 'because they move themselves and eat things,' and that others are plants 'because they make their own food,' the child must make the meaning of 'animal' more complex and more precise. It then turns out that some plants can move themselves, that some plants eat other organisms, and that some animals do not move themselves; at this point, a much more complicated definition must be developed of what it means to be a plant or an animal. This definition contains so many disjunctions and qualifications and overlapping rules and exceptions to rules that no single image can approximate it — not even a fuzzy or generic one. Just as with the transition from the imagistic to the complex and abstract concept of 'enemy,' confusion and frustration arise as the child tries to refine the old generic image so that it can carry the precision and complexity of the abstraction. Or, to consider another of Piaget's examples, the same thing happens with the concept 'to the left of.' The very young child (at age four, for example) cannot understand that Mary is to the left of Bill even though both are facing us and Mary is on our right. Here again, there is merely a *vague image* of how it would appear (to the child) if Mary were in the left part of the visual field, rather than an *abstract concept*, 'to the left.'

At this point in Piaget's reasoning, a crucial question arises: If the child does not *already* understand that there is *another* concept of 'enemy' at work besides her egocentric image of a malicious, menacing person, then why should she sense any inadequacy about this image? Inadequate to what? At some level, the child must already have some sense that there are two concepts of 'enemy,' that there is some relation between the two, and that failure to make sense of this relation thwarts the child's attempts to understand the environment. It would thus seem that the insight that the child has when she finally forms the genuinely abstract concept 'enemy' (as opposed to a mere fuzzy image of an enemy) is *not* that she recognizes for the first time that not all enemies are evil and malicious, but rather that she realizes that the word 'enemy' as applied to mean, malicious persons is not a mere homonym of the word 'enemy' as applied to pairs of people who are merely on opposite sides of a conflict, as in a sporting event or a fistfight between two normally friendly boys (a concept of mutual opposition which the child surely understands by this age); the child begins to understand that it is possible to have one single concept which is applicable to both situations. Moreover, the child is repeatedly confronted with questions that cannot be made sense of without the help of such a unified and finely-tuned concept. In order to cognize such a concept, however, the child must learn to perform a mental operation which is much more subtle and complex than the imagining of any single mental image, even a fuzzy or generic one.

Phenomenologically speaking, it would seem that what the child must undergo at this stage is a gradual process in which, each time the 'evil, menacing' image is applied, the child also asks herself whether the *other* 'enemy' image — the image of a mere member of a mutual opposition — might not be the one that applies to the case at hand. (She is helped in this process, by the way, by a language which has sedimented this achievement on the part of past generations by applying the same *word* to both images.) At this stage in the child's thought process, there develops a kind of *internal dialogue* in which the child virtually splits herself into two self-talk personae, one of whom questions the other. The image at this point remains the predominant way of cognitively operating, but exceptions begin to be made. Normally, an enemy is still a malicious, menacing person, but there are exceptions. The questioning of the image, in this case, thus leads to the use of a rudimentary *disjunctive* concept which more resembles a combination or association of *alternating images* than an abstraction. One half of this disjunct — the 'normal' or 'usual' half — is the same old image that was previously operative; the other half is the exceptional case in which certain aspects of the image are erased and others added. The same thing happens with the early childhood 'animal' image and the later exceptional cases which are seen under microscopes or described in books. Similarly, 'to the left' for an eight-year-old *usually* means (as it did when she was four) 'to *my* left' or 'in the left half of a visual image,' but again exceptions begin to be made. Sometimes I must imagine how the scene might look if I were facing in the same direction as Mary and Bill who are both facing me, in order to imagine that one is 'to the other's left.'

As this disjunction of images is employed, and as the self-questioning process continues, the child sooner or later hits on the 'essence' of what it is to be an enemy (or an animal, or to someone's left). I.e., she drops from the first half of the disjunct any of the distinguishing features (i.e., those that distinguish it from the second half of the disjunct) which can *conveniently* be dropped without reducing the domain of instantiations covered by that image, and at some point is able to answer the question: What is it that both these disjuncts have in common with each other, and without which they would not remind me of each other? Aha! *That* is what it means to be an enemy (or an animal, or to someone's left).

What is required, in concrete terms, for the mind to go through all these operations? *First,* there usually needs to be a *name* for the image, because the name facilitates pulling up different images in order to ask questions about them; when I say the Devil's name, the Devil's image appears. As Berlin and Kay (1969) demonstrated, for example, memory for colors is largely a function of color naming. The child must have names for images like 'eat,' 'move,' 'animal,' etc., in order to 'pull them up' into awareness in the needed order to see how they relate to each other to make up the abstract notion of 'animal.' Thus the left (or dominant) hemisphere and the right (nondominant) hemisphere must be differentiated and integrated, since forming visual (and auditory, etc.) images heavily involves right brain parietal and frontal function (Hoppe 1977; Springer and Deutsch 1989; Posner and Rothbart 1992), whereas the manipulation of verbal symbols is best performed by the left brain frontal area (Luria 1973: 238-240, 156ff; Sperry 1966: 60-70; Gerow 1986: 74-75). (Notice that this differentiation between left and right frontal and parietal functions is not substantially obliterated by very recent research which emphasizes the interrelatedness of left and right brain functions — as summarized, for example, by Richardson 1991.) This differentiation between left and right brain functioning is not substantially complete until around age 10-11 (Luria 1973: 270; Edwards 1979: 59).

The *Second* requirement is that there must be a *motivation* to question the inadequacies of the images when they lead to antinomy, confusion, or failure to master one's environment. This motivation's power to direct mental operations, of course, presupposes the development of the frontal lobe, with its elaborate neuronal connections to the limbic region and to all parts of the cerebrum (see Buck 1988; Petersen 1989; Winson 1985: 58; Fuster 1980: 128). As an example of the extensiveness of prefrontal area connections to diverse brain areas, here is a summary by Winson (1986):

> The prefrontal cortex . . . is defined by its connections to a particular assembly or nucleus of cells in the underlying thalamus called the mediodorsal nucleus. . . The thalamic nuclei are information relays to the neocortex. The thalamocortical systems may be sensory — vision, hearing, touch — or they may govern movement. The prefrontal cortex is different. It is neither sensory nor motor but carries out some higher-order function. Its connections with the rest of the brain give an idea of the complexity of this function; all of the higher-order sensory information that reaches the hippocampus also reaches the prefrontal cortex. In addition, it has direct information from the amygdala and many other subcortical brain structures, sends information back to almost all areas from which it receives information, and, lastly, transmits signals to the subcortical area called the basal ganglia, which are believed to be involved in final motor action (Winson 1986: 58).

And Fuster (1980) writes,

> The most crucial constituents are the attentive acts that 'palpate' the environment in search of significant clues, the intentional and elaborate movements, the continuous updating of relevant information to a cognitive scheme of the overall structure and its goal. The prefrontal cortex not only provides the substrate for these operations but imparts to them their active quality. In that active role . . . one may find some justification of the often espoused view of the prefrontal cortex — 'the executive of the brain' (Fuster 1980: 128).

Patients with lesions of the frontal lobe fail to solve cognitive tasks because they are unable to ask themselves the right questions at the appropriate point in their thought process (Luria 1973: 219 and *passim;* Sperry 1966; Joseph 1982). The frontal lobe continues to grow and develop until about age 14, but has achieved most of its growth by about age 8-10 (Luria 1973: 87, 270).

   *Third,* there must be a continuing, dialogically-structured kind of *self-talk* within the person's stream of consciousness. I.e., once the initial question is asked, if the ensuing answer is not satisfactory, a continuing dialogue takes place between the questioning persona and the questioned persona, in which the problem to be solved is never completely lost track of and continues to direct the flow of consciousness (perhaps interspersed with some digressions). The child's self-talk seems to reach the capability of such ongoing dialogue around the age of 8-10, probably because that is when connections to the frontal lobe are complete enough to facilitate it.  Prior to that point, if the child's first answer to a question is inadequate, she does not rethink the answer, does not 'reflect' on the thought process, but becomes distracted or merely fabricates a new answer with so little reference to the original one that she now claims to have known the new answer all along, and forgets that she ever believed something contradictory (Piaget 1928: 142; Luria 1973: 319). Self-talk at this earlier stage consists only of isolated expressions, such as brief recriminations against oneself, rather than two-way, continuing dialogue. Most of us can remember the development of this extended dialogue between the opposing personae in our childhood self-talk, so the way in which it developed can be regarded largely as a phenomenological datum.  One persona in a ten-year-old's self talk may ask, 'Why did you miss that problem on the math test?'  The other responds, 'I couldn't study because we went to the airport last night.'  The first counters, 'You should have been able to figure that out without studying,' etc.

The importance of this kind of internal speech for the development of thinking ability has been emphasized by Don Tucker (1981), Rhawn Joseph (1982), Stuart Dimond (1980), and by the Russian psychologist Lev Vygotsky (1962) who strongly influenced Luria.  According to these researchers, thought processes seem to evolve during childhood as primarily left-hemisphere 'internalizations' of self-directed talk, which results only with the maturation of nerve pathways interconnecting both cerebral and subcortical brain structures, including the corpus callosum and the frontal lobe-lymbic system connections.  Vygotsky emphasizes the role of *emotional* speech as motivating the self-questioning process, and suggests (consistently with Tucker) that self-talk evolves initially as a kind of truncated action.   I.e., a crucial developmental process occurs when the interpretation or evaluation of an imagined action precedes its actual execution, so that the action's consequences can be (subjunctively) imagined.   In this way, the self-questioning of the frontal lobe evolves out of the truncating of motor behaviors, resulting in the ability to question images.  This is also consistent with the frontal lobe's well-known ability to inhibit the tendency to simply respond in habitually established ways (Restak: 10).  Young (1988: 106) characterizes this directive role of the frontal lobe's questioning process as an attempt to confirm or disconfirm hypotheses about the environment.

A *fourth* requirement seems to be that the person must be able to recall and review the disjunctive variations of the generic image *in rapid enough succession,* and in such a question-directed way, that the appropriate comparisons and contrasts *between and among the images themselves* can be made. Like Socrates in the *Parmenides,* we must be able not only to compare the particular with its idea, but also ideas with each other. I.e., we must be able not only to compare a specific person to a prototypic image of 'conservative,' but also to compare each of the alternative prototypic images *with each other* (for example, 'businessman preoccupied with self interest,' 'macho man upset about homosexuals,' 'religious person upset about abortion and prayer in schools,' etc.), in order to evolve a genuinely abstract concept of 'conservative' which would be capable of applying to all the disjunctive prototypes. At this point, one of four things happens:

(a) The superfluous elements of all the disjuncts are dropped until the disjuncts are all equivalent to each other. In this case, I am left simply with an image many of whose features are left fuzzy or indefinite — in short, a refined generic image modified by a reflective operation. An example is the concept 'chair.' Obviously, this type of concept is no different from the fuzzy or generic images which the child has enacted since early infancy.

Or (b) the disjuncts *cannot* be made to match, in which case the conscious thinking of the concept — say 'animal' — consists simply in preparing my efferent receptors in such a way as to be geared up to attend to *any* of a widely-discrepant group of alternative afferent patterns should any of them occur, and to ignore any afferent patterns that do not approximate any of these alternative patterns.

Or (c) at an even more complex level, I realize that the word whose 'concept' I am trying to consistently grasp does not refer either to a refinement, a conjunction or a disjunction of specific mental images, but refers rather to the pattern of resemblances, differences and connections between various images and/or concepts. More precisely, I compare the similarities and differences *between different images* in order to sense the similarities and differences between and among *those* similarities and differences. For example, in music, the concept of an 'interval of a fourth' is learned in something like the following way: I sense the similarity and difference between C and F, and then sense the similarity and difference between E and A, and eventually realize that the patterns of (efferent) reaction which these two sets of similarities and differences set up in my consciousness all remind me *of each other* in a certain way which I can subjectively sense through phenomenological reflection (for example, they both sound like the first two notes of Wagner's Wedding March, but in different keys). And to cognize this particular way in which those similarities and differences remind me of each other is in essence to cognize the concept 'interval of a fourth.' By narrowing our focus (i.e., 'looking-for') to specific combinations of notes while ignoring others, we learn that the same note can be both a fourth lower than another and a fourth higher than still another *at the same time.* In this way, we master *relational* concepts with their difficult element of *reciprocity* — the trouble that always befell Piaget's 8-10 year olds when they tried to work with relational concepts. For example, Mary must be either to the left or to the right; she cannot be to the left of one person and *at the same time* to the right of another (Piaget 1928: 107ff).

(d)    At the highest level of abstraction, we evolve concepts like 'president' or 'algebraic function.' In these cases, as we saw in section 1 above, the *use* of the concept (say, 'president') entails a feeling that we could, if needed, elaborate a long and complicated story which would explain what makes someone a president, and this story would require that the right images be called up in the right pattern, just as when we execute a piece of music. The entire process is not undergone each time we use the concept, but the image of the name of the concept functions as a sort of filing label which could enable us to make all the needed associations, or some subset of them, whenever necessary. This *ability* to explicate the meaning of a concept must also be accompanied with a *feeling of confidence* that we *could* do so if necessary.

The *fifth* and final requirement for converting images to concepts seems to be that, in order to compare different similarities and differences between images, the child must not only enact the different images in rapid succession, but moreover, the one image must produce a 'feeling of recognition' or 'feeling of familiarity' by virtue of which the one image reminds the child of the other. And, similarly, when the more complex proprioceptive image of 'what it would be like to enact the consciousness of that similarity' (for example, between the notes E and A) is compared with the proprioceptive image of the other similarity (for example, between C and F), the second of these two imaginary enactments must produce a 'feeling of recognition' by virtue of which it reminds the person of the first one.   The 'feeling of recognition' functions very similarly to the way it does in memories generally, and I shall discuss it more extensively when we come to Chapter 6, which explores memory in detail.  I bring it in at this point to show how extensively distributed throughout the brain the processes are which are necessary to convert childhood 'generic images' into concepts in the purely abstract sense, i.e., in a sense whose meaning cannot be exhausted by enumerating the generic images that went together to make up the concept.  We know, for example, that hippocampal functioning is crucial to the 'feeling of recognition' in memory functions.  So the hippocampus must be added to all the other brain areas which we have just seen are necessary to convert a generic image into a pure abstraction.  Note that, *before any logical relations can be executed* in the brain's cognitive functioning, these diverse brain areas all must first interact in these complex ways *just in order to form one of the several terms to be related logically*.  So it would really be backwards to think (as some cognitive architectures would require) that the recognition of images results from logical computations which are executed by some computer-like mechanism in the brain.

By combining these five at-first-very-difficult mental operations, we build up from our childish generic images the concepts we need for effective logical thought — conjunctive, disjunctive and relational concepts.  Each concept has a name, which when uttered calls up the complex internal sensation or *noesis* (Husserl 1913-1931) needed to cognize that particular concept.  For example, an interval of a fourth is recognized by the internal sensation to which any interval of a fourth will equally well give rise, and which is also used to 'look *for*' intervals of a fourth.  In essence, this internal sensation, the *noesis,* is an example of a 'proprioceptive image.'

These phenomenological observations of the way concepts are built up from generic images correlate closely to the findings of neurologists about the development of categories in the brain.  Buchwald *et al* (1994) and Lenneberg (1967), for example, have shown that the specific sounds we are able to discriminate as adults are determined by the opportunity to refine our auditory categories at the appropriate developmental stage.  (This is why children who grow up speaking only Japanese, for example, have trouble hearing the difference between the sounds 'l' and 'r'.)  Obviously, each animal is born with a small collection of images to which it is pre-programmed to respond in certain ways.  By modifying these responses through cortical inhibition, we refine and elaborate the categories (Elman 1993; Blakemore and Cooper 1970; Hirsch and Spinelli 1970; Mitchell *et al* 1973; Leyhausen 1979).  Leyhausen especially emphasizes the role of inhibition in truncating pre-programmed behavior.  When we get to Chapter 6, we will be in a position to connect this point with Don Tucker's view that, in effect, an efferent activity resulting in consciousness *is* a truncated motoric behavior in which we imagine ourselves as engaging, as a musician remembers a melody by imagining herself playing it.  This is also consistent with the finding by Aserinsky and Kleitman (1953) that humans as well as cats show firing of motor neurons during dream images; and with the above cited studies by Kimura and Archibald (1974), Studdert-Kennedy and Shankweiler (1970) and Liberman *et al* (1967) which support the view that speech evolves as a truncated motoric behavior (i.e., to think a word is largely to imagine ourselves saying the word).

### 3.  General Implications for Cognitive Theory

What can be learned from all this for cognitive theory? First, that a mental image is not an item of information that can be stored in some highly specific location such as a glial cell or RNA molecule.  We must radically reject simplistic single-neuron, single-pathway, or even highly-localized *module* theories of 'mental content storage' in the brain — the kind of theory summarized by Young (1988) in such terms as the following: "We might go further and speculate that there may be neurons that represent not only physical objects but words and abstract concepts.  It is no longer possible to ridicule the idea that there are neurons responsible for representation of the concept of representation (128)." Certainly, the fact that "there are indeed cells in the temporal cortex of monkeys that signal the presence of a particular face, and even whether or not it is gazing at the observer. . . . Nineteen cells in one particular area responded selectively to the sight of a face; this was 9 per cent of all cells examined" (Young, 126) does not imply that the consciousness of that face is 'contained in' or in any way limited to the activity of those particular nineteen cells (the 'grandmother cell' approach).  On the contrary, as Varela *et al* (1991) emphasize,

In primates, the participation of subensembles of neurons in color perception has been demonstrated in the thalamus (LGN), primary and extrastriate visual cortex, inferotemporal cortex, and frontal lobes. Most notable is a collection of neurons in the so-called V4 of the extrastriate cortex where even individual neuronal responses can be roughly associated with the color constancies of a visual field. These neuronal structures constitute a color subnetwork — a sort of perceptual 'agent,' to use Minsky's terminology. Thus nothing short of a large and distributed neuronal network is involved in our perception of color (Varela *et al* 1991: 161-162).

The image is not a passive reaction on the part of a small group of cells, but rather a complex activity of 'looking-for' which originates with the 'orienting reflex' in the limbic region, continues through the focusing of attention *via* the frontal lobe, often relies on linguistic symbols from the left brain to facilitate the focusing, and enacts a quasi-spatial anticipation of the possible perception of the imagined object in the parietal region of the right brain. The imaging of the object also includes, as Newton points out, proprioceptive imaginings of what it would be like or feel like to interact with the object in certain ways — and this certainly includes hippocampal functioning. All of these activities of the various parts of the brain are inseparable parts of the pattern of activity which corresponds to the presence in cognition of the simplest possible content-element — before any propositions and rule-governed operations involving such a content-element can even begin. The physiological activities which constitute the latter operations consist of even more complex patterns, and of patterns of patterns of patterns.

To look for these contents of consciousness in a single neuron, neural pathway, highly-localized module, or RNA molecule would thus be analogous to looking for the physical equivalent of the note 'C' in one of the air molecules through which the sound wave must 'travel.' The C is not *in* any single air molecule, but in the *pattern* of their behavior. The same is true of a given content of consciousness — an image, perception, concept, or rule. A single content of consciousness requires a complex pattern of activity in order to exist. For example, an image corresponds to a pattern of efferent behaviors which occurs when I look for the afferent pattern which normally would call forth or fulfill that efferent pattern if I were to have a perception of that object. We should therefore be searching for complex patterns of activity — wave patterns, vibrational structures, etc — which could be identified with corresponding states of consciousness. We must not assume that if we can model a system which processes the same *information* that conscious beings process, then that system can also serve as a model for the way consciousness is produced. The model must also be consistent with the notion that the status of each content of consciousness consists of a pattern of activity, not a thing-like entity such as a stream of electrons, or a constellation of synapses, or the configuration of a molecule. I should add that cognitive theorists already seem to be moving in the general direction called for by these phenomenological observations, not only in the form of connectionism but also in 'production systems' theory. The recent work of such neurologists as Luria, Posner, Aurell and Damasio, as pointed out above, also suggests that conscious content-elements are extremely complex and somewhat global activities. As Luria says, "Human gnostic activity never takes place with respect to one single isolated modality . . . the perception — and still more the representation — of any object is a *complex* procedure, the result of polymodal activity. . . (72-73)" And again, "Human mental processes are complex functional systems and . . . they are not 'localized' in narrow, circumscribed areas of the brain. . . .(43)"

It is all too easy to build machines which 'process' information. We simply include a component which detects temperature, another which detects light intensity, others which detect color, distance, movement, weight, mathematical relationships, etc. The machine can operate with these many *partes extra partes* components because it is a *non-conscious* machine. But a conscious machine such as the human brain cannot operate in this *partes extra partes* fashion, because even the simplest states of consciousness are very global and involve the interplay of various parts of the system. The more complex conscious processes, such as inference and abstract conceptualization, will therefore involve correspondingly complex patterns of interaction between the simpler patterns, which themselves are already globally distributed, higher-order patterns whose substrata are already lower-order patterns of activity and synchronization.

With regard to the developmental evidence cited for this holistic-connectionist viewpoint, it might legitimately be asked whether we have not fallen into a kind of genetic fallacy. Just because the child's brain had to enact all five of the functions listed above in order to *develop* the ability to use a concept does not imply that once she reaches the adult stage she must continue to enact all five of them every time she actually uses the concept. Obviously, there is no need for an adult to be motivated to question the meaning of the concept every time she uses it, nor to rapidly alternate between visual images in order to compare and contrast them to each other, nor even to engage in a self-questioning dialogue. The process of conceptualization may become increasingly short-cutted or truncated. (This truncating process will be discussed further in Chapter 6 when we discuss memory and related functions.)

Nonetheless, there is plenty of reason to believe that adult conceptualization still involves neural activities that are quite similar in broad contour to those which must be used in late childhood to form a concept. Perceptual experiments show that looking-for enhances perception, as we have seen. Studies of the learning process in students (for example, Slomianko 1987) indicate that students absorb abstract as well as concrete reading material more effectively if they ask themselves questions about what they read, and it now seems virtually certain that this self-questioning process heavily involves the frontal lobe (Posner and Rothbart 1992; Luria 1973, 1980). It is also well established that attention and conceptual thinking are strongly facilitated by a *motivation* to select certain features of the environment or ideational material as important. Thus, while adult neurophysiological processes probably become more efficient than those of the child, they still involve essentially as complex a set of neurophysiological activities and one which is just as extensively distributed throughout the brain. The fact that adults may learn to somewhat truncate the process of conceptualization does not really change the implications for cognitive theory of the fact that the conceptualization of any one simple content-element in any cognitive proposition already involves complex and relatively global neurophysiological processes. The cognition of logical relations and propositions will therefore inevitably involve even more complex processes which are at least as globally distributed across interacting parts of the brain.

Since the brain sciences are in a state of rapid development, the neurophysiological implications of these phenomenological observations are tentative and may change as a result of further knowledge. We do know, however, that the frontal lobe is crucial to the self-questioning function, and the efferent neurons are concentrated in the front half of the cerebrum anterior to a fairly distinct groove, the central sulcus, which divides this predominantly efferent anterior from the posterior half of the cerebrum, which is largely afferent (Young 1988: 90-91). We know also that the right (or nondominant) hemisphere is holistic and imagistic, while the left (or dominant) hemisphere is very important in logic and linguistic thinking (Richardson 1991; Springer and Deutsch 1989; Sperry 1966). And the frontal lobe, we know, is the crucial link between the limbic region, which is strongly associated with the feeling of emotions, and the cerebrum, associated with representations and logical thinking. Since the framing of a question is largely a matter of defining and delineating an emotion (i.e., identifying what it is that one '*wants*' to know about or understand), it makes sense that the frontal lobe, which bridges intellectual with emotional functions, should be an area heavily involved in the formation of questions. The formulation of a question is complete only when the appropriate images or concepts are forced to appear in consciousness. Thus the frontal lobe must get the right brain to cooperate in producing the necessary images, often by getting the left brain to cooperate in saying the name which activates the imaging of that image or the enactment of that concept. If the delineation of the question involves concepts, then the more complex operations described above as involving the coordinated effort of frontal lobe, left brain, right brain and limbic area must be used. All of these activities involve non-perceptual or pre-perceptual forms of consciousness and thus are performed primarily by means of the activity of the anterior and predominantly efferent part of the brian, and all such activities are sensed phenomenologically as types of 'looking-for'.

Naturally, the question arises: How does the organism originally learn how to 'look for' a given content by making its efferent system behave in the appropriate pattern? In a few cases, neonates may be pre-programmed to look for certain patterns, such as the human face (Winson 1986: 162ff). But it is obvious that most images are not pre-programmed. Instead, just the opposite happens. At various points during the process of learning and development, afferent signals are delivered *unexpectedly* to the posterior parts of the cerebrum, i.e., without having been 'looked for.' These afferent signals lead to efferent patterns of activity in the anterior or efferent part of the brain. Later, the organism learns to execute the skills necessary to enact these same efferent patterns without the presence of the corresponding afferent activities. The organism knows that the consciousness enacted through this efferent activity is imaginative rather than perceptual because the afferent input is missing. Phenomenologically, what is being looked-for is not being found.

The efferent activity of the anterior region must be *voluntarily* activated if it is to count as an *attentive* 'looking-for.' Thus it is obvious phenomenologically that I may stare at an object for several seconds without actually being 'consciously aware' of the object. It is very likely that some of the efferent patterning which would have been caused by the afferent input from the object the first time I ever encountered it should also occur during such a 'blank stare' at the object. Yet the *consciousness* of the object is *missing*. Thus we must say that the consciousness of the object arises not simply from the efferent pattern caused by the object (some of which occurs even during a 'blank stare'), but by the *voluntary enactment* of that efferent pattern, followed in the case of perception by its afferent fulfillment. The (attentive) consciousness of the object occurs only when, having once received the afferent input from it, I 'look again' *for* the object; if at *this* point I am *still* receiving the afferent input which the efferent activity is looking for, then and only then can it be said that I 'attend to' the object, and only at this point am I 'consciously aware' of its presence. Attentive conscious awareness thus must originate with a *voluntary* enactment of the efferent pattern, rather than with an afferent pattern's directly causing the efferent pattern to be evoked. This would explain why the amount of time it takes for a subject to be 'aware' of an image on a screen is always *longer* than it takes for the neurons in the brain to be activated by the signals from the retina (Srebro 1985: 233-246). This initial neural activation is only the *first stage* in the process through which the subject becomes *aware* of the object. The afferent activity must first cause efferent activity (probably at the point when the incoming nerve impulse passes through the thalamus as it travels on its way to the prefrontal and parietal areas), which in turn sends signals to the limbic region, where they interact with the subject's *emotional/motivational* state, where they then cause the frontal lobe to formulate the question as to whether an object of such-and-such nature is present. This then causes the parietal right brain to enact an image of the object (i.e., an efferent looking-for), which then feels itself as being fulfilled by the afferent pattern being delivered.

If the kind of object being looked for does *not* present itself in the afferent activity of the occipital lobe, then the parietal lobe at first exhibits an electrical potential of N200, apparently corresponding to the negation of the original image being looked-for (Aurell 1984). Then the efferent system adjusts to the discrepancy and looks for something more closely resembling the object being presented. The end of this process (which occurs very quickly) is a P300 potential in the upper and posterior parietal lobe, corresponding to the consciousness of the object which is now perceived. Only after all these complex processes have been completed can we say that there is 'conscious awareness' of the perceptual object. The 'consciousness of the object' must therefore include the *motivation* to be aware of the object. The presence of the motivation to attend to the object is thus the essential difference between the *conscious* processing of information and the *non-conscious* processing as it might be performed by a suitably designed machine. It also follows that only if it were possible to construct a machine with *motivations and emotions* would it be possible to construct a machine with *consciousness*.

It is interesting to note, in passing, that the standard explanation of the finding just cited — the time lag between afferent neural activation and the awareness of the object which caused this awareness — is self-contradictory. J.Z. Young (1988), for example, interprets it as evidence that neural activity causes conscious processes and not the other way around (Young 1988: 127 and *passim)*. His reasoning is that it is natural to assume that a cause should precede its effect in time. But at the same time Young, like most contemporary brain scientists, rejects any dualistic account of the relation between brain events and conscious events. But if states of consciousness are not entities distinguishable from their physiological correlates in a straightforwardly dualistic sense, then one would expect to find no time lag between the one occurrence and the other. Events which are identical should occur simultaneously. My point here is not to reject the thesis that consciousness is inseparable from its physiological correlates (a complex question in its own right which I have discussed more extensively in Ellis 1986, and will take up again in the next chapter), but simply to point out that the standard explanation here is philosophically confused to the point of self-contradiction, and thus is no explanation at all. A more realistic account hinges on understanding that the neurophysiological response to a perceptual object resulting in consciousness of the object is much more complex, and thus more time-consuming, than the assumption of a simple, passive stimulation of the visual cortex would lead one to believe.

Another implication of the approach we have been taking here is that it resolves the controversy between Posner and Rothbart (1992) and Bisiach (1992) as to whether the substrate of consciousness is completely globally distributed throughout the brain (Bisiach), or is narrowly a function of the anterior-cingulate-frontal-limbic area (Posner and Rothbart).  Our analysis implies that the anterior cingulate and other closely related frontal and limbic areas are uniquely involved in orchestrating the 'looking-for' process, without which there would be no conscious awareness of any incoming stimulus or mental content, but that without global patterns of activity this 'looking-for' would never be amplified into specific mental images, concept meanings, or emotional significances.

A possible mechanism by which this afferent-efferent architecture of patterns of conscious activity could be realized has already been developed by Gordon Globus (1987), whose proposal can be summarized as follows:

> The pattern that meets the production's conditions of satisfaction would function only to pick out that production for activation.  So productions are a set of possible actions given satisfaction of certain conditions, and depending on what's in the workspace, certain actions are actually effected. . . . The whole richly interconnected system is in continuous flux.  This fluctuating whole pattern can be conceived of as if waves were coming together moment-to-moment so as to form a complicated interference pattern. . . . The mathematical formalism for representing such a system . . . would naturally utilize complex numbers for wave amplitude and phase representation (Globus 1987: 129-131).

Globus then proposes a more specific neurophysiological substrate for this process:

> Let's consider a large set of "hyperneurons," idealized entities each conceived of as a richly interconnected group of neurons. . . . When the hyperneuron's specifications are satisfied well enough by the sensory input pattern, a region of the hyperneuron is inversely Fourier transformed, which unfolds the enfolded order and the hyperneuron outputs a pattern that well enough models the sensory input pattern. . .
>
> Thus the gosling would have genetically given hyperneurons specifying "large moving objects" and the infant would have hyperneurons specifying "faces."  Through something like adaptive

resonance during a critical period of development, the gosling's hyperneurons typically become fine-tuned to mother goose and the infant's hyperneurons to mama.

Thus the hyperneuron's specifications comprise an a priori set of possible worlds for the species, modifiable through experience. . . . When satisfied well enough by the input pattern, a good enough model of the input pattern is produced by transformation of the hyperneuronal specifications. . . . World models are produced without benefit of copies of the world or instructions from the world; they are created formatively. Certain a priori specifications within the machine are satisfied by the world and then transformed to a good enough world model (Globus 1987: 133-135).

If the realization of this process is maximally holistic, the entire efferent system including its midbrain motivational components could function, by modulating its activities in different patterns, so as to play the roles of different 'hyperneurons.' Or the hyperneurons could correspond to Gazzanigian 'modules,' which would function somewhat globally, but only in limited large brain areas. In either case, a system of 'looking for' items of motivational interest in the environment would determine which combinations of afferent activity would become attuned to the efferent pattern, and thus a state of consciousness produced corresponding to that activity. The efferent system would function, generally speaking, like a Heideggerian 'existential a priori' (Needleman 1968) in that a pre-perceptual system would first activate a selective-attentional mechanism, and then subsequently information sought in the environment would be found to match or fail to match the selected pre-perceptual focus of interest, as in the testing of a hypothesis which has already been formed. According to Needleman, neurosis or even psychosis can result when the subject is so prejudiced in favor of a preconceived hypothesis that, in Kuhnian fashion, she seeks out only confirming data and selectively ignores disconfirming data. This is a dysfunctional condition because it is predicated on the assumption that there has been a breakdown either of the organism's motivation to perceive its environment in the most effective way it can (given the obvious limitations of the method of hypothesis testing), or of its *ability* to perform some of the necessary operations.

Clearly, the task of correlating phenomenological with neurophysiological observations is just at the beginning of a long road ahead.

We have as yet to address the problems involved in accounting for the numerous facts of memory, and have not yet begun the process of exploring the question as to how this approach might help us to understand the neurophysiology of logical processes, although an understanding of the neurophysiology of concept formation would seem to be an important prerequisite to such a study. But what seems clear so far is that such a phenomenological-neurophysiological correlation must be investigated if we are to have any assurance that any proposed cognitive architecture model has any relevance to the ways in which real conscious beings process information.

# CHAPTER FOUR

# The Ontological Status of Consciousness

Suppose John Smith is a philosopher committed to a thoroughgoing reductive or eliminative materialism — and thus to the view that there is no need to talk about consciousness, since everything that needs to be explained can be explained in terms of the physical interaction of particles of matter in the brain. Suppose Smith poses to himself the following question with regard to wood as a conductor of sound: 'Is sound a pattern of wood activity?' Following the reasoning of U.T. Place (1956, 1993) in his analogous treatment of the notion of 'mental events,' our enthusiastic monist might argue that sound is, in fact, a pattern of wood activity — at least during the time when it is passing through the wood — because the vibration of the wood molecules is both necessary and sufficient for the existence of the sound wave. Thus, following Feigl (1958), he might say that the notion of a 'sound wave' is a nomological dangler, unnecessary to any physical explanation of the particular pattern of wood activity in question. Once we describe and explain the motion of each individual particle, we have described and explained all that needs to be described or explained. He might suggest that we should even go so far as J.J.C. Smart (1963, 1970) in pointing out that those who speak of a 'sound wave' are in violation of Ockham's principle of parsimony, or as far as Richard Rorty (1966), whose earlier work would suggest that people should be taught to substitute descriptions of patterns of wood activity in place of descriptions involving the superfluous notion of 'sound waves.' We might call this theory the 'theory of sound-wood identity.'

Our hard-headed physicalist is of course aware of the objections his mystical-minded colleagues could bring against this theory.  It may be the 'sound wave' originating from elsewhere which *causes* the wood to vibrate in the pattern it does, not the pattern of wood vibration which causes the sound wave.  But to this he could respond that it is meaningless to ask whether a 'sound wave' causes wood vibration or *vice versa* because sound *is* the pattern of wood vibration.

Smith is also aware of the objection from the standpoint of the relativity of process:   Nothing is what it is except in relation to other things (Ellis 1992b; Whitehead 1925; Einstein 1922-1956; Cassirer 1923-1953).  We cannot describe the location of a particle of wood except in relation to patterns of movement with which the particle is involved; thus we cannot describe, let alone explain, the pattern of a sound wave merely by conjunctively stating that this particle moves here, and that particle moves there, since these discrete movements have meaning only in relation to the pattern of the larger process. Even the 'here' and the 'there' mean something only in relation to this larger pattern.  But the materialist response is that, when we describe the movements of the various particles, we have already described them by means of measurements which by their very nature take account of the relativity of motion, so there is still no need to bring in a meta-level of entities such as 'sound waves' in order to explain the movement of the wood.  Each particle just moves because the adjacent particle caused it to move, and there is no need to speak as though this explanation were insufficient by saying that the 'pattern of the wave' causes the door to vibrate.  Why not just eliminate all unnecessary vocabulary and speak only of the location, distance and velocity of the movement of each particle?

Others might object, with Wilfrid Sellars (1965), that 'sound' and 'patterns of wood activity' do not occupy the same logical space.  It does not mean the same thing to speak of beautiful sounds as to speak of beautiful patterns of wood.   To this our reductionist colleague might respond in Davidsonian fashion that, while sound and wood activity are the same thing, it is possible to view them from two different perspectives:  One can either receive the impression of them with one's ears, or one can look at diagrams of them in physics books.  Of course, the perception of the diagram in the physics book can also be looked at from two different perspectives:  as the representation of a certain relationship, or as the discrete motions of billions of elemental particles in the paper of the book and in the brain. In each case, however, the reductionist prefers to regard the more discrete particle or movement as an 'entity,' and to regard the more continuous pattern — i.e., the pattern that focuses on the *relations between* things — as a 'nomological dangler.' To be sure, what there is in nature which brings it about that there *are* these two different perspectives, while both perspectives are 'really' the same thing as each other, is a different question. But our Ockhamite friend does not care to delve into 'metaphysics.'

There is one sense in which the theory of 'sound-wood identity' is true, but with mostly trivial consequences; and there is another sense in which it would have earthshaking consequences if true, but in this sense it is not true. It is true, of course, that sound is a pattern in the activity of its medium: but in what sense of 'activity'? The crucial question is whether the particles in the medium first act, and the reason for the pattern of the wave is *because* each of the particles acted in the way they did so that the action of the particle could serve as an *explanation* for the wave's having the shapes, contours, and rhythms that it has. Or, on the contrary, does a wave *already* having those particular shapes, contours and rhythms 'act upon' a particular medium (the wooden door), so that the pattern of the pre-existing wave would serve as an explanation for why the particular particles are moving in the pattern they exhibit? What makes the theory of sound-wood identity 'sound' so ridiculous is that it sounds as though the identity theorist were trying to explain why the sound wave has the pattern that it has by reference to the movement of the individual particles of wood. And there are some obvious problems with this explanation, three of which are especially important: (1) We cannot explain why the individual particles move in the way they do without reference to a previously existing sound wave, having the same or a very similar pattern to the one being explained; the 'explanation' therefore does not explain why that pattern existed in the first place, and in a pragmatically important sense becomes circular. (2) The pattern of the sound wave would have been the same or very similar even if those particles of wood had never been there, provided that some other usable lumps of matter had been available; at the level of what explains what, there is an important sense in which, as Ernst Cassirer (1923-1953) puts its, function is often prior to the particular substance which serves as its substratum. (3) Even from a purely ontological point of view, it is questionable whether the being of a whole pattern can be reduced to the being of its parts. For example, it is possible that each of the particles of wood could have moved in just the way it did, but in a different order and rhythm, and in that case the sound wave in question would not have existed. While it is true that each particle moves as it does only because some previous particle moved the way it did, the question as to why these movements occur with the order and rhythm they do can be answered only by positing that this order and rhythm (or a related one) already existed prior to the movement of the particles in question. 'Two singers singing the Star Spangled Banner in rhythm with each other' is not necessarily the same as 'Two singers singing the Star Spangled Banner *per se.*'

Because of these problems, it would not be surprising if we were often to hear a sound-wood identity theorist say that the vibration of the wood *causes* the sound wave — as if the cause and the effect were two different entities. The problem is that the cause-and-effect relationship is needed to give the theory its explanatory value, yet a literal ontological *identification* of the explanans with its explanatory antecedent would render the explanation inadequate.

Let us turn now to the relationship between mind and body. Many neuroscientists, having rejected a mind-body dualism, remain ambivalent about whether they believe that consciousness is *caused by* brain processes (causal epiphenomenalism), or whether the consciousness is *identical with* the corresponding brain processes. Yet these two views are crucially different from each other. The view that consciousness is *caused by* brain processes rather than being *identical with* them entails the claim that there is a difference between the brain processes and the causal effects they produce (for example, subjective states of consciousness). The attempt to easily sidestep the mind-body problem by positing that consciousness is merely a causal epiphenomenon therefore inadvertently commits itself to the very dualism that neuroscientists wanted to avoid.

But on the other hand, if consciousness is *identical with* the corresponding brain states (rather than *caused by* them), then we should be able to learn everything we need to know about what it feels like, say, to be in love, merely by examining the brain of someone who has reported being in love, and without ever having felt the sensation or anything like it ourselves. But it is well known that there is a difference between being able to *identify* an emotion and knowing what the emotion feels like. In fact, people afflicted with motor aprosodia, which is caused by damage to the right brain beneath the cerebral hemisphere (Restak 1984: 261) can readily identify the existence of very intense feelings in others but, for their own part, they cannot feel them, or at least cannot express them. Obviously, then, even if it is true that a feeling is a brain state experienced from the subjective perspective (as Davidson's 'anomalous monism' would have it), the fact remains that there is a difference between the view from within (which we call consciousness) and the view from without (the objective observation of the brain scientist). And this difference remains even if it is the neurologist's *own* brain she is observing and her *own* feeling of being in love that she is feeling. To look at a brain (even one's own) is not the same as to feel an emotion (even if the emotion is somehow 'in' the brain one is looking at). But if what can be predicated of X (that it can be known objectively) cannot be predicated of Y (which cannot be known objectively), then we need to be able to specify and talk about the differences between them. These differences obviously do exist. This means that both causal epiphenomenalism and psychophysical identity theories are inadequate in certain respects. This is probably why so many neuroscientists want to straddle the fence between them. But by accepting both doctrines, they not only run together theories whose implications are very different, but also end up with all the inadequacies of *both* theories.

The question of the relationship between consciousness and its physiological correlates is not merely an entertaining intellectual parlor game. There are instances of cognitive processes that are *not* conscious (for example, a computer's processing of information; or the registering of sensory data in the primary projection area, but without conscious awareness; or the nervous system's control of our walking movements, breathing and reflexes). And there are instances of cognitive processes that *are* conscious (as when we *want* to know the answer to a question, or when we *search* for a certain item in our environment). The differences between these two kinds of information processing — conscious and non-conscious — are crucially important for our understanding of neurophysiology, psychology, the relationship between consciousness and its physiological correlates, and even our understanding of what consciousness *is*. These issues in turn of course also affect our thinking about the etiology or causal determination of human behavior patterns and personality characteristics, which in turn affect the way we think about moral, social and political issues. The latter problems are beyond our scope here, but understanding the basic nature of human consciousness is crucial for their solution, as I have argued extensively elsewhere (Ellis 1986, 1991, 1992).

It might be possible to create a model of an information processing system capable of duplicating many of the cognitive functions that the human brain is capable of executing. Although artificial intelligence workers have been less successful in this endeavor than they had originally hoped, it is possible that a 'connectionist' system (Churchland 1989; Bickle 1993; Tienson 1987; Bechtel 1987), or a 'production system' (Anderson 1983) might eventually conceive one. Yet such a system would inevitably process information in a completely different way from the way the human brain does. The human brain generates its own questions about the environment (a process dominated by the prefrontal cortex), as motivated by emotional concerns (survival, entertainment, etc., as mediated through the midbrain, limbic system and reticular formation). These questions then 'prime' the cerebral cortex to 'look for' certain categories of stimuli by enacting patterns corresponding to the consciousness of those categories in the form of images or concepts. All these processes are functionally prior to the act of attending to a perceptual object, and they determine for the most part which perceptual objects we will attend to, and which aspects of the objects we will focus on and use in our cognitive processes. The brain in its conscious function (by contrast to some of its non-conscious functions) much more frequently searches out, motivatedly selects and acts upon sensory input than it passively reacts to the input in a 'stimulus-response' fashion.

It is of course true, as artificial intelligence workers will be quick to point out here, that computers also actively search for information. But, in the first place, the computer's having searched for the information is not an essential precondition for any input's being registered if it *is* passively received. And, more important, the computer's having consciously felt the emotion of *wanting* to receive that particular information, of being interested in it, is not an essential precondition for the computer's seeing it. I am not making the absurd claim that people never receive information that is contrary to their wishes, but rather that the act of attending to information *per se* must be motivated by a general desire to know what is going on in the environment (as we saw in Chapter 1) — a motivational desire which is not necessary in the case of computers. But this is really just another way of saying what folk psychology has claimed all along — that computers do not have consciousness.

Even as early as Stanley Kubrick's film *2001: A Space Odyssey* (1969), viewers were not convinced that Hal the computer really had consciousness until they became convinced that he (or she) had *desires and volitions*. This point will be developed further in a later context.

Another major difference between conscious and non-conscious cognition is that the 'events' which occur in non-conscious cognition can be described as first-order changes in the spacial configuration of electrical and chemical states. Conscious cognitive events, by contrast, are higher-order relationships of patterns of such changes in terms of the *temporal* configuration of these changes. 'Two singers singing in rhythm with each other' cannot be adequately described by first describing the one singer's melody, and then describing the other's melody. Nor can their synchronization be explained merely by means of what would suffice to explain why each singer sings. Minsky (1986) relates this point directly to cognitive states: "Concerns about minds are really concerns with relationships between states — and this has virtually nothing to do with the natures of the states themselves" (287).

To show that it is possible that the explanation for the behavior of the substratum of a process may not suffice to explain the process itself, consider what would happen if a wave pattern were formed out of the simultaneous occurrence of several independent causal chains of substratum events. Within each independent causal chain, the movement of each particle can be completely explained in terms of the movement of the prior particle in that chain. But, given the same causal chains, the wave pattern built up from them will have a different pattern if, say, the first causal chain begins a fraction of a second ahead of or behind the second one, or if the second one begins a fraction of a second ahead of or behind the third, etc. The only way to explain why the events in the different chains occur in the rhythm they do at any given time is that prior events in those chains were already occurring in that rhythm. I.e., the same causal chains may form a different pattern depending on the order and rhythm with which their previous histories occurred. One causal chain could have been earlier or later in relation to the others without any alteration of its causal explanation. Thus the sum total of the explanations for the movements of all the particles that make up the process does not suffice to explain why the process has the overall pattern that it has. It follows that the sum total of the movements of all the particles is not identical with the pattern of the overall process; if the two were identical, then whatever sufficed to explain the one would also suffice to explain the other. Even if there is a combination of substratum movements which is both necessary and sufficient for some aspect of the functioning of the process, this does not mean that this combination of substratum movements is the *same thing as* the corresponding aspect of the functioning of the process.

It is important to be clear about the differences between conscious functions, which are higher-order processes, and the non-conscious functions which make up the substratum for these processes. A thermostat can perform non-conscious information processing of a very elementary kind, but it cannot be conscious. Nor would an increase in the *amount* or *complexity* of the information processed by a thermostat-like gadget bring it any closer to experiencing consciousness. We have seen repeatedly in the previous chapters (and will see in still more detail later) that conscious information processing is a completely different *kind* of thing from non-conscious processing, and no amount of increase in the sheer *quantity* of the latter can render it equivalent in kind to the former, any more than the collection of a large number of violins could equal a trumpet.

Again, this is not meant to deny the reality of unconscious mental processes which in some instances function analogously to conscious ones. But, as explained in the Introduction, these sophisticated unconscious processes are derivative from earlier conscious ones through a process of habituation, as supported by the neurological findings of Posner and Rothbart (1992) and other neurologists discussed earlier.

In this chapter and the next one, I shall try to show that the relationship between consciousness and its physiological correlates is similar in some very interesting respects to the relation between a sound and the medium through which the sound is propagated. The fact that the sound could not be propagated without the medium by no means implies that the sound is a causal epiphenomenon of the medium or is equivalent to the medium. It is the temporal sequence, order, and rhythm in the movement of the particles that makes the sound a sound — not the mere fact that the particles move. Furthermore, it is at least as true, and probably more informative, to say that the sound wave (originating from its source elsewhere) 'causes' the particles to move in the order and rhythm they do, as to say that the particles 'cause' the sound wave to have the character that it has as it passes through the particular medium in question.

In the next chapter, I shall go further still and argue that the mind-body relation is also *unlike* the sound-wood relation in one very crucial respect. Consciousness is a process which is capable of appropriating, replacing, and reproducing many of the substratum elements it needs in order to maintain or expand the pattern of *its own* process, and it does this in part by imaginatively and symbolically 'representing' aspects of the desired substratum elements. If a sound wave, when it reaches the end of the earth's atmosphere, could suddenly cause air molecules to begin reproducing themselves in order to allow the wave to continue travelling, then we could envision the sound wave as being analogous to consciousness in this respect.

But first, I would like to spend the remainder of this chapter laying some ontological groundwork for conceptualizing the mind-body relation as a process-substratum relation which is neither a causal epiphenomenalism, nor an interactionism (which I shall argue would entail dualism), nor a psychophysical identity.

## 1. Formulating the Essential Ontological Problem

Perhaps the most viable version of the *identity* theory of mental events and their corresponding neurophysiological events has been proposed by Donald Davidson (1970), who suggests that the corresponding mental and physical events are the same thing as each other, but viewed from two different perspectives — subjective (through introspection) and objective (through empirical observation).   This view has been criticized by Frank Jackson (1986), Norman Malcolm (1967), Stephen Noren (1979) and others; Jackson, Malcolm and Noren therefore conclude that some sort of interactionism must be at work.   (On my interpretation of their view, this would be a *dualistic* interactionism, positing that in some instances the mental events are causally independent of any physical causation.)   But what I want to argue here is that it is not necessary to posit a psychophysical identity theory in order to make the compatibility of mechanistic and voluntaristic explanations consistent.   Nor (I shall argue) is Alvin Goldman's (1969, 1970) 'nomic equivalence' concept the only viable alternative to the identity thesis.   Rather, compatibilism only needs to establish the *inseparability* of any given mental event and its neurophysiological substratum.   This inseparability thesis is not vulnerable to the criticisms of the identity thesis which have been put forward by Jackson and others. Yet it does hold, with identity theories, that no mental event, $M^1$, could occur without a corresponding neurophysiological event, $N^1$.

It is important to be clear about the inescapable fact that the impressive correlativity of mental and corresponding neurophysiological events does present a problem for the compatibility of physical explanations with mentalistic or 'intentional' ones: Suppose that a conscious mental event $M^1$ is accompanied by neurophysiological event $N^1$, and that a subsequent conscious mental event $M^2$ is accompanied by neurophysiological event $N^2$, as in the following diagram:

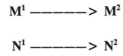

$$M^1 \text{ ------} > M^2$$

$$N^1 \text{ ------} > N^2$$

If $N^1$ 'causes' $N^2$ in the way that we normally say that physical events are 'caused,' and if $N^1$ is necessary and sufficient for $M^1$ (since it is an observed fact that the two regularly correlate in well-controlled empirical studies) while at the same time $N^2$ is necessary and sufficient for $M^2$, then it becomes very difficult to say how it can make sense that $M^1$ acts as a reason for, or in some sense brings about $M^2$. As I emphasized in my *Ontology of Consciousness* (1986, esp. Chapter 2), this problem is aggravated still further when we try to formulate which items are 'necessary' and 'sufficient' for each other in any causal relation. Suppose we want to hold that a cause is necessary and sufficient, under certain given circumstances, to bring about a certain effect. Then we would have to grant that, if neurophysiological event $N^1$ is sufficient to produce neurophysiological event $N^2$, it follows that mental event $M^1$ cannot be necessary to produce it (since, if one antecedent is sufficient, then no other antecedent can be necessary). But since $M^2$ and $N^2$ are necessary and sufficient for each other, this means that $M^1$ also cannot be necessary for $M^2$. At the same time, if $M^1$ is sufficient to produce $M^2$, then $N^1$ would not seem to be necessary to produce it. But, here again, since $N^2$ and $M^2$ are necessary and sufficient for each other, this would mean that $N^1$ would not be necessary to produce $N^2$. Similarly, if $N^1$ is necessary to produce $N^2$, then $M^1$ would not seem to be sufficient to produce it (and thus $M^1$ would not be sufficient to produce $M^2$); whereas if on the other hand $M^1$ is necessary to produce $M^2$, then $N^1$ would not seem to be sufficient to produce it (and thus $N^1$ would not be sufficient to produce $N^2$).    And finally, if $N^1$ is both necessary and sufficient to produce $N^2$, then $M^1$ would seem to be neither necessary nor sufficient to produce it (nor therefore could $M^1$ be necessary and sufficient to produce $M^2$); and in the same way, if $M^1$ is both necessary and sufficient to produce $M^2$, then $N^1$ would seem to be neither necessary nor sufficient to produce it (nor therefore could $N^1$ be necessary and sufficient to produce $N^2$ in this case).    Therefore, either $M^1$ would not produce $M^2$ or else $N^1$ would not produce $N^2$.

And yet it seems impossible to escape the fact that, if we want to hold in any sense that A causes B, then we mean that A is at least *sufficient* to produce B under certain given circumstances.    And it also seems unavoidable that we want to hold that A is *necessary* for B under these given circumstances, at least in the sense that we could say, 'If A had not happened, or had happened differently, then B could have been avoided.'    When it comes to conscious choices, for example, we want to mean that 'If the agent had chosen differently, then she would have acted differently.'    We are therefore faced with two equally unworkable options:  (1) Neurophysiological event $N^1$ causes neurophysiological event $N^2$, which in turn generates the conscious state $M^2$; in this case conscious event $M^1$ is a causally irrelevant epiphnomenon caused by $N^1$.    Or (2) conscious event $M^1$ leads to conscious event $M^2$ by means of reasoning or some other connection between the *ideas* present to consciousness in its successive conscious acts; in this case $N^1$ would not be sufficient for $N^2$, and thus consciousness would have to be capable of contra-causal, metaphysical (or, as Gilbert Ryle says, "ghostly") powers to prevent the principles of physics from operating in their usual way in the case of neurophysiological processes. The first alternative seems unacceptable because we cannot reconcile it to the common observation that we do seem to have the power to act on the basis of rational or at least conscious decisions. (Note that this is not easily reconciled with the epiphenomenalism of option (1) above even if we are prepared to give up the 'freedom' supposedly attaching to the conscious decision).    The second alternative, on the other hand, seems to contradict some very obvious facts that now have been learned about neurophysiology; it has simply been demonstrated in too many empirical contexts that the brain viewed in its physiological dimension functions according to the regular principles that govern all chemical and physical phenomena, and that these physiological events correlate regularly with the corresponding conscious events.

The most tempting aspect of psychophysical identity theories is that they can solve this problem by positing that mental event $M^1$ and neurophysiological event $N^1$ are really the same event viewed from different perspectives. This view has been criticized with some justification, as we shall see. I suggest, however, that a compatibilist resolution for the problem can be preserved without positing the identity of $M^1$ and $N^1$. It is only necessary to posit that $M^1$ and $N^1$ are *inseparable* — that is, that they are necessary and sufficient for each other in some sense other than one's being the cause of the other. For example, they could both be caused by a third thing. Or one could be subject while the other is predicate, as Feuerbach puts it. Or one could be a wave while the other is its substratum or the medium through which the wave is propagated. There are a variety of different alternative ways in which $M^1$ and $N^1$ could be inseparable without being identical and without causing or being caused by each other. But it is only necessary that they be inseparable — not that they be identical — in order for compatibilism to make sense. If conscious event $M^1$ and neurophysiological event $N^1$ are inseparable without being identical, while the same is true for $N^2$ and $M^2$, then $M^1$ may be necessary and sufficient for $M^2$ *and* $N^1$ may be necessary and sufficient for $N^2$ *and* $N^2$ may be necessary and sufficient for $M^2$, all at the same time and without entailing any contradiction. We shall see that for $M^1$ and $N^1$ to be inseparable and therefore necessary and sufficient for each other without being either identical or the cause of each other is perfectly natural and unparadoxical, and that in this sense two events can *each* be both necessary *and* sufficient for some third event, but only if the first two events are necessary and sufficient for each other. The terms 'necessary' and 'sufficient' in the context of causal theory tend to lend themselves to a certain ambiguity and can become misleading in this respect. But when they are adequately clarified, we shall see that the problem for compatibilism mentioned above — which forms the essential core of the main criticisms of compatibilism offered by interactionists like Jackson, Malcolm and Noren — vanishes. I shall attempt to show through this clarification that the whole situation can make sense only if we view 'mind' as a *process* which takes physiological events as its substrata.

The two following sections will therefore attempt to establish two basic clarifications:

(1) The confusion about the compatibility problem results partly from the 'necessary-and-sufficient' relations implied by the meaning of the word 'cause.' In cases where events A and B are *inseparable*, the principle does not apply which says that if A is necessary for C then B cannot be sufficient for C.

(2) A little clarification of the meaning of the term 'cause' and of the nature of 'necessary-and-sufficient' relations in general can help us understand more effectively the fourfold interrelation of mental event $M^1$, neurophysiological event $N^1$, mental event $M^2$ and neurophysiological event $N^2$: $M^1$ may be necessary and sufficient for $M^2$ while at the same time $N^1$ may be necessary and sufficient for $N^2$, yet neither a causal relation nor an identity relation exists between $M^1$ and $N^1$. We shall also see that certain criticisms of the identity theory are well-taken, although the dualist/interactionist alternative they seem to imply is equally unacceptable. I shall then attempt to describe the sense in which $M^1$ and $N^1$ can be inseparable without being either identical or the cause of each other. It will turn out that the process/substratum model of the mind-body relation is the only workable compatibilist resolution for the problem.

## 2. Why Theories of Interactionism and Causal Epiphenomenalism Have Failed

It will be helpful to begin by ruling out several possible solutions which fail to work. One solution that can be quickly rejected is interactionism, the thesis that $M^1$ causes $N^1$, which causes $N^2$, which causes $M^2$, which causes $M^3$, which causes $N^3$, etc. The problem here is that the causal self-sufficiency of the physiological chain $N^1$, $N^2$, $N^3$, etc. would be destroyed, since $N^2$ would not be *sufficient* to cause $N^3$ without the 'ghostly' intermediary, $M^3$. Moreover, we would be forced to posit that each time one of these *'free'* mental events occurs, still another rupture is created in the supposedly universal laws of physics. If $M^1$ is free, then $N^1$ has no physical cause, and similarly for $M^3$ and $N^3$.

One is tempted at this point to simply deny that a cause must be both necessary and sufficient for its effect, thus getting rid of the counterfactual conditional which states that if the cause had not occurred, then neither would the effect. This option appears plausible at first because it is true that there may be more than one possible cause for some events; but, on closer inspection, this appearance proves misleading. *In a sense*, it is often false to say in the case of a causal connection that 'If A had not occurred, B would not have occurred,' because something else might have stepped in and caused B if A had failed to cause it. But *in another sense* — the sense really intended in the definition of 'cause' — it is always true that in any *specific context*, given all other circumstances exactly as they in fact are, except for the deletion of A, then B must fail to follow or else A does not qualify as the cause of B. The fact that in other possible contexts (and other possible worlds) C, D, or E might also be capable of causing events like B is irrelevant. So in this sense, A must be necessary for B *in the given circumstances* if it causes B.

Of course, the problem remains that if 'A causes B' were to mean nothing *more* than that A is necessary and sufficient for B, then B would also be sufficient and necessary for A, which would imply that if A causes B, then B must also cause A, as Taylor (1962, 1963, 1964, 1964b), Sharvy (1963) and others have pointed out. But this need not pose any grave difficulty for our purposes. As J.L. Mackie (1974) suggests, it is only necessary to add to the necessary-and-sufficient stipulation some additional stipulation designed to insure the directionality of the causal relation.

Mackie has explored some of the possible stipulations that might be added in order to convey the sense of directionality in the causal connection. He clearly shows problems with most possible stipulations that have been proposed to meet this problem (such as, for example, stipulating that the cause must precede the effect in time); his conclusion is that a present event may be "fixed" in a sense that can never apply to the corresponding future event for which it is necessary and sufficient. Unfortunately, as I discussed in more detail elsewhere (1986, 1991), Mackie does not adequately answer the objection that if the present event is fixed and is necessary and sufficient for a future event, then the future event by the same token becomes just as 'fixed' as the present one. Nor does he explain how this concept defines the direction of causation when the cause is simultaneous with the effect.

This is why I have suggested (1986, 1991) a slight modification of Mackie's view: Suppose we define the direction of causation in such a way that, if A causes B, then any experimental manipulation of A under appropriately controlled circumstances will lead to a corresponding change in B, whereas an experimental manipulation of B in the same circumstances will not necessarily lead to any corresponding change in A. This is in essence the way empirical scientists normally determine which of a correlative pair is the cause and which is the effect. If A is the necessary and sufficient cause of B in the given circumstances (i.e., absent the experimental manipulation), then to change the circumstances so as to alter B does not necessarily alter A; whereas to change the circumstances so as to appropriately alter A will necessarily alter B (unless we simultaneously introduce still another change in the circumstances so as to purposely *avoid* altering B). For example, if turning a switch (A) in the appropriate circumstances causes a light to come on (B), then not only is A necessary and sufficient for B (and *vice versa*) in the given circumstances (i.e., a good bulb appropriately wired, etc.), but also the direct experimental manipulation of A necessarily affects B, but not *vice versa*. I.e., in the given circumstances, if the switch is flipped the light will come on, and if the switch is not flipped the light will not come on. But we do *not* say, if the circumstances are altered so that something other than flipping the switch causes the light to come one, that this in turn will *cause the switch to be flipped*. Hence the causal relation is asymmetrical even though *under the given circumstances* the cause and effect are both necessary and sufficient for each other. In this way, we can preserve the sense that a cause is necessary for its effect in the kinds of examples where we want to say this, without falling into the trap of making the causal relation symmetrical (so that the consequent could just as well qualify as the 'cause' of its own antecedent). And this strategy remains equally workable even in the case of a simultaneous cause and effect.

Someone might object here that by introducing the experimental manipulation of B which fails to affect A, we are merely demonstrating that A is not really necessary for B in the first place, even though it was the cause of it — thus refuting the notion that a cause must be necessary for its effect. But our claim was, more precisely, that a cause is necessary and sufficient for its effect *under the given circumstances,* and that *if* the circumstances were *altered* through an appropriate experimental manipulation, *then* A would no longer be necessary for B. 'A causes B' posits both that A is necessary (and sufficient) for B under the actual, given circumstances, *and* that A would *not* be necessary for B under certain experimentally altered circumstances. This simply means that a causal claim is a claim about what would or would not have happened if certain circumstances had been different from the way they are.

I shall save a more detailed analysis of this concept of manipulability until another time, since it is only marginally relevant to the problem we are considering here. (I have discussed it more fully in Ellis 1991). In our context here, it is only necessary to establish that there are certain examples in which both the 'necessity' and the 'sufficiency' stipulations are necessary to the concept of cause (as we have already seen), and that with the addition of some stipulation to make the causal relation asymmetrical (such as the notion of manipulability), the necessary-and-sufficient characterization makes enough sense that we can still analyse the fourfold interrelation of consecutive mental events with their corresponding consecutive neurophysiological events in terms of which of these events are necessary and sufficient for which others.

What we must understand, then, is how it can make sense that no contradiction is involved in saying that mental event $M^1$ is necessary for mental event $M^2$ while at the same time neurophysiological event $N^1$ is necessary and sufficient for neurophysiological event $N^2$, which in turn is necessary and sufficient for mental event $M^2$.

## 3. Process and Substratum: How Consciousness and Its Physiological Correlates Can Be Inseparable yet Different

In many contexts, it seems reasonable to suppose that the necessary-and-sufficient relation is 'exclusive.' That is, it seems that, if A is sufficient for the occurrence of B, then C cannot be necessary for B, and *vice versa*. We have already seen that much of the appeal of physicalism, and consequently much of the rejection of the causal relevance of consciousness, stems from the seeming inevitability of this assumption. If some physical antecedent is both necessary and sufficient for every (physical or mental) event, then no conscious or 'intentional' state can ever be causally relevant to any (physical or mental) event.    But when we carefully examine this 'exclusivity' assumption, we find that it involves a number of difficulties.    One obvious problem (essentially, the same one that was pointed out by Alvin Goldman) can be illustrated with the following example.    Suppose three dominos are lined up such that the first falls, causing the second to fall, causing the third to fall.    Let's call these three events A, B and C.    Then according to the axiom that if A is necessary and sufficient for B then C can be neither sufficient nor necessary for B (the 'exclusivity principle'), we find the following perplexing state of affairs:

(1)    If A is necessary and sufficient for B, and if B is necessary and sufficient for C,

(2)    then A is necessary and sufficient for C.

(3)    But if A is sufficient for C, then B is not necessary for C.

(4)    And if B is sufficient for C, then A is not necessary for C.

(5)    Furthermore, if A is necessary for C, then B is not sufficient for C.

(6)    And if B is necessary for C, then A is not sufficient for C.

Obviously, the conclusion of the conditional in each of (3), (4), (5), and (6) contradicts (1) in some respect, even though each of them follows directly from (1).    Goldman tries to avoid this kind of problem by proposing that the causal relations involved are 'nomologically equivalent' with each other and therefore that the 'exclusivity' principle of the necessary-and-sufficient relation does not apply.    I.e., we must deny in such cases that if A is necessary and sufficient for B, then no other event can also be necessary and sufficient for the same event.    But not all instances of non-exclusivity can be gotten out of so easily.    Consider the following more serious dilemma:    Suppose the dominos are lined up so that if the first falls (event A), it causes the second and third to fall (events B and C) by striking them both simultaneously. In this case, the following relations would obtain:

(1)  If A is necessary and sufficient for B, and if A is necessary and sufficient for C,

(2)  then B is impossible without A, which entails C, and C is impossible without A, which entails B; therefore B is necessary and sufficient for C and *vice versa*.

(3)  But if C is necessary for B, then A is not sufficient for B.

(4)  And if B is necessary for C, then A is not sufficient for C.

(5)  Furthermore, if C is sufficient for B, then A is not necessary for B.

(6)  And if B is sufficient for C, then A is not necessary for C.

Just as in the earlier example, the conclusion in each of (3), (4), (5), and (6) contradicts (1), even though each of them follows directly from (1). And in this case too, the problem results from the 'exclusivity' principle of the necessary-and-sufficient relation which was presupposed by the inferences. It thus seems that we must deny that if A is sufficient for B then no other event can be necessary for B, and we must also deny that if A is necessary for B then no other event can be sufficient for B. But in this case, Goldman's 'nomological equivalence' explanation does not work. We cannot regard the relationship between A and B as equivalent in any sense with the relationship between A and C, although in the given circumstances the two relationships are inseparable.

At the same time, we cannot simply give up the exclusivity principle. In most cases, we want to hold that A's being necessary for B *means* that nothing other than A can be sufficient for B. In this sense, to give up the claim that the sufficiency of A precludes the necessity of any other event for the same purpose seems to strip the words 'necessary' and 'sufficient' of all meaning.

Luckily, we do not have to give up the exclusivity principle in all cases. We can allow that if A is necessary and sufficient for B, then C can be neither sufficient nor necessary for B, *unless A and C are inseparable*. In the case of the three dominos, the exclusivity principle is not applicable because the causal connection between the first and second dominos is inseparable (in the given circumstances) from the causal connection between the first and third dominos (even though these two relationships are neither identical nor nomologically equivalent). In general, we can call X and Y 'inseparable' whenever neither a causal nor an identity relation exists between them, yet the two are necessary and sufficient for each other (in a given context) — e.g., by virtue of being simultaneously necessary and sufficient for some third event.

We have seen that X and Y lack any direct causal relationship unless the directionality of this relationship can be established in some such way as outlined in the last section (i.e., by performing experimental manipulations). When it comes to consciousness and its physiological correlates, however, this directionality cannot be established, because to manipulate a conscious event is *ipso facto* to manipulate its physiological correlates and *vice versa*. The relationship between them must therefore be either one of identity or one of inseparability. The remainder of this book will develop a type of inseparability theory: the process-substratum approach. In my view, a process may be non-identical with its substratum, yet the process and the substratum can interrelate in such a way that process events are inseparable from corresponding substratum events. For reasons that will become increasingly obvious, I believe it is often misleading, and in many instances false, to think (with the strict identity theorists) that what explains the elements of a given substratum is thereby sufficient to explain the corresponding process.

## 4. The Multiple Realizability Problem

The objection has often been raised against psychophysical identity theories that, if a given state of consciousness could be realized by means of any one of several different underlying physiological mechanisms, then it makes no sense to equate the state of consciousness with a particular underlying mechanism. Horgan (1992) has made the case for the possibility of multiple realizability, and has suggested that it raises these kinds of problems for the reducibility of mental to physical events. While the inseparability thesis is not reductionistic in some important senses — for example, it does maintain the possibility of distinguishing between what is meant by a state of consciousness and what is meant by its underlying physiological substratum, and leaves open an epistemological role for the 'privacy' of subjective experiences — still, it might be worried that the same kind of problem might arise for the inseparability thesis. If a state of consciousness is inseparable from its underlying physiological substratum, in the sense that the two event-patterns are 'necessary and sufficient' for each other, then the possibility of multiple realizability might seem to present a problem. If the conscious state could have been realized by several different physiological substrata, then the actually-occurring substratum would not seem to be *necessary* for it, and therefore would not seem to be *inseparable* from it.

Luckily, the solution to this problem has already been developed by John Bickle (1992). Consider the reduction of thermodynamics to statistical mechanics, for example.

> When you think in terms of the velocity and momentum of each individual molecule, you will see that there are an *indefinite* number of ways for a given aggregate of molecules to realize any given temperature. . . . Here, again with a vengeance, is multiple realizability of 'the same individual across times' — an indefinite number of distinct possible micro-realizations of a given macroscopic phenomenon in the same molecular aggregate (Bickle 1992: 53).

Yet, Bickle argues, no one would raise this as an objection against explaining thermodynamics in terms of statistical mechanics, or of saying that a given temperature is inseparable from certain conditions which could be stipulated with regard to the underlying mechanics — that a certain mathematical relationship must obtain between the velocity and momentum and the density of particles within a given volume.

Even if a given temperature is realizable by an indefinite number of mechanical patterns, we can still say that that temperature is both necessary and sufficient for one of a disjunctive set of alternative patterns. Similarly, if a state of consciousness can be realized by means of a multiplicity of physiological substrata, this would mean, according to the inseparability thesis, that the state of consciousness, $M_1$, can occur if and only if at least one of a disjunction of physiological  states of affairs obtains.  I.e., $M_1$ will occur if and only if ($P_1$ or $P_2$ or $P_3$ or $P_N$ ) obtains.  And, as another way of saying the same thing, ($P_1$ or $P_2$ or $P_3$ or $P_N$ ) will occur if and only if $M_1$ obtains. Moreover, if the *given background conditions* are such that $P_2$, $P_3$ and $P_N$ *do not* occur, whereas $P_1$ does, then in the given circumstances $M_1$ will occur if and only if $P_1$ obtains.  And (again as another way of saying the same thing) $P_1$ will occur if and only if $M_1$ obtains.

Horgan is correct in that this does not imply that $M_1$ *means* the same thing as $P_1$, since it is still *possible* that $M_1$ could have been associated with $P_2$, $P_3$ or $P_N$ if some of the circumstances had been different.  But Bickle is correct in that, *under the given* circumstances, $M_1$ can occur only if $P_1$ does. If Einstein had not been the discoverer of the theory of relativity, then someone else probably would have been; thus 'Einstein' and 'the discoverer of the theory of relativity' do not *mean* the same thing, any more than 'Clark Kent' and 'Superman' do.  If circumstances had been different, Clark Kent might have been Batman or Zorro instead of Superman.  But, given the circumstances which actually did obtain, Einstein and the discoverer of the theory of relativity *were* the same entity, just as Clark Kent and Superman were.

Bickle's reasoning seems to work equally well as a defense against the multiple realizability problem for either the inseparability thesis or for certain types of psychophysical identity theories .  However, the inseparability thesis does not necessarily entail psychophysical identity, and I believe there are strong reasons to refrain from taking the step from inseparability to psychophysical identity.  These reasons will be the subject of the next section. Then the next chapter will systematically develop a theory of inseparability which is not a theory of psychophysical identity.

## 5.  Why the Process-Substratum Model Is Not a Psychophysical Identity Theory

There seem to be certain problems that we encounter if we try to simply equate a conscious process with its neurophysiological substratum — or even with the *activity* of the substratum.  Davidson maintains that the *apparent* differences between consciousness and brain activity are attributable to the fact that we can view the same phenomenon from two different perspectives — subjective or objective. But this move only transforms the problem rather than solving it. The question remains: Why is there a difference between *what is known* from subjective introspection into my own consciousness on the one hand, and on the other hand *what is known* from objective empirical observation of my own brain? If the subjective and the objective perspectives are two different ways of knowing the same thing, then why is that which is known different in the two cases? If a neurologist had never experienced anything like a headache, she could never learn what it feels like to have a headache from any amount of empirical observation of someone's nervous system. But if the facts that are known when we know our own consciousness are still different from the facts that are known when we know our own brains *no matter how much of both types of information we acquire,* then these facts must not be the same facts (although the two types of facts must be very intimately interrelated or even completely inseparable by their very nature).

This is why many computer-based cognitive theorists feel compelled not only to adopt a reductive materialism, but also to insist that, if only we had enough empirical scientific information, we could *translate* any 'folk psychological' statement (for example, 'I have a headache') into an equivalent but much more accurate empirical scientific statement (for example, 'the firing of certain neurons with excessive buildup of negative charge inside the cell walls is depleting certain neurotransmitters in my limbic system, thus causing still further electrical imbalances in the midbrain'). I.e., they feel compelled to insist that the *meaning* of these two types of statements must be the same, although presumably one is a more vague and the other is a more precise statement of this same meaning. In their view, this would be like saying that Clark Kent is Superman, and thus that if we learn everything we can about Superman, we also know everything that can be known about Clark Kent.

But this is just why Jackson and Malcolm, representing the extreme opposite side of this dispute, say that one of the main differences between mental event $M^1$ and corresponding neurophysiological event $N^1$ is that any objective observer can experience and measure $N^1$, whereas only the person who directly and subjectively feels $M^1$, and who is identified with the series $M^1$, $M^2$, $M^3$, etc., can experience $M^1$ as such. As Newton (1993) points out, one implication of the 'problem of indexicals' is that anyone can empirically observe anyone's brain, but only I can feel my own feelings. Conversely, the most complete subjective knowledge of $M^1$ does not guarantee any knowledge whatever of $N^1$. Husserl's unpublished manuscripts comprise at least 50,000 pages of phenomenological description (in shorthand, no less), but hardly any neurophysiology at all. In fact, if conscious state $M^1$ is multiply realizable, then one could not even *infer* from it to its physiological correlates without the assistance of some empirical assumptions at the physical level. Moreover, the subjective description of $M^1$ (from a phenomenological point of view) would not make the appropriate kind of sense, i.e., would not *be* an adequate description, unless described in terms of references to other items in the series $M^1$, $M^2$, $M^3$, etc,; whereas a description of $N^1$, $N^2$, or $N^3$ *can* frequently be adequate without references to other items in the series $N^1$, $N^2$, $N^3$, etc. — especially to items in the series which have not yet occurred at the time of the one which is to be described. Michael Simon (1979) stresses this point, concluding that consciousness sometimes makes sense only holistically, whereas the physical interactions between the particles of its physiological substratum can usually make sense in *partes extra partes* fashion, as Merleau-Ponty (1942-63) argues in detail.

If there are real differences between what we mean by subjective consciousness and what we mean by its objective correlates, then Davidson's notion that the only reason for the difference is that $M^1$ and $N^1$ are the same event *but viewed from different perspectives* leaves the central question unanswered. The main problem with this solution is that the 'perspectives' which are supposed to be different would not in fact *be* different if $M^1$ and $N^1$ were not different in the first place. If $M^1$ and $N^1$ were not different, then Sartre would be right in his preposterous assertion that Peter can have just as intimate an intuition of Paul's emotions as Paul can. The qualitative difference between Paul's experiencing of his own emotions and Peter's apprehension of them is a phenomenological datum. This difference would remain even if we are comparing Paul's experiencing of his own emotions with Paul's objective observation of his own brain.

The point is that, just as $M^2$ and $N^2$ can both be explained by $N^1$ (since $N^1$ is necessary and sufficient for both $M^2$ and $N^2$), so $M^2$ and $N^2$ in principle could also be explained by $M^1$ (since $M^1$ also is necessary and sufficient for both $M^2$ and $N^2$). However, either explanation taken by itself tends to be misleading because it either denies the existence of one or the other of the '$M^1/N^1$' pair, or else it interprets one as the cause of the other. But neither can be the cause of the other, since to manipulate either one would be *ipso facto* to manipulate the other, thus no causal directionality can be established. The only viable solution is therefore to find a way to regard the two as distinguishable but necessarily *inseparable* events.

Other philosophers, such as Vivian Weil, have tried to save compatibilism from this kind of objection in a different way. The problem to be overcome of course, is that the anti-identity theorists' way of *distinguishing* between mental and neurophysiological events seems to entail a dualism. Weil maintains that when Malcolm says that if mechanism were true a man would move up a ladder whether he wanted to or not, he confuses the event to be explained — the 'action' of climbing a ladder (purposely climbing it) — and the unconscious or sleepwalking climbing of a ladder which is not an 'action' at all. Weil says, "We regard mental components as essential to actions. Holding that reasons are components of actions makes it possible to avoid the bog of the reasons-causes debate." But it seems inescapable that Weil is only dodging the question here. Malcolm's contention is precisely that the *action* of climbing a ladder cannot be explained mechanistically; if compatibilists want to deny Malcolm's contention, they must show, not merely that if no purposes are present then the event is not an action, but that even if the event *is* an action, there is no contradiction in accounting for it both mechanistically and purposefully.

Let me be clear about the sense in which I am arguing that consciousness and its neurophysiological substratum are not literally the same thing as each other, and in what senses I do not mean to argue this. We say that a transverse wave — for example, a wave in the ocean — is not identical with the up-and-down oscillation of certain specific drops of water. The wave travels for miles whereas the water drops do not. The wave has a certain shape and contour, whereas none of the water drops have this shape and contour. Most important, if the up-and-down oscillation were to take place just as it does, but in a different order and rhythm, then the contour of the wave would be different even though the movements of the individual drops would be the same. If certain things that can be said about the wave cannot be said about the water drops or about the movement of the water drops, then there is a sense in which the wave is not the same thing as the water drops or of the movement of the water drops. There is a sense, of course, in which the movement of the water drops can be identified with the movement of the wave, if we take the *rhythmic pattern* of the movements of all the drops into consideration. But, what if the wave would still be the same wave even without the presence of those particular water drops, and what if the wave were capable of *appropriating and reproducing* water drops in order to use them as its substratum in cases where it found itself to be missing the number of drops needed to have a medium through which to propagate itself? Then the notion that the wave is just identical with this particular substratum would lead to very misleading and even false consequences, as I shall show in detail in the next chapter. If a process determines its own substratum by appropriating and reproducing its own substratum elements when needed, then the process is no more identical with its substratum than a computer program is with its hardware, or than a symphony is with its notation on a stack of music paper or with a particular performance of it. This was the original conceptual distinction that motivated the functionalist approach in neuroscience to begin with. As Putnam said in a recent paper at the American Philosophical Association (December 28, 1993), part of his original motive in proposing functionalism was the 'compositional plasticity' of mental states. If mental states are compositionally plastic, he reasoned, then 'what else could they *be* but functional-logical contents?' (What I am suggesting here is that they are not merely 'computational' organizations, but rather higher-order processes which take neurophysiological activities in relation to the organism's environment as their substratum.) But, because neuroscientists could find no way to explain the causal interrelations we have been discussing without positing a strict identity between consciousness and its neurophysiological substratum, they ultimately ended up destroying the original distinction that Putnam and others were trying to maintain between software and hardware — or between patterns of information and the material medium through which they are instantiated.

In the next chapter, I shall try to show that consciousness is different from a wave in the ocean in just this respect. The problem of the relationship between process and substratum is not a difficult issue if we choose to equate the wave with a 'pattern of activity' in the drops of water which oscillate only up and down, because the 'pattern' of this up-and-down oscillation can be described at the same level as the separate up-and-down patterns of the individual particles. There is no worry that the wave itself may create additional water drops just so it can have water drops through which to move.

In that case, it would be seriously misleading to equate the wave with the water drops which it had created. But since consciousness *does* appropriate, replace, and reproduce the substratum elements needed to continue being conscious — since material which comes into its systematic functioning tends to be used for this purpose — then there is a problem with merely equating consciousness with its substratum. To do so is to make it seem that the overall pattern of the changes in all the individual particles is only an accidental byproduct of the movement of the individual particles, which interact only in *partes extra partes* fashion. We shall see in the next chapter that this is not the case with regard to consciousness and its organismic substratum.

If two events are inseparable, yet they are not identical, and there is no directionality for a causal relation between them, then the only remaining explanation would seem to be that the one is a complex *process* while the other constitutes a *substratum* for the process. Obviously, since carbon, oxygen, hydrogen and nitrogen atoms would behave according to the same predictable laws whether associated with a human organism or not, their activity must be the substratum for the more complex process which is consciousness, and not the other way around. On this hypothesis, then, consciousness would become a process, or a higher-order wave-pattern in some sense to be further clarified, which could not possibly exist without some substratum through which to move; conversely, the particles which make up the substratum could not possibly move in the pattern they do without the wave's existing with the particular character and properties it has.

I shall go further in the next chapter and argue that, in the case of consciousness, it is not the motion of the individual particles, each acted upon by other individual particles, which 'causes' the wave to have the pattern it has. It may be possible that consciousness has the capacity to find and use other substrata to perform its functions if some particles which had been used suddenly become dysfunctional or unavailable. For example, to a certain extent the brain in Kurt Goldstein's experiments was able to replace cells that had been destroyed and to incorporate other cells into the needed functional continuity.

This view is similar in some respects to James' idea that 'consciousness is not an entity but a function,' although precisely what James means by an 'entity' would remain to be clarified. However, given James' rigorous empiricism (exemplified by his dramatic statement that consciousness "does not exist") he seems to reduce consciousness to the status of an epiphenomenon which is more or less 'caused by' its underlying physiological correlates. (Hence, in his view, I am depressed because I cry rather than crying because I am depressed.) In light of the foregoing analysis, however, we must agree with him at least in saying that consciousness has the ontological status of a process rather than a stasis — more like a wave than its substratum. A pattern or process is as different from its substratum as the activity of walking down the street is different form the street itself and the feet which walk on the street.

Let us therefore explore further the notion that consciousness exists with the ontological status of a complex process constituted by interrelations among simpler or lower-order processes. This would be entirely consistent with the fact that consciousness makes contact with the world in this same realm of complex processes, where the 'things' we perceive are not really 'things' at all but rather relationships among 'things' (a visual object, obviously, is a complex relationship resulting from the activity of subatomic and simpler kinds of beings; as Restak 1984: 58ff and other neurologists have pointed out, the eye is sensitive not to light or to dark, but to the contrast between them — a point whose philosophical significance was pursued by Merleau-Ponty 1942-1963). If we could ever arrive at simple 'things' (if there be such), we would first have to carry out complex analyses of the processes with which our perceptual processes are capable of making contact.

An example of these kinds of ontological relationships can be seen clearly in the case of music. In this case, what we mean by 'form' or 'relationship' and what we mean by 'substratum' are obviously relative. If we regard the form of a musical composition as its overall structure, such as sonata or fugue, then the individual parts — the themes and the development sections — become the substratum elements for this form. But if we regard a melody as a form, the chord progressions and phrases that make up the melody become substrata. If we regard a chord progression as a form, the chords become substrata. But if we regard a single note as a substratum, then a single chord can be a form. Any element can be either a substratum or a form, depending on the ontological level or degree of formal complexity we choose to bring into focus. Even the 'simple' tone in itself can be analysed, if we wish, into still lower-order substrata — the vibrations of molecules, which in turn can be analysed into atoms, etc.

Any relation can also be one of several substratum elements which together form a higher-order relation. The term 'substratum' implies no metaphysical concept of a simplest-possible-substance. Yet the logical relationship between substrata and relations can be maintained. For example, the fact that a 'wave' is a process (therefore a relation) to be distinguished from its 'medium' (or substratum) does not imply that the medium itself may not also be a process in its own right. The wave theory of light, therefore, does not imply the existence of a material ether. The ontological status of the medium of a wave might itself consist of a set of 'relations' among other substratum elements, while at the same time serving as substratum for the relation which is the wave.

Thus the relationship between 'subject' and 'predicate' does not imply a metaphysical relationship between 'thing-in-itself' or 'substance' on the one hand and 'property' or 'relation' on the other; nor does it imply that relations could necessarily ever even in principle be analysed into simplest-possible, self-subsistent entities or things-in-themselves. Formal logic therefore is not dependent on any metaphysical concept of its terms. It can just as easily stand for 'relationships' among 'substratum elements' (which in turn may be relationships themselves) as it can stand for 'substances' and their 'properties.' We can thus designate lower-order and higher-order predicates, processes or relationships even if no lowest-possible-order relationship or simple substratum of the relationships exists. If A and B are both relationships, but A is a relationship between B and some other substrata, then B is a substratum element for the relationship A and therefore is a lower-order relationship than A.

It is also possible for A to be a lower-order relationship than B in one respect, while B is a lower order relationship than A in another respect. For example, 'walking down the street' is a relationship between someone's body and the street, whereas the person's body is a relationship between some other substrata (cells, atoms and subatomic particles) and the bodily processes which include, for example, walking-down-the-street. To say that 'my body walks down the street' therefore does not imply that my body is ultimately either a lower-order or a higher-order predicate than walking-down-the-street. It can be both simultaneously, but in different respects.

It is therefore possible to preserve the compatibility of mechanistic explanations of mental events on the one hand, and on the other hand the possibility that conscious choices and other conscious states have power to bring about actions. All that is needed is a workable conception of the way a mental event and its physiological correlates can be necessary and sufficient for each other without one's acting as the cause of the other — and to show that if A is necessary and sufficient for B, it does not follow that C cannot also be necessary and sufficient for B, as long as A and C are inseparable. (Without such a conception, we could not make sense even of a straightforward case of falling dominos.) If Jackson and Malcolm are right in distinguishing consciousness from its physiological substratum, the possibility that they can still be inseparable remains if we hold that consciousness is a higher-order process which takes the lower-order activities of the nervous system as its substratum. To deny such an ontological status for consciousness would seem to render us unable to solve the paradox of the fourfold necessary-and-sufficient relation among conscious states $M^1$ and $M^2$ and neurophysiological states $N^1$ and $N^2$, or else being forced to deny that consciousness exists at all. But we have already seen many reasons not to deny that consciousness exists, provided that we do not elevate it to the level of a dualistic 'soul-substance' (which is what James wanted to avoid). The only workable option therefore seems to be that consciousness has a process nature and takes physiological events as its substratum. To elaborate this process theory of consciousness more fully, and in more concrete terms, will be the task of the next chapter.

# CHAPTER FIVE

## The Priority of Process over Substratum: Consciousness as an Organic Phenomenon

We know from empirical observation of the electro-chemical transactions between neurons (for example, Kandel and Schwartz 1981; Restak 1984: 234ff; Ornstein and Thompson 1984) that at least one precondition for the existence of conscious *desires* in living subjects is that many micro-'desires' in the non-conscious sense set up a pattern in which the fulfillment of one 'desire' leads to the creation of another. For example, when a more negative than usual ionization exists inside the cell wall of a neuron, tiny gates pop open in the cell membrane so that positively charged sodium ions can rush into the cell and neutralize the charge through a chemical reaction with the negatively ionized proteins inside the cell. Because these chemicals 'want' to achieve electrical neutrality — i.e., 'want' to either fill or empty the outer energy shells of each ionized atom — there is a "very strong electrical force *trying* to pull sodium ions into the cell" (Ornstein and Thompson 1984: 77, italics added). Each of these little 'desires' is a 'desire' only in the non-conscious sense, but the total constellation of them somehow feels *desire* in the conscious sense. At what point does the 'desire' become conscious?

It seems clear — again from empirical observation of the way nerve impulses 'travel' when feelings are phenomenologically experienced — that the total constellation can feel *desire* in the conscious sense only because homeostasis cannot be achieved in one part of the system (for example, in one neuron) without disrupting it in another part (for example, in an adjacent neuron). It is not enough that an electrical imbalance *exists* within the system if a conscious pain or desire is to be felt. If this were so, the creation of ionization in a flask of liquid would result in a conscious pain or desire — or, for that matter, the movements of electrons in a metal wire would feel consciousness. It would therefore be too simple to say that the feeling of a pain is merely a consciousness that disequilibria exist within the system. On the contrary, the feeling of the pain must be in some way a consciousness that the resolution of one such disequilibrium cannot be achieved without creating another. Pain is a consciousness that only by changing the larger *context* in which these inter-neuronal conflicts are inevitable can the conflicts be resolved.

For example, it is easily observable that the tissues of a dead frog or eel will respond electrically (Restak 1984: 30ff; Ornstein and Thompson 1984: 77ff), showing that they have 'desire' (in the sense that their molecules still 'want' to achieve electrical neutrality), but this cannot add up to *desire* in the conscious sense, because experience teaches us that dead animals do not show the important signs of consciousness, such as the ability to learn from experience and to engage in apparently purposeful behavior (as Max Scheler 1928-1968 took the trouble to show in a detailed way). Our question, then, is this: How are those natural systems in which many 'desires' produce a *desire* (such as living human nervous systems) different from those in which many 'desires' are *not* sufficient to produce a desire in the conscious sense?

I shall focus here on two of the main differences. Section 1 will try to work toward an understanding of how it is that many lower-order 'desires' can function together in such a way as to produce a *desire* whose aim is not the same as the aggregate sum of all the lower-order 'desires.' This difference naturally leads to another, which will be discussed in Section 2: How are organismically structured systems different from merely 'mechanically' interrelated systems? And this, as one might suspect from our previous discussions, will in turn lead to the topic of Section 3: In what sense can we say that in 'organic' systems the overall process of the system 'causes' the substratum elements of the system to behave in the way that they do, rather than allowing the behavior of the individual substratum elements to determine the pattern of the overall process? This is a much more difficult question for us than it was for Aristotle when he wrote *de Anima,* and in fact more difficult than it was for Merleau-Ponty when he wrote *The Structure of Behavior,* because we are now so much more successful in explaining the activities of living organisms in scientifically reductive ways — reducing the biological to the organic-chemical level, the organic-chemical to the inorganic-chemical, and the inorganic-chemical to the subatomic-physical level.

I shall argue, however, that there *is* an essential difference between organic and inorganic phenomena, and that this difference hinges on what Varela *et al* (1993) call the 'self-organizing' nature of living systems (see also Umilta 1988; Pribrum 1980; Dewan 1976; Gleick 1987). There does seem to be a sense in which process as a self-perpetuating pattern of a system as a whole dominates the behavior of substratum elements in living beings, and I shall try to show that this inverted relationship between process and substratum is one of the necessary conditions for consciousness; even systems in which 'desires' exist at the lower level still cannot feel *desires* in the conscious sense unless this condition is met.

## 1. How Does 'Desire' Become *Desire?* Internal Conflict as an 'Ecological' Problem

Our goal is to understand how a conscious *desire* is different from the mere aggregation of many 'desires' in the non-conscious sense. To work toward an understanding of this structural difference, an analogy might be useful in showing that it is possible, at least, for a higher-order desire to have a completely different aim and intentional object from the lower-order desires that function as substrata for the higher-order desire. Imagine a tired man after driving for twelve hours to reach his destination. He arrives to find that he must sit on the floor to hear a lecture. He sits in an uncomfortable position, feels a pain in his left ankle, immediately shifts to another position only to feel a pain in his right ankle, shifts again and immediately experiences discomfort in his knee, etc. No matter what he does to relieve one pain, he can do so only by creating another. At length he realizes that the problem cannot be solved unless he changes the *total situation* in which *each of these little pains is unavoidable without thereby creating another.* He realizes that he must go to a quiet room where he can get seven or eight hours of sleep to change the overall condition of the entire organism. Then if he must sit on the floor the next day, at least he can find a *temporarily* tolerable position from which he can shift after a few moments to relieve the pain in an ankle without thereby *immediately* creating an intolerable pain somewhere else.  While it is still true that there is no such thing as a *permanently* comfortable position, at least there are temporarily comfortable ones which can be alternated without inevitably and immediately creating discomfort elsewhere in the system.

The example just given involves a relationship between a *conscious* desire at one level, and many lower-order yet still *conscious* desires at a more 'fundamental' or 'immediate' level.  Although both these types of desire are conscious, the relationship between them is instructively analogous, in certain respects, to the relationship between any *conscious* desire and the lower-level, non-conscious 'desires' (such as a cell's 'desire' to regain electrical neutrality) which serve as the substratum for the conscious desire.  At least it shows that the aims of the lower-order 'desires' may not constitute the aim of the higher-order conscious desire in a simple, additive way.

Suppose we think of the relationship between 'desire' and *desire* by analogy to the condition of the man in the example.  The man's total situation (sitting on the floor to hear a lecture) does not become intolerable just because he has a pain in his ankle, provided he knows that he can relieve this pain without creating another.  What makes the total situation intolerable is that he cannot relieve the pain in his ankle without immediately creating another one somewhere else.  Similarly, an important difference between 'desire' and *desire* is that 'desire,' at least in principle, can sometimes be satisfied without reference to whether doing so thereby creates more and more 'desires' within the same organism.  *Desire,* on the other hand, is not merely a critical mass of 'desires.'  It arises rather from the 'desire' of the total organism that the total situation of the organism be changed in such a way that the satisfaction of one 'desire' does not immediately and inevitably create another.  Organisms do not want to be in the position of a cat on a hot tin roof when it comes to reducing various 'pains' and fulfilling various 'desires.'  *Desire* arises from the 'desire' of a total organism that *internal conflict* among the 'desires' of each of its parts should not remain inevitably irresolvable.  *Desire* thus arises from the futility of internal conflict among 'desires' given a certain context.  And the object of *desire* is different from that of a 'desire.'  *Desire* wants not merely to fulfill a collection of 'desires,' but to change the total situation in such a way that internal conflict among 'desires' not be inevitable.  I.e., it is concerned not so much with reducing specific electrical imbalances, but with reducing an internal conflict.  As a simple example, an organism faced with an environmental situation in which it cannot resolve the internal conflict between the 'desires' of its component cells will often change this larger environmental situation by moving the entire body to a new environment which does not render those micro-conflicts (inabilities to achieve aggregate intracelular neutrality) irresolvable — by moving closer to a fire or away from an intense smell, for instance.

Of course, there are obviously some disanalogies between the lower level pains experienced by the man in our example (as they interrelate to form the higher-level pain of his general discomfort), and on the other hand the lower-level 'pains' in his neurons (as they interrelate to form the higher-level *pain* he consciously feels). In our example, the man does consciously feel the pain in his ankle, whereas we do not consciously feel the 'pain' in a neuron. We therefore cannot understand what makes a pain or desire *conscious* merely by means of this analogy. But the analogous aspect is this: Just as the man's general discomfort results not from the mere aggregate sum of little pains, but rather from the way in which these little pains *interrelate* with each other (i.e., in a mutually conflicting way), so also a pain or desire in the conscious sense does not result from the mere aggregate sum of 'pains' or 'desires' in the non-conscious sense (i.e., electrical imbalances), but rather from the way in which these little 'pains' or 'desires' interrelate with each other (i.e., here too, in a mutually conflicting way). What the *disanalogy* between the two situations shows us is that the point we have just made is not a sufficient explanation of how a 'pain' or 'desire' becomes a *pain* or *desire*. The fact that the object of a *desire* is to resolve the conflict *between* the requirements for eliminating 'desires' (i.e., electrical imbalances) is a *necessary* condition for something to count as a *desire* rather than merely a 'desire,' but it is not a *sufficient* condition for explaining this difference. But exploring the necessary conditions for a phenomenon often leads to an understanding of its sufficient conditions. So let's continue in this direction for a step or two further.

There is an important sense in which *desire* is less adamant in its demands than 'desire.' 'Desire' can never be satisfied until maximal electrical neutrality is achieved. *Desire,* on the other hand, is willing to tolerate some electrical imbalance, as long as temporary balances can be achieved without *immediately and inevitably* setting up additional imbalances elsewhere in the system. In logical terms, if R1, R2, R3, etc., stand for the relief of 'pains,' then the object of *desire* is not to bring it about once and for all that

$$R1 \ \& \ R2 \ \& \ R3$$

but rather to remove or change a condition in which

$$R1 \longrightarrow (\sim R2 \ \& \ \sim R3),$$
$$R2 \longrightarrow (\sim R1 \ \& \ \sim R3),$$
$$R3 \longrightarrow (\sim R1 \ \& \ \sim R2),$$

and so forth. I.e., the organism as a whole could temporarily tolerate $\sim R1$ or $\sim R2$, but it cannot tolerate a permanent state of affairs such that R1, R2, R3, etc., inevitably conflict with each other. It is the incompatibility of R1, R2, etc. that disturbs *desire,* not merely the factical *presence* of the specific electrical imbalances involved.

Although *desire* is less demanding than 'desire' in this respect, there is another respect in which *desire* is more difficult to fulfill than most 'desires' are. It may be easy to correct a particular electrical imbalance by introducing an appropriately charged substance; but a total situation in which the conditions needed to satisfy one 'desire' will immediately and inevitably create another one *ad infinitum* is more difficult to resolve. This is one reason why those organisms which evolve more and more complex and sophisticated 'central processing units' (i.e., brains) are the ones that seem to have the higher degree of consciousness. The conflicts between the 'desires' of an amoeba are not complicated enough in their interrelatedness to require a very sophisticated internal conflict resolution capability.

So it seems obvious that the consciousness of those beings which have consciousness is always oriented not just toward achieving the well-being of the cells of the organism, in the sense of restoring their electrical neutrality, but toward the holistic harmonization of all the 'desires' of all components of the system. As Merleau-Ponty suggests, an organism will rearrange the overall configuration of its parts if an imbalance is created in one part which disrupts the functioning of the whole. "We will say that there is form whenever the properties of a system are modified by every change brought about in a single one of its parts and, on the contrary, are conserved when they all change while maintaining the same relationship among themselves" (Merleau-Ponty 1942-1967: 47). For example, in cases of development of a 'pseudo-fovea,' the eyes change the functioning of the cones and rods from their original anatomical programming. In cases of hemianopsia, the subject is rendered blind in half of each retina, so that he now has the use of only two half retinas.

> Consequently one would expect that his field of vision would correspond to half of the normal field of vision, right or left according to the case, with a zone of clear peripheral vision. In reality this is not the case at all: the subject has the impression of seeing poorly, but not of being reduced to half a visual field. The organism has adapted itself to the situation created by the illness by reorganizing the functions of the eye. The eyeballs have oscillated in such a way as to present a part of the retina which is intact to the luminous excitations, whether they come from the right or the left; in other words, the preserved retinal sector has established itself in a central position in the orbit instead of remaining affected, as before the illness, by the reception of light rays coming from one half of the field. But the reorganization of muscular functioning, which is comparable to what we encountered in the fixation reflex, would be of no effect if it were not accompanied by a redistribution of functions in the retinal and calcarine elements which certainly seem to correspond point for point to the latter (Merleau-Ponty 1942-1967: 40-41).

Merleau-Ponty also notes the finding by Fuchs (1922) that all the colors are perceived by the new fovea even though it is now situated in a retinal area which in a normal subject would be blind to red and green. "If we adhere to the classical conceptions which relate the perceptual functions of each point of the retina to its anatomical structure — for example, to the proportion of cones and rods which are located there — the functional reorganization in hemianopsia is not comprehensible (41)." Here we have an excellent example of Merleau-Ponty's principle that in organisms the whole will readjust the functioning of some of its parts when other parts are disrupted in order to maintain the original function of the whole. Similarly, desire intends to remove the inevitability of conflict not by eliminating this or that electrical imbalance, but by changing the *context* which renders the conflict inevitable. Other examples of self-directed neurophysiological reorganization following localized brain injury or trauma can be found in Restak (1984: 360ff). Kandel and Schwartz (1981) also place great emphasis on the 'plasticity' of the brain in reorganizing itself to accomplish its objectives by getting around disruptions in one way or another.    They find, for example, that if brain cells of an embryo are transplanted to a different region of another embryo, they are transformed into cells appropriate to that region.    This plasticity in the realizability of the mental functions of living beings has been emphasized by Putnam (1994), Horgan (1992) and Bickle (1992), as discussed earlier.

Eliminating electrical imbalances *per se* is not the aim of *desires,* although it is often the aim of 'desires.'    For example, death would be one way to eliminate electrical imbalances within the organism (as Freud points out in *Beyond the Pleasure Principle),* but death is not usually the way to homeostasis intended by *desire.    Desire* wants not just homeostasis (which could be achieved by suicide), but rather to exist *qua* consciousness, but in a condition relatively free of completely irresolvable internal conflicts (i.e., it does not want to be a cat on a hot tin roof).    This is also consistent with the finding of Roffwarg *et al* (1966) that internally generated excitation is necessary for the normal development of the brain.    This means that the organism wants  cognitive stimulation, not just the reduction of electrical imbalances to a state of 'homeostasis' conceived as neutralization of ionized charges.    Freud's earlier thinking was centered around just such an electrostatic reductionism, but he rejected it later in life when he wrote *Beyond the Pleasure Principle* (although many of his own followers ignored this radical change of heart).

I have said so far that *desire* arises from the 'desire' that the internal conflict between and among various 'desires' be removed.    As long as the organism is too near to the fire, then the ionization in one neuron cannot be neutralized except by creating a similar ionization in the adjacent one (i.e., the extra charges cannot be absorbed by adjacent neurons, so the signal continues to 'travel'); the hopelessness of resolving the conflicts among the 'desires' of neurons for electrical neutrality is one of the hallmarks of a conscious experience of pain.    But this 'desire' for internal conflict resolution itself is not a sufficient condition to produce desire in the conscious sense; it is only a necessary condition.    Lower organisms and sometimes even inanimate systems also 'desire' that conflict between specific 'desires' be removed, but in many of these cases they still do not feel this desire in a conscious sense.    For example, a homing device on a missile may be wired in such a way that its components can all simultaneously achieve electrical neutrality only when the missile is aimed toward its target, and mechanisms may be arranged to allow the missile to continually maintain this holistic balance by keeping it pointed in the right direction. But no one would say that the missile experiences consciousness. Not just any 'holistic' feedback mechanism, such as a thermostat or an electric-eye door, is a conscious being. Moreover, there are many living beings which *do* meet Merleau-Ponty's criteria for organicism — for example, plants and microscopic organisms — yet are not conscious in the sense we are discussing here.

If genuine consciousness is to occur, rather than just non-conscious holistic functioning, then what is necessary, in addition to the 'intention' of removing internal conflict, is that this total situation — i.e., the inevitability of interneuronal conflict given a certain ecological context — must somehow be 'represented' as a totality. Desire intends to remove a burning sensation by moving the fire away from the organism or by moving the organism away from the fire. This entails that the organism must be able to represent to itself not only the internal conflict among its various 'desires' (which itself is a complex operation), but also the ways in which the total ecological context of the situation contributes to the inevitability of the conflict, and the ways in which changing this context might render the conflict less inevitable and less permanent. The organism must 'know' in some sense that proximity to the fire is the problem that must be solved if the internal conflicts between the various electrochemical 'desires' in its cells are to be harmonized.

It follows that a central processing system for 'desires' and 'representations' must be present in order for desire or representation to become conscious. And, furthermore, this central processing system must be able to sense the larger patterns set up by the overall interrelations of 'desires,' and it must sense the ways in which groups of these larger patterns interrelate *with each other.* Thus there is no consciousness in an ordinary household electrical circuit, even though the movement of a charge from one atom to the next immediately and inevitably sets up an electrical imbalance in still another atom, etc. *ad infinitum.* There is no desire in the circuit (although there are 'desires') because the circuit does not grasp in a unified act the inevitability of its own internal conflict. Even if we include a voltmeter in the circuit, which can serve as an 'indicator' of the conflict, the circuit as a whole is still not grasping its own condition. The voltmeter does not 'care' about imbalances in the rest of the atoms in the circuit any more than the other atoms 'care' about the imbalances in the voltmeter. The interests of the parts are not subordinated to the interests of the whole, but rather each part pursues its own interests exclusively, and the overall pattern that is set up is purely a causal result of the *partes extra partes* interaction of each part's seeking its own electrical balance.

We have seen that the intentional object of a desire or pain is not simply the aggregate of the intentional objects of all the 'pains' and 'desires' within the organism. Pain and desire intend not the reduction of this, that, and the other 'pain' or 'desire,' but rather they seek to eliminate the inevitability of internal conflict between and among all the 'pains' and 'desires' by changing the larger ecological context in which the organism must exist. Desire intends that something about the total organism must be changed: Either it intends a change in its location (for example, to move further away from a fire); or a change in its own substratum (for example, by obtaining nourishment through the introduction and assimilation of appropriate physical materials into the organism, which then can serve as the substratum for its continuing processes); or a change in its own condition in terms of the patterning of its processes (for example, by resting or sleeping in order to rebuild the strength of its processes to maintain their primacy over these various substratum elements).

At this point, we might pause to reflect that this view of the relation between 'desire' and *desire,* combined with the ontological considerations of the previous chapter, and our 'whole-brain' analyses of perception, imagination and conceptualization in Chapters 1 and 2, apparently implies a system of neurophysiological substrates which has often been referred to as 'holistic.' Lashley (1950) and Pribram (1971, 1974) are prominent examples of this kind of approach to neurology, although they have notably failed to find a viable explanation for just how the whole brain accomplishes its functions (the goal we are working toward here). J.S. Young (1988) characterizes all such holistic approaches in this way:

> There have been repeated efforts to treat perception and memory in terms
> of the operation of whole masses of nervous tissue rather than of the
> individual cells or groups of cells. This is a healthy reaction in so far as
> large numbers of cells undoubtedly work together even in a simple
> response, such as when an octopus decides to attack a vertical rectangle;

many times more cells are involved in human recognition of a face. . . It is not popular to consider that the brain is a sort of homogeneous soup or jelly, traversed by fields and gradients. It may yet turn out that this scepticism is unwise. It may be a product of the fascination that physiologists have felt for their microelectrodes over recent decades. At present there is a growing interest in the variety of small peptide molecules, such as enkephalin and 'substance P', that are released by nerve cells. Further knowledge about the diffusion of the effects of these substances may produce an altered picture, perhaps of groups of nerve cells united by chemical or electric fields as well as by nerve impulses (Young 1988: 160).

In any event, as far as our present discussion is concerned, although the realization that desire holistically intends the reduction of internal conflict (rather than merely the *partes extra partes* elimination of electrical imbalances) may help us to understand the difference between 'desire' and *desire,* it is not by itself a sufficient explanation. It is conceivable that an organism could accomplish all the ecological conflict-resolution functions we have been describing here, yet without having what we experience phenomenologically as *consciousness.*

The next section will try to go a step further. Why do some higher-order 'desires' become conscious desires whereas others remain merely 'desires' existing at a more complex or global level in the functioning of the organism? For example, the regulation of the heartbeat has as its object the resolution of internal intercellular conflicts, yet is not a conscious desire. We can of course say that consciousness is a *type* of higher-order pattern or process, and this is not a useless piece of information (since many theories would reduce it either to a mere epiphenomenon of lower-order activities, or simply to the aggregate of all the lower-order activities); but this information does not enable us to understand what consciousness is in a precise enough way. To do so requires that we develop a more specific understanding of the way a 'desire' and a 'representation' interact within the context of organisms. This will be the aim of the next section.

## 2. The Relationship between Consciousness and Organicity

I would now like to propose and defend the hypothesis that consciousness is a process which is capable of appropriating, replacing, and reproducing elements of its own needed substratum by growing to include an imaginative representation of the missing elements or of ideas related to them.   If a 'desire' is capable of reproducing its own substratum in this particular way, the inverted commas can be removed, and the 'desire' becomes a desire in the consciously aware sense. I.e., the organism is aware of desiring something. The fact that something is desired is not merely 'represented' (in the metaphorical usage), but is *represented in consciousness.*

To see how different this kind of process is from inorganic and non-conscious processes, imagine what would happen if a sound wave, travelling to the edge of the earth's atmosphere, were to somehow cause the air molecules to begin reproducing themselves so as to provide a few miles of additional medium through which the wave could continue being propagated, because it could somehow tell that this is what it would need in order to continue being propagated.   It seems absurd to imagine a sound wave accomplishing such a feat, but this is precisely what the process that constitutes consciousness does in relation to its own substratum all the time. The process has as its main 'purpose' to continue being propagated in patterns similar to those constitutive of its existence up to that point in time; in order to continue allowing such patterns to transpire, it reproduces and transforms the substratum needed for these patterns to occur.

The way consciousness reproduces the substratum for this continued process is analogous to the way a crystal forms.  It begins with the shaping of a form virtually empty of matter (although of course it cannot be completely immaterial), and then additional material naturally moves in to fill out the pattern that has been set up by this initial form.   Concretely and literally speaking, what happens here is that, in order to continue being conscious, consciousness needs, for example, to have nourishment introduced into the body which is serving as the substratum of the consciousness.   Without the needed nourishment, consciousness is lacking in the physical substratum for its continued process. At the same time, biochemical deficits result from the lack of nourishment, and these deficits 'desire' (in the metaphorical sense) to be returned to homeostasis. (Ultimately, this means that all the atoms within the system 'desire' to have their outer energy shells filled.) This 'desire' then leads consciousness to grow until it includes an imaginative representation of some aspect of *what it would feel like to get something to eat*. In higher forms of consciousness (for example, humans), this leads to a conscious process of 'looking for' fairly specific categories of things — the muscle tissue of edible animals, fruits, nuts, etc. The patterns of consciousness set up by the forming of these images in the imagination (i.e., in the secondary sensory areas and the relevant areas of the parietal lobe as they interrelate with the 'looking-for' processes of the prefrontal cortex and the limbic system) then causes the primary projection area and the other areas just mentioned to synchronize the pattern of their activity so that a perception of the desired object (for example, a fruit hanging from a branch) becomes a very pronounced and decisive pattern of activity in the brain, and the consciousness constituted by this pattern is intensified still further when synchronization is achieved, not only between the primary and secondary sensory areas and the parietal association areas, but also with the thalamus and other parts of the midbrain. By assimilating the pattern of sensory input from the physical environment, the organism's initial 'desire' for nourishment has reproduced the physical substratum of which a conscious *desire* in the full sense can be predicated.

Of course, little or no new *matter* has been introduced into the brain in this process (except perhaps a few stray photons that impinge on the retina and a few extra acetylcholine molecules that get assimilated in the process, as Kretch *et al* 1960, 1962, show). Reproduction never involves the creation of new matter; that would be physically impossible (for all practical purposes in our present context). What reproduction does do is to take old matter and give it a new shape, take elements which previously were lying idle, and recombine them so that they form entities that previously did not exist as such-and-such a type of entity.

This is what consciousness does when it 'reproduces the substratum needed' for a given conscious process or state of consciousness. It does this by creating new nerve pathways, or re-activating nerve pathways that had begun to disintegrate (because of the 'extinction' of old 'learning,' in behavioral jargon). In this way, new entities are produced, similar but not identical in pattern to those which already existed in the stream of consciousness, thus making possible the imaginal 'looking for' and finally the 'looking at' of some particular content of consciousness. This content is the *representation* in consciousness which results from the *desire* previously present in consciousness. The act of representing the imaginary object (or concept) is in effect the desire's method of reproducing its own substratum. A residual cumulative effect of this continual process can be seen in the dissected brains of laboratory rats.      Rats that participated in learning experiments while alive show alteration not only in the structure, but also in the chemical composition of their brains, which contain significantly more acetylcholine and a larger number of glial cells (Kretch *et al* 1960, 1962).

One very readily visible example in which a neurophysiological process grows to include the needed substratum is described by Ornstein and Thompson (1984): "The song region in the brain of the male canary grows to double its normal size in the spring as the bird learns its song to attract a female.   After the mating season, the song area shrinks and the song is forgotten. Next spring, the song area grows again as the canary learns a new song (69)." This example is of course atypical, but only because the 'growth' involved is growth of the mass of a brain area as a whole.  More typically, a pattern 'grows' to include related emotive and representational activity in other parts of the brain, even though the size of each brain area, considered purely as a lump of physical material, remains the same.

Some readers might wonder at this point why a conscious desire would want to maintain and reproduce its substratum so as to continue existing as a state of consciousness.  After all, is not the aim of a desire to *cease* existing as the state of consciousness that it is?

It is not really necessary to get bogged down in the theory of motivation (which I have discussed elsewhere, 1986, 1992, and will touch on in the next chapter) in order to answer this question. For present purposes, it should be sufficient to observe that consciousness does not desire the *cessation of consciousness* when it experiences a desire; what it desires is a change in the pattern of consciousness which is occurring.  And the ultimate reason for the desire for this change is that, if the organism were to continue as it is (i.e., in the painful condition), the continued existence of consciousness at its optimal level of intensity would be threatened in some way.   For example, failure to eat deprives the organism of some of the materials it needs to serve as the substratum for its continued conscious activity.  Or, to use a seemingly very different type of example, failure to achieve the right kinds of social relations cuts off resources needed for consciousness to express itself through concretely symbolic media (language, sexual behavior, etc.). These social contacts which facilitate concrete symbolization are needed in order for consciousness to embody itself in a physical medium (such as language) to enough of an extent to enact the patterns of consciousness with optimal intensity. The threat of loss of some such social opportunity therefore deprives consciousness of some of the resources it needs to be optimally stimulated and active, so that extended failure to make a desired kind of social contact begins literally and in a very direct way to choke off the continued existence of large chunks of the organism's potential for conscious activity.

Organisms, unlike computers, robots, thermostats and thermos bottles, behave in such a way that materials that enter into them are to a great extent *assimilated* to the pattern of activity which already exists. Moreover, unlike inorganic systems in which some such assimilation also occurs (such as whirlpools, certain kinds of wave patterns, and certain kinds of feedback loops), organisms actively seek out and reproduce the needed substratum elements. As a standard neurology text puts it simply, "The brain is often likened to a computer, but the analogy is not very accurate. The brain is living — it can grow and change, but a computer can't. . . . To appreciate just how extraordinary the nerve cell is, we must look at the nature and evolution of all biological cells" (Ornstein and Thompson 1984: 61-62). *Conscious* organisms (to the extent that they are conscious) sometimes accomplish this purpose of reproducing the needed substratum motivated by its desires by forming representations related to the objects of these desires. In organisms, protective devices are also used to keep out materials that cannot be assimilated to the organism's definitive pattern. One of the main devices used by humans to ensure this protection from materials that cannot be assimilated is consciousness itself. I.e., conscious problem solving enables us to figure out how to protect ourselves from the danger of having our definitive patterns disrupted by alien materials. We consciously know to let in materials that can be successfully assimilated to the pattern (such as edible foods) and to avoid invasion by those which cannot (such as inedible foods, axe blades, bullets, or falling rocks).

In *'purely mechanical'* (i.e., non-organic) systems, alien materials injected into the system do not step into the flow of the pre-existing pattern and allow themselves to be incorporated as elements participating in it as part of its substratum. Instead, they disrupt the pattern, change it, break down its organization, or stop it from functioning altogether. The aftermath of the introduction of this alien material is in this case determined more by the alien material itself than by the organizational pattern in the flux of the organism. An odd electric charge introduced into a computer circuit, for example, often blows the circuit or causes it to go haywire. With organisms, within certain limits, the introduction of an odd electric charge will at first disrupt the pattern of functioning, but the organism will then readjust the functioning of its various constituents so that the alien presence can be assimilated (again, as Merleau-Ponty continually emphasizes). An alien presence that is difficult to assimilate produces illness, and its eventual assimilation or elimination results in healing. It is true that a 'fix' may be put on a computer so that it resists a virus or resists having its circuit blown. But even in these cases, the computer does not assimilate these alien elements and expand its own operation to use them as additional substrata; and, even if it did, it would not do this in the service of its own desire for internal conflict resolution, but rather because of one particular lower-level 'desire' (for electrical neutrality in a specific circuit) that a technician has inserted into it in *partes extra partes* fashion. I shall return to these disanalogies between organisms and 'purely mechanical' systems in a moment.

It is also true that scientifically reductive explanations can be given for even an *organism's* processes of growth and assimilation, and even for a conscious organism's processes of motivation and representation; these will be considered in some detail in the next section. For example, psychological processes can be explained biologically, biology can be explained in terms of organic chemistry, organic in terms of inorganic chemistry, and the latter in terns of subatomic physics. This, however, does not prevent processes from appropriating and reproducing substratum elements. As the next section will show, to explain the process that characterizes a system, it is not sufficient to cite the mechanical interactions of the substratum elements *within that system.* One must refer to processes going on *outside* of the system, which in turn cannot be explained purely by citing the behavior of the external system's own substratum elements. Ultimately, an adequate causal account must refer both to the mechanical interaction of elements outside of the system *and* to the tendency of certain patterns in nature to maintain themselves. But, before entering into a full discussion of this difficult issue, I would like first to further clarify the concept of 'organicity' that seems to be crucial to the possibility of conscious (rather than merely non-conscious) information processing.

In many ways, the notion that consciousness reproduces elements of the substratum for desire sounds similar to the way Aristotle defined 'organisms' in *de Anima,* but there are some important differences. Like Aristotle (and also like Merleau-Ponty in *The Structure of Behavior),* I am suggesting that an organism, insofar as possible, will purposely rearrange some of its parts if that is what is necessary to maintain the desired functioning of the whole, given a disruption of the functioning of one of its parts. One part will 'compensate' for the dysfunction of another. There are obvious examples of this in the brain. If a right hemispherectomy is performed early in life, the left hemisphere will take over many functions that otherwise would have been handled by the right brain. After a stroke, new nerve pathways will be developed to 'circumvent' the ones that have been destroyed, insofar as this is possible and insofar as the attempt is made. (It is well known among stroke rehabilitation specialists that one of the main determinants of speech restoration after a stroke is that the patient must continually *make an effort* to say the sounds corresponding to the destroyed neural connections — for example, see Restak 1984: 256; Springer and Deutsch 1981: 173-212.) As Aristotle would have it, the guiding purposes of the organism as a whole allow some of the parts to rearrange themselves so as to maintain the desired functioning of the whole.

Aristotle also emphasizes that organisms have as one of their main guiding purposes to grow toward the achievement of a certain 'mature form,' and will actively seek out environmental conditions that are useful for this purpose. The actual patterns of activity in an organism are determined largely by a potential pattern to be achieved later. Only if the organism's search for appropriately facilitative environmental circumstances (nourishment, etc.) fails to turn up the needed materials will the organism fail to achieve the potential 'mature form' toward which it is trying to grow. We can see this process at work in many aspects of brain functioning. The brain needs to form acetylcholine in order to perform more and more sophisticated cognitive activities. If the organism's diet is severely deficient in the B vitamin choline (contained in lecithin and eggs), the needed acetylcholine cannot be formed in the brain (Restak 1984: 339ff). But in this case, the organism will readjust its orientation to its environment. The person will notice a sudden appetite for lecithin-containing grains or eggs. Especially if the person is aware of the relevant nutritional information, he or she will actively and purposely set about to ensure that adequate choline-containing foods or vitamin supplements can be obtained.

But, in order to follow Aristotle just *this* far in his thinking about the difference between organic and non-organic phenomena, it is not necessary to distinguish between them as radically as he did. Most importantly, it is not necessary to claim, as did Aristotle, that some organic processes cannot be explained in terms of 'efficient' causes, and should be explained *only* in terms of 'final causes' — i.e.; teleological goal orientations. Contemporary brain scientists and cognitive theorists (and most contemporary philosophers) want to hold that the *same principles of physics* which describe the behavior of materials in a non-organic context can also be used to describe the behavior of those same materials in an organic context. For example, nerve impulses flow through the nervous system by means of the reduction of a negative charge in a neuron, which then causes a negative charge to be conveyed to the next neuron, and so on. There is nothing here that cannot be fully explained by citing the relevant principles of physics and the relevant efficient causes which occurred as antecedents of each successive event. None of the principles of the behavior of these electrically charged particles are any different from the principles that would guide those same particles in a non-organic setting — in a household electrical circuit, for example. It has been calculated, in fact, that if all the electrical potentials in the human nervous system were linked together in a continuous circuit, the voltage would be more than enough to electrocute a person (Ornstein and Thompson 1984: 77). The same principles of electricity used to describe household circuits are still at work here. This means ultimately that everything that happens in the physiological functioning of organisms can be explained in terms of the principles of *inorganic* chemistry and physics.

Organisms (in which 'final causes' are supposed to predominate over 'efficient causes' in the Aristotelian theory) are in this respect no more or less explainable in terms of efficient causal mechanisms as are non-organic, purely mechanical phenomena. But this does not mean that the distinction between organic and purely mechanical phenomena is a useless or untenable distinction. What it means is that we must make the distinction in a way that makes sense in terms of what is known about the relation between organic and inorganic chemistry. We must say that organic systems are a subset within mechanical systems in general, and that inorganic systems are another subset. Inorganic systems are *'purely* mechanical,' whereas organic systems exhibit patterns of organization that *'purely* mechanical' systems lack. I.e., they exhibit an ability to reproduce the physical substratum needed to maintain a form or pattern of activity, and to shape and replace elements of their substratum according to whether those elements serve well as substrata for the form of activity that is being maintained. Inorganic or 'purely mechanical' systems are systems that lack this particular ability. So it seems necessary to grant that organic systems are no less mechanical than *'purely* mechanical' systems, in that they do conform to all the principles of physics and chemistry that govern all mechanical systems. They are different only in that they possess certain specific capabilities which inorganic systems lack. Organic systems are not *non*-mechanical, but are a subset *within* mechanical systems in general, the latter being divided into 'purely mechanical' phenomena on the one hand, and 'organic' phenomena on the other.

I should also mention that the 'non-mechanical' nature of 'quantum mechanics' does not in any way contradict what has just been said. Searle (1984) expresses this point well:

> The statistical indeterminacy at the level of particles does not show any indeterminacy at the level of the objects that matter to us — human bodies, for example. . . . It doesn't follow from the fact that particles are only statistically determined that the human mind can force the statistically-determined particles to swerve from their paths. Indeterminism is no evidence that there is or could be some mental energy of human freedom that can move molecules in directions that they were not otherwise going to move (Searle 1984: 87).

What I am suggesting, then, is that conscious processes (i.e., conscious in a literal rather than a metaphorical sense — thinking, knowing, seeing, desiring, etc.) can exist only in organic systems. They cannot exist in *'purely* mechanical' systems in the sense just defined. The reason is that, although 'desires' may exist in a thermostat, 'memory' in a thermos bottle, and 'vision' in a robot or an electric-eye door, none of these processes can become states of conscious awareness unless the thermostat, thermos bottle, robot or electric eye door is capable of reproducing elements of its own substrata in order to maintain, continue, or expand its particular pattern of 'cognitive' activity when the availability of an adequate substratum becomes a problem for it; and it must do this because of an internal motivation resulting from its own *desires,* not as the result of an externally imposed process. For example, if a mother organism reproduces elements needed to maintain the functioning of, let us say, a one-week fetus, this does not mean that the one-week fetus is yet a complete organism or a being capable of consciousness in the literal sense. It is the *mother* in this case that is an organism capable of consciousness. The fetus is not yet responsible for reproducing elements of its substratum *via* a representation of missing elements and as the result of its own internal motivational processes, but instead the *mother's* motivational processes are necessary to determine this effect. Similarly, if a neuroscientist engineers a robot in such a way as to systematically replace its own parts as they become dysfunctional, this does not mean that the robot is an organism or is capable of consciousness, because it is not the robot's *own* desires (or even its own 'desires') that motivate the replacement, but rather the neuroscientist's desires. Thus it is the neuroscientist, not the robot, that qualifies as an 'organism' in our sense, and as capable of consciousness.

This does not mean at all that it would be impossible in principle for a neuroscientist to build a mechanical system which would qualify as an organism and would be capable of consciousness in the literal sense. But, in order to do so, the neuroscientist would have to construct an *organism* and not a purely mechanical system as we have been using these terms here. There is nothing logically incoherent about the story of Frankenstein. Already, scientists have succeeded in mixing inorganic substances in the right conditions to create organic tissues. Probably in the near future, scientists will be able to mix together certain inorganic substances under the right circumstances to generate tissues that are not only organic, but also capable of growing to reproduce the substratum for their own states of consciousness as governed by their own desires, and these organisms may well then possess some degree of consciousness. But these would be *organic* beings, not purely mechanical ones, and their pattern of information processing would include the patterns we have been discussing here under the heading of *conscious* information processing and would not be limited to the kind of information processing used by what we now call ('purely mechanical') computers or robots. In plain terms, they would be the mature adults grown from fetuses nurtured in laboratories and originally constructed in test tubes; they would be flesh-and-blood creatures, not nuts-and-bolts ones. In a sense, many neuroscientists have already created such intelligent beings: They have done it by engaging in sexual activity, resulting in pregnancy and childbirth.

## 3. The Process-Substratum Relation: A Closer Look

We must consider carefully some very cogent objections that might be raised against the notion that a 'process' can 'cause' its substratum elements to participate in its already established pattern. I have suggested that there seem to be in nature processes which tend to incorporate new substratum elements into a previously operative pattern. For example, when a microphone membrane is introduced into an area where a sound wave is operative, the membrane begins to vibrate in the pattern of the wave. When a leaf floats into a whirlpool in a river, the leaf follows the pattern of the whirlpool. When a satellite goes into orbit around a planet, it also follows that planet's orbit around its sun, and that solar system's path in relation to other planetary systems. When food is introduced into a living organism, it is assimilated in such a way as to participate in the patterns of activity which are already operative in that organism.

But at the same time it would be implausible to deny that, in each of these cases, the domination of the process over the substratum elements can be explained through the workings of efficient mechanisms at a reductively lower level of scientific explanation. For example, we can explain the vibration of the microphone membrane by examining the way the movement of particles in the medium of the original wave pattern cause the movement of particles in the membrane, and this causation is purely mechanical. Since the movements of the individual particles constitute the substratum for the wave, and since an explanation for the movement of the individual particles is sufficient to explain the pattern of the wave, it seems to follow that an explanation for the substratum is sufficient to explain the process as well. So there seems to be no sense in which the process has 'primacy over' its substratum or 'dominates' its substratum. The process would thus appear to result from the movement of the individual particles, not the other way around.

But let's explore this type of reductive explanation a step further. When we explain a wave pattern by reference to the movement of the particles of its medium, we are explaining a pattern in terms of the movement of its constituent components. By doing so, we appeal to component movements which in turn can be explained only by reference to other patterns or processes. For example, why does a stone fall to the earth? In Einsteinian terms, the explanation is that all massive objects follow geodesics which describe the shortest possible distance through space-time when travelling through space-time which is affected by the mass of other objects, remembering that the relative movements and inertias of the two objects affect the length of the spacial and temporal distances within the reference systems of those objects (see Einstein 1922-1956; Pauli 1958; Calder 1979). In Newtonian terms, we would say that a 'force' called 'gravity' causes the object with the lesser amount of inertia to change its inertia because it is affected in some way by the fact that the neighboring object has tremendously more inertia than it has (Pauli; Calder). But *what are we saying* when we say (1) that an object in motion has 'inertia,' and (2) that this inertia will be changed in predictable ways when it enters the vicinity of another object which has substantially greater 'inertia'? Is (1) not merely describing the fact that an object in motion relative to other objects will tend to maintain its pattern of motion relative to the other objects unless it is affected by the differing pattern of objects in its vicinity whose 'inertia' (defined in similar terms) is much greater? And is (2) not saying that an object with a great deal of 'inertia' in this sense is engaged in a stronger pattern — one which is more resistant to change or disruption — than is an object with a lesser degree of 'inertia'?

The ultimate first premise of any system of physics must in one way or another posit that an object or system tends to maintain its inertia — i.e., a previously established pattern of motion or activity — unless it comes into relation with another object or system whose inertia affects it in some way — i.e., an object or system with a *stronger* previously established pattern of motion or activity. And this is just a way of saying that some processes are stronger than others, and that the weaker process will be more disrupted by the stronger one than the stronger one is by the weaker one. One factor that determines the strength of a process is the 'mass' of the objects that constitute its substratum. Another factor is the particular spatio-temporal configuration of the pattern of movement in which these objects are engaged. This means that, even at the simplest, most reductive level of explanation, the causation of the movement of substratum elements must be explained at least partly through reference to processes in which they are involved. This part of Whitehead's metaphysics seems unavoidable, even if we reject other parts of his system (such as, for example, his notion that the future is not completely determined by the past). I have discussed these issues in detail in separate articles (1991, 1992b, 1983) and do not want to get any more involved in them here than is necessary. The main point for our purpose here is that one may explain patterns by reference to the action of substratum elements, or one may explain the action of substratum elements by reference to the pattern in which they are involved.

But what would be really misleading, and in fact downright false, would be to explain the higher level process within a system by reference to lower level substratum elements within the system (which subserve the process for that system), when the truth is that the higher level process must be explained by reference to both lower level and higher level events *outside the system* being explained. This is the kind of falsehood that would occur if we were to explain the vibration of a wooden door in the pattern of Tchaikovsky's Sixth Symphony by saying that the movements of the individual molecules in the door are sufficient to explain what causes the door to vibrate in that particular pattern. In truth, the cause of the door's pattern of vibration is that the pattern was operative for molecules of air *outside* of the door; and these patterns were caused by patterns of vibration of a speaker, which transmitted a similar pattern from an orchestra, and in turn from Tchaikovsky's score, and in turn from Tchaikovsky's brain, and in turn form the somewhat depressing structures of reality as Tchaikovsky saw it — including certain lamentable facts of life such as the fact that we must die and the fact that meaningful social contacts with significant others are difficult to establish. (So depressive was the pattern of Tchaikovsky's consciousness at this time that he apparently committed suicide three days after the first performance of the symphony.)

Part of the reason Tchaikovsky saw reality in such a negative light is probably that there were serious chemical imbalances in his brain. But we should also note that part of the reason why Tchaikovsky's brain enacted this depressed pattern was that *it is true* that we must die, and *it is true* that meaningful social contacts with significant others are difficult to establish. As Gurwitsch (1964) continually emphasizes, part of what determines a state of consciousness as what it is is its 'saliency' as a representation of reality. Thus the pattern of activity in Tchaikovsky's brain was determined in part (at a certain level of explanation) by the truth of these statements about reality, in much the same way that the motion of the earth is determined in part (at a certain level of explanation) by the truth of the statement that $F = MA$. At this level of explanation, it is false to regard the motion of the molecules in Tchaikovsky's head as a sufficient causal account of what happened in his consciousness, because it is necessary to go outside of the system to be explained (Tchaikovsky's consciousness) to find certain substratum elements which are also necessary for the explanation of the system (for example, the truth of the unfortunate facts just mentioned did not exist only in Tchaikovsky's head). Similarly, a cue stick's striking a billiard ball is not a sufficient explanation of the billiard ball's motion without assuming the additional condition that $F = MA$. But the statement that $F = MA$ describes a larger process in which both the cue stick and the billiard ball are subsumed. Reference to this larger process is tacitly presupposed when we explain the billiard ball's motion by reference to the cue stick.

J.L. Mackie (1974) contributed a great deal to the clarification of this kind of discussion when he emphasized that nothing is ever necessary or sufficient for anything else except *given certain background conditions*. And one of the background conditions that is always assumed for this kind of statement is the regularity and resistance to disruption of certain patterns in nature — in other words, laws of physics. Applying this principle to the problem we are considering here, we can see that there are two very different kinds of situations:

(1) **A** is the cause of **B** given certain background conditions.

(2) **A** is the same thing as or inseparable from **B**, so that we must look to the background conditions for an explanation of **A** *and* **B**.

In the case of the action of the cue stick (**A**) and the action of the billiard ball (**B**), we can distinguish between **A** and **B**, so it makes sense to explain **B** by citing **A** as its cause, given certain background conditions (**C**) — including the fact that $F = MA$. On the other hand, in the case of the sound wave permeating the wooden door and the movement of the door's molecules in a certain pattern, the sound wave permeating the door (A) and the vibration of the door's molecules (B) are inseparable from each other. Extensionally, we cannot distinguish them, although intentionally we can. (In one sense, they are the same thing as each other. They are like the temperature and the pressure of a gas in this respect, to use Bickle's example.) So, in the case of the wave (A) and its substratum (B), we cannot say that A causes B, no matter what background conditions we recognize. We must go outside of the system to find the causal explanation for its process, and when we do we find that the explanation is that this same process (or a very similar one) *already existed,* and then somehow came to appropriate the new substratum elements for an extension, continuation or expansion of that same process. In this case, the process cannot simply be relegated to part of the 'given background conditions' for the causal relation. It must be cited as the *causal antecedent* for the consequent being explained. More simply put, we cannot explain what causes A by saying that B causes it if A and B are not distinguishable and separable events.

Consider the example of an emotional event. Suppose a relative of mine has just died and I am depressed. And suppose I am depressed not so much because this particular person dies, but because reality is such that everyone must die, that each of us is, as Shakespeare says, "a poor player who struts and frets his hour upon the stage and then is heard no more." A causal epiphenomenalist would say that my depression is caused by certain chemical reactions in my limbic system. A psychophysical identity theorist would say that my depression just *is* this limbic activity. Both would say that the limbic activity is caused by optic stimulation of the occipital lobe which sets off 'learned' association activities in the temporal and parietal lobes, and these physical structures are caused by prior physical movements of particles in the environment in certain stimulus patterns interacting with certain chemically determined response patterns. Thus, in these types of theories, everything can be explained at the 'purely mechanical' level.

The process-substratum theorist, on the other hand, will begin with the notion that chemicals 'want' to reduce their electrical charges (in the non-conscious sense). This is a way of *describing* (not explaining) one of the ultimate process structures of our universe. And when patterns are set up in nervous systems such that these patterns become organismically structured, the reduction of one electrical imbalance can be accomplished only on the condition of creating another, unless the organism can 'envision' a change in its ecological position such that this internal conflict could be reduced. The organism thus has a higher-order pattern in which it 'looks-for' ecological conditions in which these conflicts can be reduced and the organism can continue existing as a conflict-reducing entity. This higher-order pattern results from the fact that (1) the lower order patterns of chemical activity 'want' to have their charges reduced, and that (2) a certain pattern of organization subsumes these lower order processes. At this point, the organism is 'looking for' situations in which it can realize its higher-level conscious aim, to continue existing as an organism. But then, in the example of depression we are considering (in which the depression is precipitated at least partly by unpleasant facts about reality), the organism encounters resistance from the environment: It turns out that reality is patterned in such a way that all organisms must die. This too is a fact about the process structure of reality. The one process, my organism, interacts with the other process, the fact that everyone must die (as exemplified by concrete instantiations of the fact), and causes another process — a depressed form of consciousness. And this depression continues until a resolution can be found for the internal conflict — for example, by achieving a pattern of consciousness in which the value of being can be fully appreciated in spite of its fleetingness.

All of these processes are inseparable from their embodiment in substratum elements. Therefore, we cannot explain why one process occurs by saying that its own substratum 'causes' it to have the pattern that it has. The pattern of the process can be *causally* explained only by reference to prior processes, which in turn are inseparable from their own substrata.

A process, then, cannot be explained as a causal result of its own substratum. And the substratum for a process cannot be explained as the causal result of the substratum of some prior process unless some prior or more basic process is also assumed as one of the 'background conditions' for that causal relation. There is always a sense in which a process is implicated in the total causal explanation for any substratum activity, just as some prior substratum activity is always implicated in the total causal explanation for any process.

But the difference between 'organic' and 'purely mechanistic' systems is this: An organism is structured so that at first a process has certain material elements as its substratum; then, because the organism either 'wants' or *wants* to maintain a similar pattern in the future, it finds other material elements to serve as the future substratum for the continuing process. In physical terms, organisms are very 'strong' processes in this regard: They are structured so that when they come into contact with material elements which previously were engaged in weaker processes, either the weaker process is broken up so that the material elements are caused to take over the pattern of the organism's process (i.e., they are 'appropriated'), or at least the organism avoids a disruption of its process by the pattern of the weaker process.

## 4. Conclusion

We have reached the position that desire differs from 'desire' in two important respects. (1) The aim of desire is not the aggregate of the aims of all the 'desires' that make up the substratum for the desire; instead, the aim of desire is to remove an irresolvable internal conflict by changing the overall condition of the organism. And (2) a conscious desire is a process which is capable of appropriating, changing and reproducing elements of its own substratum in order that the process not only may continue, but also may expand in scope; it accomplishes this purpose by imaginatively representing the missing elements or ideas related to the missing elements.

Have we said enough to define the essential differences as well as the interrelations between *desire* and 'desire'? I believe we have. The crucial type of case that still was not accounted for at the end of section 1 was the case of autonomic nervous system activity. The brain regulates many bodily process, such as heartbeat, temperature and breathing, without conscious awareness. In these cases, condition (1) above is met. I.e., the aim of the organism in regulating heartbeat is not merely to resolve numerous electrical and chemical imbalances, but rather to remove or avoid irresolvable conflicts among these many 'desires.' But condition (2) is not met by autonomic activities. I.e., even though the 'desire' to maintain a regular heartbeat *does* maintain its overall process by regulating elements of its substratum, it does not do so by representing the desired state of affairs or related ideational material.

We can see the difference this makes in the case of those autonomic activities which are also subject to voluntary control. Normally, we do not consciously desire to regulate our breathing, although we do unconsciously 'desire' to. But when we learn relaxation techniques, we learn to regulate our breathing in a different way. We learn to take a deep breath, exhale, and then wait an instant before inhaling. During that instant, we imagine our hands or feet as relaxing (an imaginative representation in a mostly tactile and kinaesthetic modality). By imaginatively representing what certain elements of the substratum would need to do, we subsume them within the desired pattern or process.

In other relaxation techniques, we may imagine words or visual images which have for us a 'relaxing' pattern, and thus cause our own substratum (our muscles, blood pressure, etc.) to be subsumed within a correspondingly relaxed pattern. Thus we say that we 'consciously' make the effort to relax. Here too, the representations involved make the difference between a conscious effort and a non-conscious one.

We can see, then, that a 'representation' (for example, in the coordination of parietal and primary sensory areas) must be motivated by a corresponding 'desire' (for example, a conscious or non-conscious 'interest' which leads us to consciously or non-consciously 'look for' certain types of objects or object relations) in order to become a *representation* in the conscious sense. Similarly, a 'desire' (for example, love) must motivate a corresponding 'representation' (for example, the image of the absent beloved person as it begins to dominate the activity of the parietal lobe) in order to become a *desire* in the conscious sense. This view, which we have arrived at through primarily phenomenological considerations, is consistent with the findings of neurologists about the activity of the midbrain and the cortex when consciousness is present. "Activities [of the midbrain alone] seem to allow for identification of the position and main features of objects even in the absence of the cortex, but they are not accompanied by consciousness" (Young 1988: 132). Desire in the conscious sense always involves the use of representations. Sometimes the representations are visual or auditory, at other times tactile or sensorimotor ones; sometimes they are vague, at other times clear ones; sometimes they are very accurate, at other times less accurate ones; sometimes they are direct representations of the object of desire, at other times less direct symbolic representations; sometimes they are positive, at other times negative ones, as when we envision only the fact that something we need is missing before pinpointing what it is — for example, when we say 'Something is missing here — ah, yes, Jacques should be here!'

A 'desire' may be very strong but not very conscious — for example, a self-aggrandizing or narcissistically disturbed person's desire for everyone's unqualified praise and approval. In this case, the 'desire' becomes more conscious at times when the narcissist represents the missing elements of the needed substratum for the narcissist's own self-congratulatory form of consciousness, but the necessary elements are usually represented only in negative form. I.e., there is a sense that something needed is missing, and a vague sense that this missing factor has to do with other people's behavior; but the person does not go so far as to positively represent an image of the missing element — praise or approval. If the narcissist were to represent this, the 'desire' would then have moved from a predominantly unconscious to a predominantly conscious status.

In some cases, we represent the object of a 'desire' only in its negative form. For example, when we burn our hand, the hand 'desires' that certain serious electrical imbalances in its nerves (and resulting imbalances in the limbic system) should be corrected. But in this case what we represent is the negative of what the 'desire' wants — i.e., we represent 'heat' — the feel of a hot surface, or the way it feels to have the hand against a fire or hot surface. Even in this case, though, something is being represented, and the content of this representation is related to the aim of the corresponding desire. We focus on negative stimuli as well as positive ones because we are keenly interested in them, and we represent them to ourselves for the same reason.

In many emotional contexts, it is easy to see from a phenomenological perspective that we represent what the emotion is 'about' (i.e., its aims and objects) only in negative terms at first, and then move toward a positive characterization of what the emotion wants. For example, we may at first feel only a vague discomfort or dissatisfaction which we associate very generally with our relationship to our social environment. Representing to ourselves the images of people who have treated us rudely or acted distant then somehow moves us closer to understanding what the feeling is 'about.' Finally we hit on phrases like 'I feel alienated,' 'My interests are irrelevant to everyone I know or interact with,' 'People don't want me to relate to them unless I wear a very alien mask,' etc.; at the end of this process we may finally realize what it is we are missing — a sense of social community. At this point we have moved toward a positive and specific rather than only a negative and vague characterization of what the 'desire' wanted when it first began to be felt as a conscious feeling. To the extent that it was consciously felt, what it wanted was to change the ecological situation in order to make possible the resolution of internal conflict between certain constellations of 'desires' within the organism.

A desire always begins with only a vague and negative representation of what it is about — of what the missing substratum elements are which would facilitate the continued successful existence of the organism as a conscious being. But then with the help of a series of neurophysiological processes, the vague sense that something is missing is refined to form a more or less definite image or concept of *what sort of thing it is* that is missing.

In animals with simple brains (lacking the vast prefrontal cortex and pronounced left-right differentiation that humans have), the desire or interest is translated into a 'looking-for' category of images with which it is compatible by means of patterned neural connections which are partly genetically pre-programmed, and partly learned through simple associations of images (including generic as well as specific ones, and including tactile and sensorimotor images as well as auditory and visual ones). In humans, this translation of motivational interests into an understanding of what the interests are 'about' is accomplished in a more refined and versatile way. The function of the prefrontal cortex makes it possible for us to *formulate questions* to ourselves about a desire or representation, using subjunctive images and concepts, and using a calculative control of symbolic images and concepts made possible by the left-right brain differentiation. Our category system is refined enough, thanks to the sophistication, abstraction, and flexibility it is able to achieve, that the prefrontal cortex can play a successful game of charades with the limbic system. 'Is it something edible?' 'Does it have to do with social relationships?' 'Is it related to the need for intellectual stimulation?' etc. Eventually, what began as a vague and purely negative representation of the ideas associated with missing substratum elements is systematically interrogated with the help of the prefrontal cortex (whose main cognitive function is to help us formulate questions to ourselves) until a match is found with more specific and positive images and concepts.

Apparently, a very similar process occurs in even the simplest perception of a visual object. I mentioned in an earlier chapter that neuroscientists who study the correlations between electrical potential in different parts of the brain (for example, Aurell 1983, 1989) have found that, when the subject is prepared to see one object, and then is presented with a very different one instead, the first thing that happens, after the stimulus signal passes through the thalamus and reaches the primary projection area, is that a negative potential arises in the anterior portion of the parietal lobe which is measured at N200. Then, after a noticeable time lag, a positive potential of P300 is evoked in the more posterior portion of the parietal lobe. Aurell hypothesizes that the N200 potential corresponds to the realization that the object which was expected is not the same as the one presented, before a conscious awareness of the object which *is* presented occurs; and that the subsequent P300 potential corresponds finally to the subject's conscious awareness of the object which *is* presented. This would suggest that the subject first searches for the object which is expected (which, as is now well known, produces 'expectancy waves' — see Libet *et al* 1983), and when an unexpected object is encountered instead, the mind first realizes that what was expected is missing, then arrives at a more and more definite consciousness of the ways in which the object presented is different from the one expected, until a match is achieved between what the subject is attuned to 'look for' (to use my own term for this process) and the pattern of activity which is taking place in the primary projection area of the occipital lobe or the temporal lobe (depending on which sensory modality the expected and presented objects correspond to).

Undoubtedly, the pioneering attempts by neuroscientists to correlate conscious processes with neurophysiological ones will be vastly refined by future neuroscientific research using increasingly sophisticated methods of recording neural activity. But they generally show that an understanding of the difference between conscious and non-conscious processing of information (along with the various vague and somewhat amorphous semi-conscious processes which lead from one to the other) is now at least possible in principle and in rough outline. Organisms undergo conscious processes by appropriating, reproducing, or changing substratum elements needed for their own continued appropriate activity and existence as such. Unconscious organisms, which lack nervous systems, may 'sense' which substratum elements are missing, but do not *sense* them. The function of the nervous system is to further unify the organism in relation to 'needed' elements by ensuring that one part of an organism cannot unilaterally achieve its 'desires' without immediately disrupting the balance of another part. This, as we have seen, is what happens in the nervous system. The aim of a conscious desire is therefore to bring harmony to the conflicting elements, and the nervous system cannot achieve such a harmonizing of its 'needs' without taking account of the total situation of the organism considered as a whole. The idea that the aim of *desire* is to resolve internal conflict thus fits in with the notion of organisms as systems in which the process reproduces its own needed substratum elements, and with the notion of consciousness as a system in which the process accomplishes this reproduction of substratum elements by creating representations related to the missing elements.

# CHAPTER SIX

# Memory, Emotion, and Symbolization

The goal of this chapter is to work toward a coherent accounting of the working of memory, emotion and symbolization in terms of the theoretical framework we have developed so far. But the approach I shall take requires getting a good deal of phenomenological description out on the table before we can weave the various elements into a unified theoretical accounting. The first two sections will consist primarily of phenomenological description and related neurological data. The purpose of these descriptions and data is to provide the groundwork for a unified accounting, in sections 3 and 4, of memory as it relates to emotion and symbolization.

## 1. Toward a Process-Substratum Approach to Memory, Emotion, and Symbolization

An understanding of memory functions must take account of at least seven aspects of the phenomenological experience of memorizing and recalling something: In memorizing a melody, I (1) move my fingers in such a way as I would if I were to *play* the melody; (2) imagine the way the notes would sound; (3) train myself to expect each successive note as the image of the previous one lights up in my consciousness; (4) develop a 'feeling of familiarity' which is associated with certain combinations of notes; (5) combine two or more sensory modalities (for example, a series of auditory images with a series of visual images and sensorimotor firings) to create an *intersensory intentional object* which *makes sense* in terms of all the sensory modalities at once — i.e., an intentional *meaning;* (6) use a system of symbols to help 'pull up' the associated images and meanings — for example, 'b-flat minor,' 'interval of a fourth,' etc.; and (7) think about the way each note 'makes sense' in the context of what I understand about music. For example, in the key of b-flat minor, a d-flat 'makes sense' in a way that a d-natural does not. To a great extent, it is the *meaningfulness* of the whole that allows me to remember the parts.

Consider an extreme example of the difference this last point makes: Claudio Arrau, the famous concert pianist, was interviewed at the age of 90, when his career was still fully active. At that time, Arrau had enough music committed to memory that, if his physical strength would have permitted, he could have played non-stop, 24 hours a day, for *six months* without ever referring to a single sheet of music. This amount of memorization is not atypical for concert pianists. At the level of technical difficulty of the music in Arrau's repertoire, there could be an average of about 20 notes per second (in both hands combined), which would come to 1800 notes per minute, 108,000 notes per hour, or over 2.5 million notes per day. This means that Arrau can recite a series of about 450 million notes without error. And when we consider that he must remember not only the pitch of each note, but also its duration, the series of memorized items comes to about an even billion. And this does not include the expression markings, the pedalling, and the fingerings of the various patterns of notes.

Now imagine what the result would be if we were to ask even a gifted mnemonist to memorize a list of a billion randomly generated numbers or nonsense syllables! Even the mnemonist of Luria's famous case study (1968) could never perform such a task. And of course the reason is obvious. It is much easier to memorize meaningful than meaningless information. That is why psychologists invented nonsense syllables for their memory studies in the first place — to control for the variable effect of the meaningfulness of the material. But *why is* meaningful material easier to remember?

Consider another well-known fact. When the Harvard education department developed its 'Learning to Learn' program, the main strategy they found to be helpful in improving students' study habits (and subsequent grades) was a very simple one: In the margin next to each paragraph in a textbook, the student is supposed to write the question to which the information contained in that paragraph would constitute the answer. Instantaneously, the grade point average of these students increased by an average of 1.5 on a 4.0 scale — a tremendously greater increase than among students using other tutoring methods (Slomianko 1987). And the improvement was just as dramatic in courses emphasizing rote memorization as for those which stressed critical thinking.

Why such a dramatic increase? The Harvard team theorized that the improvement was attributable to students' adopting a critical, questioning frame of mind rather than a passive, receptive one. And we now know from Luria's and Sperry's work on the prefrontal cortex that, when we ask ourselves a question — and especially when we *formulate* a question *for ourselves* (as opposed to merely responding to someone else's questions) — this is precisely when the prefrontal cortex increases its level of electrical and chemical activity. It is also obvious from PET scans and other such measures of brain electrical activity, and from the anatomy of neuronal connections, that when the prefrontal area is activated, the rest of the brain quickly follows suit. What seems to be happening, then, is that we remember information more effectively when we ask ourselves questions about it during the learning process, and this formulation of questions about information is a primary aspect of the process of 'making sense out of' the information.

One aspect of memorization therefore is obviously the development of an ability to make some sort of sense out of what we memorize. To a certain extent, this applies even to nonsense information. Personally, when I memorize a phone number, I do so by remembering the musical melody spelled by the notes of the scale to which the numbers correspond. Each phone number has its own musical sound and emotional meaning, and of course some phone numbers lend themselves more easily to this method than others. A similar familiar technique is the one where the mnemonist associates people's names with a meaningful image or idea which the name calls to mind, and then combines that image in a meaningful way with another image which reminds us of the person's face or some other salient fact about the person.

This brings us to the second important aspect of memorization — the one most emphasized in Luria's astounding case study: The items memorized are recalled most effectively if they can be associated with mental images. Luria's mnemonist showed an unusual degree of overlapping and interconnection between different sensory modalities. For him, every sound evoked the image of a certain specific color. This is true to a certain extent for everyone; we tend to associate the timbre of each instrument of the orchestra with color images (Restak 1984: 68-69; Marks 1978). The same is true for the vowel sounds of words, and consonants seem to evoke shape or boundary images. Also, studies show that when one sensory modality is stimulated by an object, the other modalities are also to a certain extent activated by the patterns of stimulation which that object would elicit (Marks 1978). For example, a musician hearing a melody moves his fingers slightly, or at least fires some of the motor neurons involved in those finger movements. We know that congenitally blind people form mental maps of the space around them. There is now even an invention which allows blind people to 'see' their surroundings by stimulating the nerves of a certain patch of skin in patterns corresponding to the patterns of light from nearby objects (Restak 1984). For the blind person, the resulting experience is like 'seeing' one's surroundings in something like braille. Merleau-Ponty also describes the blind man's 'seeing' or 'visualization' of the data from his stick (Merleau-Ponty 1962).

One difference between most of us and Luria's extremely gifted mnemonist in this respect is that the mnemonist's 'imaging' patterns are much more readily and sharply set off by corresponding patterns elsewhere in his brain. Everything for him evokes a powerful constellation of images, often in more than one sensory modality, and including the 'kinaesthetic' and 'sensorimotor' modalities. (For example, he describes laboriously how he visualizes every detail of scenery on the streets near his apartment and associates items to be remembered with those images as he 'walks down the street' in his imagination. More obviously, as we have already seen, a musician remembers a melody more easily if he can associate it with finger movements.)

But we have also seen that connecting different sensory modalities with each other is part of the process of 'making sense' out of what we perceive. And much of this process involves counterfactuals or subjunctive imagination. I.e., Piaget's infants learn to perceive objects by understanding what *would* happen *if* they were to grasp the object, throw it, rotate it, feel its surface, etc. And to know what would happen in each of these imaginary cases is to answer a question which one has implicitly put to oneself: What would happen if I were to *do* so-and-so with this object? Questions and counterfactuals are closely related forms of cognitive functioning. (We know this through the phenomenological observation of our own consciousness as we use these forms of expression.)

Experiments which we discussed earlier also show that kittens allowed visual but not sensorimotor contact with their surroundings during early development become functionally blind, even though their eyes and occipital lobes are perfectly normal (Held and Hein 1958; Blakemore and Cooper 1970; Hisrch and Spinelli 1970; Mitchell *et al* 1973; Leyhausen 1979). Since the kittens are strapped into carts pulled by other cats, so that they can receive visual input from objects but cannot manipulate the objects by touching them, they do not learn to put to themselves the implicit counterfactual questions of Piaget's infants: 'What would happen if I were to pounce on this object, bite it, etc?' But it will become increasingly important in our discussion that humans are equipped with a much more prodigious questioning apparatus than cats (the prefrontal cortex) as well as a greater preponderance of inhibitory neurotransmitters. This enables us to make much more sophisticated discriminations — to make more sense out of more information — so that our memories are correspondingly much better than those of cats. In this connection, Mark Johnson (1987) has developed even further Piaget's idea that we learn to perceive by learning what actions could be performed on which type of perceptual object (throwing, dropping, etc.). According to Johnson, ways of categorizing things (i.e., concepts) evolve from 'kinaesthetic image schemas.' These schemas originate in bodily experience, and are used to structure our perception, imagination, and thinking — for example, through the 'part-whole schema,' the 'container schema,' the 'source-path-goal schema,' etc. Similarly, Rosch *et al* (1976) argue that "The basic level of categorization [is] the most inclusive level at which category members (1) are used or interacted with by similar motor actions, (2) have similar perceived shapes and can be imaged, (3) have identifiable humanly meaningful attributes, (4) are categorized by young children, and (5) have linguistic primacy in several senses" (as summarized here in Varela *et al* 1991: 177). But it is also crucial to remember that all these combinations and refinements of 'generic images' (as I called them in Chapter 2) can lead to the relatively precise concepts needed for adult thinking and problem solving only when the generic images are further questioned through motivated prefrontal activity and an extended self-talk process which later becomes truncated. (Later in this chapter, we will have to understand more clearly how this truncating process can come about.)

Remembering thus involves a process of making sense of the data by interrelating different sensory and sensorimotor modalities in response to questions we put to ourselves. Obviously, it therefore involves diverse areas of the brain — prefrontal, parietal, temporal, sensory and motor areas. And there can be little doubt, from brain-damage studies, that the hippocampus and other midbrain areas are very heavily involved as well. For example, see Winson (1985: 210ff); Morrison (1979, 1983). Memory is a whole-brain activity.

This leads us to a third important aspect of memory function. Memory is something that I *do* — a behavior of the efferent aspect of the brain and, to a lesser extent, of my whole body (as when I move my fingers in the attempt to remember a melody). Behaviors are largely conditioned responses. When I learn a melody, I condition myself to respond with a certain behavior (say, hitting a certain piano key) when I have previously hit a certain other piano key in a certain context. To a great extent, Claudio Arrau knows each of his 450 million notes because each note is a conditioned response to the previous note in context. (I shall return to the 'in context' aspect of this later, in connection with Gendlin's notion that our bodies 'imply' certain contexts, projected actions, and understandings of holistic situations we are in.) So, in a sense, it is no more mysterious that Arrau remembers all those notes than it is that someone who develops a nervous twitch — which occurs only, let us say, every time he is in an anxiety-provoking situation — 'remembers' to twitch just that particular muscle in that particular way in that particular context. (What is more mysterious, and must be considered later, is that we not only can *re-enact* an efferent behavior that has previously been enacted, but also that we *know* that we enacted it before — i.e., the 'feeling of familiarity' which now accompanies the enactment.)

Arrau's responses, however, are much more 'finely tuned' than in the muscle twitch example. They involve sophisticated discrimination learning of which animals without extensive prefrontal cortex are incapable. When it comes to very simple combinations of sensory images, lower animals exhibit quite remarkable memories. For example, I once took my dog back to a neighborhood in which she had lived for a few months two years earlier. When we were still a block from the apartment, she unhesitatingly crossed the correct street, ran in the right direction up the steps of the building, and began scratching at the door. (Later in this chapter, we shall be in a position to understand what there is in a dog's — or human's — brain that facilitates this kind of simple recall.)

But when confronted with complex discriminations, lower animals cannot remember at all. Even as intelligent an animal as a chimpanzee cannot learn to discriminate conditioned and unconditioned stimuli whose association depends on the interconnection of three or four contingency variables in certain regular combinations (Premack 1988). For example, they can learn to respond to triangles as opposed to squares, red as opposed to black, or loud as opposed to quiet. But they cannot learn to associate a reinforcement with a red square when the noise is loud but a black triangle when it is quiet, or to respond to a triangle when followed by a black square but to a square when followed by a red circle. Of course, these are the kinds of multiple-contingency discrimination skills needed to master abstract concepts as opposed to simple combinations or disjunctions of mental images, and just these kinds of concepts are needed to understand the meanings of terms in modern human languages. This brings us to the connection between memory and language — or, more generally, 'symbolization' in the sense we have been using in previous chapters.

To the extent that complex discriminations are needed for effective memorization, the prefrontal cortex seems to supply the needed brain area for this function. And to the extent that language requires multiply-discriminative concept formation, the prefrontal cortex is also responsible for language development. Of course, this also leads to increased left-right brain differentiation, in which one half of the brain is used to coordinate both finely-tuned motor functions (for example, writing, throwing) and fine discriminations, while the other half increasingly specializes for holistic functions such as recognizing the Gestalt of an image or a melody. But this differentiation seems to result largely from the prefrontal lobe's need to appropriate a division of labor for its purposes, since the expansion of the prefrontal cortex is the crucial jump in evolution from animals unable to use abstractions to those able to use them (Springer and Deutsch 1981: 345ff). There seems to be something about the specialized way in which neurons are organized in the left brain (the so-called 'vertical' stacking that has now been explored by brain scientists — for example, Woodward 1968) that makes it more amenable to fine discrimination learning and appropriation for symbolizing purposes. But we have seen already that the prefrontal cortex in response to the motivation of the organism orchestrates this entire process by putting the appropriate questions to the rest of the brain.

We have already seen that the prefrontal cortex facilitates transforming generic images into logical concepts by allowing us to question the images by which we operate as children through an extended self-talk process, which finally becomes very truncated as we learn to use the results of it habitually. If self-questioning is crucial for complex discrimination, and the latter is crucial for effective memorization, it follows that self-questioning is crucial for effective memorization.

We thus come to a very pivotal question: What does it mean to formulate a question? What *is* a question? As phenomenologically experienced, a question is midway between a thought and a feeling. It is a *desire* to know or represent something, or to represent it in a more adequate or accurate way.

As Husserl points out in the *Logical Investigations*, a question normally contains implicit assertions. 'What is that object?' implies that some sort of object is there. 'Is there anything there?' implies a 'there,' a spacial context defined by the presence of other background objects or the location and orientation of my own body in perceptual space (see Merleau-Ponty 1962, 'The Body and Motility'). What the question is saying is that I have managed to achieve in my consciousness some sort of vague or fuzzy representation which I desire to make more adequate in some respects. But adequate to what? As Meno asks Socrates in the *Meno,* must we not already know the answer to our question if we are to hope to recognize it when we find it? But if we already know the answer, there is no need to look for it.

The answer to Meno's question is that we already have some vague sense of what it is that we are looking for, but the sense is too vague for our (motivational/emotional) purposes. I.e., our desire has come into relation with a vague representation associated with the missing elements, but the representation is not accurate enough. We want to have an image or a concept which would enable us to understand *exactly* what is missing. The representation of the missing element, if we could successfully elaborate it, would serve effectively as the subsratum for our consciousness of the desire. But the desires of a complex organism are themselves too complicated for a simple representation of missing elements to serve as their subsratum. So the desire strives to appropriate substratum elements in more and more subtle ways. It evolves 'symbolization' as a technique for self-clarification. We use a symbolizing behavior — for example, playing a certain piece of music — to enable us to pull a feeling into clearer focus and thus explore what the feeling is 'about.' The 'symbol,' in this sense, is neither a sign nor a codified signification. It is rather a mental image or concept or motor behavior (or merely motor firing) whose enactment in the brain works well to explicate the meaning of a certain feeling — i.e., what the feeling 'wants' or 'is about.' (Recall the studies by Kimura and Archibald 1974, Studdart-Kennedy and Shankweiler 1970, and Liberman *et al* 1967, showing that language develops as a truncated motor response.) As I give symbolic expression to a 'feeling,' it becomes more and more a *feeling,* because it is able to appropriate the right pattern of substratum elements for its 'amplified' and 'equalized' enactment (in the senses discussed earlier). The symbol serves as substratum for the desire, whose first motive is to find a substratum in which its pattern of activity can be enacted. Consciousness is, in effect, a process looking for a substratum in which to move; thus physical symbolization — through words, images, movements or music — effectually provides the needed substratum. And we have seen that this symbolization process is part of the process of providing ourselves with the cues needed to re-enact the images and associations of our memories.

A memory, then, is a truncated behavior of the body and especially of the efferent aspects of the brain, which is elicited through conditioning to a very complex set of cues to which the organism is able to respond because of the abstract capability facilitated by the self-questioning directed by the prefrontal cortex.

Notice the similarity between the way symbolization facilitates the process of activating *emotions,* and the almost identical way in which symbolization evokes *memories.* Notice also that both emotions and memories at first crucially involve the functioning of the hippocampus and limbic system, and then spread through the prefrontal cortex to involve symbolic behavior, primarily by means of left temporal lobe syntactic activity and imaging activities in the right parietal lobe. And of course it is well established that emotional/motivational interest is one of the main determinants of the strength of a memory (Restak 1984: 182ff).

Still another remarkable similarity between memory and emotions can be observed phenomenologically. When we exert an effort to remember something, often the memory will not respond to our voluntary effort to remember, and then suddenly it dawns on us all at once, as if involuntarily. The same thing happens when we try to identify the meaning of a difficult emotional feeling. At first we try to understand what the feeling means — what it is really about, what it wants to happen — but it eludes us, or we continue to misconstrue it in terms of inadequate categories. For example, we may feel very agitated in response to someone's not taking the garbage out, when we know very well that such a trivial incident alone would not normally evoke such a strong feeling. Yet at first we cannot understand what we *do* feel so strongly about, if not the garbage incident. There is often a process through which we attempt to understand what the feeling is about, apparently to no avail, and then suddenly, all at once and with a feeling of non-voluntariness, the true meaning of the feeling comes to us whole. For example, the feeling turns out to be one of frustration at the way our career is going, not anger at the person who did not take out the garbage.

In this sudden 'Aha!' experience, whether it occurs in an instance of memory or of emotion, what we undergo is essentially the Wurzburg phenomenon of 'insight' or 'creativity' (Hunt,1985). The feeling or memory does not respond directly to a voluntary intention, but neither would the insight have come had we *not* exerted the effort. There is a sense of 'not knowing how we do it' (Dennett 1991). Winson (1985: 210) also stresses this point, hypothesizing that the frontal lobe must continually reorganize the information implicitly present in other parts of the brain before we can be consciously aware of it. Until this reorganization occurs, Winson believes, a memory cannot 'pop up' from the unconscious. This is also consistent with the findings of Aurell (1989) and Posner and Rothbart (1992) discussed earlier.

In both cases — memory and emotion — there is first an implicit sense of what we are trying to represent in our consciousness, but we need a process of using images and symbols to facilitate a questioning process so as to 'amplify' and 'equalize' the implicit body sense by making the interaction of various brain functions serve as an appropriate substratum for the implicit sense, which becomes explicit once it has attained access to this more elaborate substratum.

In both memory and emotional explication, the implicit body sense tells us whether each representation we try out is the right one. We know when a wrong guess is wrong. Suppose, for example, that the emotion is a 'restless' feeling. We might first try applying the word 'depressed' to what we feel. But 'depressed' does not work as a symbol for the feeling because it does not 'resonate' with the implicit sense of the feeling (to apply Gendlin's 1981 term 'resonate' in a neurophysiological context). Similarly, in the case of memory, 'Bob' dos not work as the forgotten name because the implicit bodily sense of what we have forgotten is used as the criterion even when we cannot yet say what the correct name *is*. Just as in Aurell's perception studies (1983), we can negate a 'wrong' match before we can locate a 'correct' one. (I.e., the N200 potential precedes the P300 potential.)

The implicit bodily sense of what we have forgotten is not precise. It is fuzzy and amorphous. I may feel that the name is 'something like Bob,' but not know exactly what it is. It may be 'Bill' (same first letter, same number of syllables) or 'Rob' (rhyme and same number of syllables) or 'Robert' (different first letter, different number of syllables but same vowel sound and related in meaning). Or it could be 'Steve' ('one of those short, common and typically American names'), or it may be 'Rauschenbach' (the name of someone who was once in the same circle of friends with someone named 'Bob'). Just as in the interpretation of the meaning of emotions, the prefrontal cortex must play a game of charades with the limbic system to find the right category in terms of which 'Bob' is like the name I am trying to remember. When the right name comes, there is a holistic feeling of closure, all the demands of the implicit body sense are satisfied at once, and the newly hypothesized name 'feels right.' There is a 'feeling of recognition' or a 'feeling of familiarity' about the way the name fits into the overall situational context into which it is supposed to fit. The fit is somewhat analogous to the mental image which is activated in the parietal and secondary areas and the matching afferent data in the primary projection area when we have a conscious perceptual experience. The 'looking for' which is implicit in the body has a feeling of recognition when it finds a match with what is happening in the brain activity corresponding to the 'amplified' and 'equalized' image. (Later in this chapter, we shall be ready to understand the neurophysiological substrate for this 'feeling of recognition.')

To see more clearly what I mean by 'amplified' and 'equalized,' think of an incident in which you tried to remember the name of an actor in a film, but could not. You could remember vaguely what the actor looked like, but could not remember the name, though it was on the tip or your tongue. Then the film began, you saw the actor's face on the screen, and before the name was given you suddenly remembered it, just because you had seen a clear perceptual image of the actor's face (rather than merely a vaguely recollected mental image). The difference between the vague image in your imagination and the precise image as you saw it on the screen is analogous to the difference made by 'amplifying' and 'equalizing' the pattern of brain activity that makes the image possible. Apparently, the more precise ('equalized') and vivid ('amplified') image is better able to dredge up the memory than is the vague and weak one.

We saw earlier that, when an electrochemical signal travels from the stimulated optic nerve to the primary projection area in the back of the occipital lobe, it first passes through the thalamus, which alerts the reticular formation to a consciousness of arousal or vigilence, and this in turn arouses the prefrontal cortex to begin asking questions about what sort of thing the object might be. This in turn leads to hypothetical image patterns associated with parietal lobe activity. But if we imagine the brain in this example as lacking a cerebral cortex altogether, then what we are left with is merely a stimulated thalamus and reticular system. In this case, the animal has *only* an 'implicit bodily sense' — unamplified and unequalized. Thus the animal knows only very vaguely that 'there is something emotionally important out there' — for example, dangerous, or sexually arousing. But the animal could not specify *what there is about* the object that makes it dangerous or sexually arousing. Nor, according to the analysis of consciousness presented in the last chapter, would such an animal experience much *consciousness* in the literal sense — only a vague feeling of 'desire' or 'fear' in their metaphorical senses, along with a very vague, amorphous 'representation' of some gross feature of the object (for example, 'dangerousness') which never attains the level of an image. Again, this is consistent with the empirical data provided by Young (1988: 132) which we discussed in the previous chapter, where we saw that midbrain activity without the normally interrelated cerebral activity is not accompanied by conscious awareness. We must therefore say that amplification and equalization of the implicit bodily sense of a situation is the cerebral cortex's way of transforming the implicit sense into an explicitly conscious experience.

If only we could understand how this implicit bodily sense works, we would have the most elementary building block for building up an understanding of how memory, learning, symbolization, and emotional explication operate on the implicitly felt sense to amplify and equalize it, thus providing the needed substratum for the corresponding forms of conscious activity. As a beginning in this direction, I would now like to explore the way a very astute phenomenological cognitive theorist, Eugene Gendlin, has already developed the notion of the 'implicit bodily sense.' Then, in the following sections, I shall build on Gendlin's idea to form a theory of memory and complex discrimination learning as ways of modifying 'natural unities' in efferent behavior, through interrelations of cortical excitation and inhibition.

## 2. Gendlin's 'Implicit Bodily Sense'

Suppose, as I am about to go to sleep at night, someone in the apartment upstairs drops one shoe on the floor. I wait for him to drop the other one (as he does quite loudly every night), but the sound is not forthcoming. There is a tension in my body in preparedness to hear the other shoe drop. My mind wanders to other things, but the tension in my body is still there. It will not release until the other shoe drops. As I toss and turn, unable to get to sleep, I wonder why my body is tense; I then remember, simply by noticing the way my body feels, that it is still in a state of preparedness for the other shoe to drop. The particular way in which the muscles are tensed contains the implicit information 'waiting for the other shoe to fall.' This is part of the way I know why I cannot get to sleep, and it is the main factor that causes me to remember (repeatedly) that the other shoe still has not yet fallen.

This bodily tension which 'implies' the anticipated (auditory) image of the other shoe falling (and with reference to which I am repeatedly *reminded* that the other shoe has not yet fallen) is a simple example of what Gendlin calls the 'implicit bodily sense' of a situation. It is 'implicit' because the body's orientation 'implies' information about the situation toward which it is oriented, and because we need not be 'explicitly aware' of it in order for it to be there. We can attend to it explicitly if we choose to, but it is still 'implicitly' there whether we are consciously aware of it (paying attention to it) or not. And the implicit sense of the situation is 'bodily,' because it is physical, and I need not be consciously aware of it in order for it to be there. Yet it is still a *sense* (or 'sense,' if unconscious) of the situation because it contains information *about* the situation which was obtained through the way the situation affected the orientation of my body.

In this section, I want to explore the implications of Gendlin's notion of an 'implicit bodily sense' not only for interpreting motivations, emotions, and the lived sense of situations, but also for the processes of memory and symbolization as they function in the brain. I shall try to show that recovering a memory involves neurophysiological activity very similar to what the brain does when we try to identify the meaning of an emotion. Gendlin underscores the similarity between these two operations in an example he uses to show how we refer to the body's 'implicit felt sense' of a situation. He describes 'the odd feeling of knowing you have forgotten something but not knowing what it is,' as follows:

> You are troubled by the *felt sense* of some unresolved situation, something left undone, something left behind. Notice that you don't have factual data. You have an inner aura, an internal taste. *Your body knows but you don't.* . . . You find a possibility. "Helen's party! I forgot to tell Helen I can't come to her party!"
>
> This idea doesn't satisfy the feeling. It is perfectly true that you forgot to tell Helen you would miss her party, but your body knows it isn't this that has been nagging you all morning. . . . Your body knows you have forgotten something else, and it knows what that something is. That is how you can tell it isn't Helen's party. . . . Then suddenly, from this felt sense, it bursts to the surface. The snapshots! I forgot to pack the pictures I was going to show Charlie! You have hit it, and the act of hitting it gives you a sense of sudden physical relief. Somewhere in your body, something releases, some tight thing lets go. You feel it all through you (Gendlin 1981: 38-39).

But now let's follow this idea of the implicit bodily sense a step further. In an unpublished paper, Gendlin suggests that there is a sense in which even organisms without nervous systems 'perceive' their environments. Of course, this is not the usual sense of *consciously perceiving* something. But Gendlin, like Merleau-Ponty (1962), believes that this 'latent' or 'implicit' intentionality of the body, which is prior to any perception in the conscious sense, is a necessary building block which is presupposed by the act of perceiving in the conscious sense.

> To begin philosophy by considering perception makes it seem that living things can contact reality only through perception. But plants *are* in contact with reality. They *are* interactions, quite without perception. Our own living bodies also *are* interactions with their environments, and that is not lost just because ours also have perception. . . . Our bodies . . . interact as bodies, not just through what comes with the five senses. . . Merleau-Ponty . . . meant perception to include (latently and implicitly) also our bodily interactional being-in-the-world, all of our life in situations. . . The body senses the whole situation, and it urges, it implicitly shapes our next action. It senses itself living-in its whole context — the situation (Gendlin 1981: 4-5).

The body not only 'implies' information about the environment; it also implies what we want to do about it:

> . . . Your body-sense includes more than we can list, more than you can think by thinking one thing at a time. And it includes not only what is there. It also implies a next move to cope with the situation. . . . Suppose you are walking home at night, and you sense a group of men following you. . . . Suppose among the moves you can think of the only hopeful one is to turn a corner and quickly enter a building, but suppose that this idea gives you a trapped feeling in your body. Suppose you cannot figure out why it feels that way. Should you do it? I would say no. . . . From one ancient bone one can reconstruct not only the whole animal, but from its body also the kind of environment in which it lived. . . . The body even as a dead structure still contains all that implicit information about its environment. . . . My warmth or hostility will affect your ongoing bodily being whether you perceive it or not. You may find it there; if you sense how your body has the situation (Gendlin unpublished: 7-13).

We can relate these phenomenological observations to the way in which 'desires' in the non-conscious sense produce 'representations' so as to make consciousness possible as a process capable of reproducing its own needed substratum elements. Making this connection will enable us in turn to see how symbolization, emotions, and memory relate to the cognitive functions we have explored so far.

In order to show this connection, it will be helpful to examine a bodily feeling whose object is at first unclear. Suppose we take a vague feeling of restlessness as our example. In this example, we lack a clear knowledge of what the feeling is about. In the terms outlined in the last chapter, we could say there is a sense that something needed is missing, but we cannot understand what it is.

We might automatically go to the kitchen and get something to eat, then notice that something to eat was not what we wanted. The feeling of emptiness is still there. What we wanted must be something else. We pour a cup of coffee, but this is only a habitual response. We have alleviated the feeling somewhat by getting *something* we can enjoy, but we still have not identified what it is we want. (An extreme example of this kind of situation was related to me by a friend who smokes. He felt that he wanted a cigarette, and then realized that he was already smoking a cigarette.)

Finally, we walk to the window and look out — and suddenly we understand what the 'desire' wants: a change of scenery. Now that we are able to associate the right representation with the feeling, what was only a vague sense becomes a sharp feeling. 'Dammit!' we say to ourselves, 'I want to get out of this house.' In this way we bring the 'desire' from an almost completely unconscious level to a completely conscious level. It is now a conscious desire because the whole brain is involved in appropriating the needed substratum for a conscious (and not merely unconscious) process. The mere fact that the body needs something constitutes a 'desire' in the sense that something is missing, and finally a more and more accurate imaginary representation of *what* is missing brings the 'desire' to the level of a state of consciousness. Since my total ecological environment functions as part of the substratum for the process which is my consciousness, changing the environment (i.e., a 'change of scenery') can facilitate forms of consciousness which are desired by providing part of the needed substratum (as we saw in the last chapter).

There is usually an intermediary step in this process which I omitted from the above example — the step in which we attempt to *symbolize* the 'desire.' Suppose we sense this feeling of uneasiness so strongly that we feel a need to call a friend and talk. Already we have begun the symbolization process by using the word 'uneasiness.' It may be that, in the instant when the word 'uneasiness' occurs in our thinking, the feeling begins to seem important enough that we need to call a friend and talk — i.e., already it is becoming more and more conscious. Also, by imagining the idea of discussing it with our friend, we are *representing* part of what the feeling wants (to symbolize itself more adequately by using words to help toward a representation that will connect the 'desire' with what is missing in a more specific way).

As we discuss the feeling, we find that the use of words either increases or decreases the level of conscious awareness of the feeling. We say the word 'uneasy,' and that sharpens the feeling a little. But then we say 'tired' and its level of consciousness drops; we almost lose the sense of what we are referring to when we use a completely wrong word. Yet at this point we also increase our *negative* consciousness, our awareness of what the feeling is *not*. 'No, that isn't it,' we say. Then suddenly the word 'bored' occurs, and we feel the desire stirring again. Finally we hit on 'restless,' and suddenly we know specifically what the desire wants — to get out of the house. A bodily release of tension tells us that we have hit the nail on the head. Simultaneously, we can now represent to ourselves the image of getting-out-of-the-house, which is the 'intentional object' of the feeling.

In the various cases of finding the right symbols, correctly interpreting the intentional object of a feeling, and remembering something we have forgotten, there is a common element: In each case, we feel the same 'sense of release' or 'feeling of recognition' when we have hit on the right word, image, description of a situation, or memory. We can now proceed in the remainder of the chapter to explore the way this 'bodily felt sense' forms the basis for remembering, how the bodily sense is evoked along with an image or association 'stored' in the brain, how this image or association *is* 'stored,' and how this information along with the 'feeling of recognition' is retrieved, in both phenomenological and neurophysiological terms.

### 3. How the Brain Learns to Recognize and Re-enact Efferent Memory-Behaviors

We saw earlier in this chapter that a memory is a behavior, not a configuration of spatially-describable *things* which would be 'stored' in some molecule or configuration of molecules in the brain. This behavior consists of an efferent neurophysiological activity in which an image is activated (prefrontal, parietal, temporal and/or motor areas are involved here) along with a feeling of recognition. This behavior is usually a conditioned response to a cue which consists of another efferent behavior which precedes the one to be cued. This prior efferent behavior usually consists of a prior image (visual, auditory, kinaesthetic or motoric) or a symbol (which includes both an image component and a number of sedimented associations from prior learning, as discussed in Chapter 2).

But now we come to the crux of the whole question about memory. How is it that the brain knows to *execute* this particular pattern of efferent behavior in response to the right cue rather than the wrong one, often after many years of inactivity on the part of that particular image, and often following only a *single initial presentation* of the stimuli to be associated? Here we have, if not exactly the same question, then a transformed version of the age-old cognitive problem: What is a memory 'trace' or 'engram,' and how is this 'trace' 'recorded' and 'stored' in the brain? We have rejected the idea that the 'trace' could be a quasi-permanent, spatially-describable fixture in the brain (as in computer storage). But then what is it, and how does it operate?

Let's begin by examining phenomenologically certain aspects of that which is to be 'stored' or 'recorded.' Let's begin first with an obvious example to illustrate the problem of identifying what '*a*' memory really consists of. (As Coulter 1983: 79-81 asks, how do we divide up the flow of memory-consciousness to decide which elements in it constitute the separate, isolable units to be 'stored'?) When I remember what my wife's face looks like, how do I remember that this particular mouth goes with those particular eyes? Why do I not, for example, erroneously remember my present wife's mouth as going with my ex-wife's eyes, and my ex-wife's mouth as going with my present wife's eyes? Must there be a reinforcement schedule to teach me to remember to associate the right mouth with the right eyes?

Of course, this is a ridiculous question. When I activate the mental image of my wife's face (i.e., when I execute this behavior), I am activating *one unitary* image (executing *one unitary* behavior), and both the eyes and the mouth are contained in this one execution. There is no need for a conditioning schedule to condition me to associate them. There was never a time in the 'learning history' of this image that it was not *one unitary* image. Thus the memory of it counts as *one* memory rather than as three (i.e., as the mouth, the eyes, and the fact that they go together, as if these were three separate 'memories' to be 'stored').

And yet, the perception of the parts of the face, when originally presented, was not one simultaneous, homogeneous look. On the contrary, our eyes focus first on one point, then another, then another, until they have covered the entire face. It is well known that the eyes see an object not all at once, but by scanning it sequentially (Helmholtz 1962). Through this scanning operation, consciousness perceives an image as a *whole* image, not as a number of partial images which we must 'remember' to associate with each other.

A unitary 'act' of consciousness is something that *takes time* to occur. There is no such thing as a consciousness which could be contained in an infinitesimal instant of time. The reason for this is purely logical and ontological: Consciousness *is* a process, and a process (unlike a physical thing) does not exist in each instant of its occurrence, but exists only when enough time has elapsed for its pattern to have developed in the activity of the substratum. In Husserl's (1905-1966) terms, a conscious act is *'erstreckt'* — 'stretched out' over time, just in the sense that a musical melody cannot exist in a discrete instant.

A state of consciousness, such as the enactment of an image, then, is a behavior which consists of a *sequence* of actions which can be counted as 'unified' in some sense. We say that my wife's face is a single image, but we do not say that my wife's face and my ex-wife's face together constitute a single image which can be broken down into two 'parts.' Nor, when one wife's face is flashed on a screen rapidly followed by the other's face, do I regard all of this as 'one' image.

What is the difference between a single image which can be analysed into several parts (for example, focusing on one point, then another and another), and on the other hand a series of successive images which occur in rapid succession?    This question also presupposes the answer to a prior question: Since enacting an image is a complex efferent *behavior* of the brain and nervous system, we must also ask what the difference is between a unitary behavior and a rapid sequence of 'different' behaviors.

Consider a baseball player swinging a bat.  The swing of the bat seems to be an example *par excellence* of a behavior that must be considered a *single* behavior, and not a collection of discrete movements which are pieced together to make a whole swing.  So unitary is this behavior, in fact, that once the swing has begun, the player virtually *cannot* stop it until it has reached completion in the habitual follow-through of his swing.  Somehow, because of the way the principles of physics operate on the player's body, it is more 'natural' to complete the swing than to inhibit it once it has begun.  It might be reasonable to suppose that there are also sequences of neurophysiological activity which it is more 'natural' to complete than to inhibit once they have begun, and for a similar reason — because of the way the principles of physics affect the body (including those very delicate parts of the body which are in the brain).

Now suppose a father is teaching his little son to bat correctly. Suppose the father stands behind his son with his hands over the son's hands on the bat.  He leaves it up to the son to start the swing, but he is concerned that his son is not 'following through' in the right way with his swing.  He therefore gives the bat an extra push at the end of the swing.  In this case, the son will experience the swing not as one behavior but as two.   First he executes his normal swing, then he follows through with the swing in response to his father's push.

Analogously in the case of executing mental images, we could say that an image is unitary when from beginning to end of its execution it is guided by its own self-movement as it interacts with the principles of physics.  And the execution is considered a series of discrete executions pieced together if, at several points during its duration, the smooth momentum of a naturally flowing movement is interrupted by some opposition extraneous to the movement — either a purposeful interruption from within (such as, for example, changing my mind about which face I want to imagine), or an *external* source (such as an image being flashed on a screen, or someone saying a name).

Sometimes this is a subtle distinction and one of degrees. Suppose, for example, that I am memorizing a Chopin piece. It is well known that Chopin often repeats the same melody within a piece but with different embellishments. It is very difficult for the performer to remember which embellishment goes with which repetition of the melody. When memorizing the piece, therefore, the performer may keep on the music stand a little summary of the order of the embellishments, while playing the rest of the piece from memory. When the relevant point is reached in the music, the 'natural' tendency is to play the note without embellishment, but because of the afferent data coming from the 'summary sheet,' the performer inhibits this 'natural' tendency and plays the embellishment. Over time, the embellishment becomes a 'natural' response to the previously played note in its context, so that the performer no longer needs to think about it or look at the 'summary sheet.'

But, in principle, there are 'natural' behavior sequences which must be explicitly inhibited if they are to be stopped midway. And on the other hand there are discrete behaviors which must be purposely conjoined because an external stimulus causes them to be conjoined. And it is possible to distinguish these two types of situations. In the one case, inhibition is called for; in the other, excitation (Springer and Deutsch 1981: 350ff).

But each 'natural unit' of experience — say, the image of my wife's face — contains more than just that image. It also contains the total experiential context which was being experienced simultaneously with the image. For example, after meeting my wife for the first time, the memory of the face also was naturally conjoined with other information which was also part of the 'natural whole' of that moment — the content of what she was saying to someone when I first walked over to them, the location of the room in the apartment at which the party was being given, the smell of her perfume, the vague feeling of apprehension because someone had brought a live bird to the party, the general mood of the party as a whole, and the general feeling of the way my life was going at that time. All of this was part of a unitary experience, so that in recalling her face, it is also very easy to infer 'when' that was in my life history — especially since this was the only time I was ever in that apartment. *Places* are important components of memories because the place is experienced through the body's overall 'felt sense' of its situation, and it is this overall felt sense that is enacted as a natural whole — although usually in truncated form — when we dredge up the memory. (Bartlett, *et al* 1932 show how all the affective and various perceptual modalities are entertwined in memories when they are first 'recorded.') As the re-enactment of the image recurs again and again, it becomes increasingly truncated according to the purposes of the re-enactments, so that eventually the smell of the perfume may drop out, along with what she was saying as I walked up, and the vague apprehension due to the bird's presence. But, if I had met the person only once, I would need to re-enact as many of these aspects of the experience as I could in order to get the image of the person's face to light up as vividly as possible. This is why we have a more vivid 'feeling of recognition' when we actually return to a place than when we merely re-enact it in the imagination or see a photograph of it.

The natural whole of an experience contains all sensory modalities at once. It is only through the truncating process through re-enactments that some of the modalities drop out. And this is one reason we remember better when we include several sensory modalities in our re-enactment. The person's name 'naturally' 'implies' the image of the face which was part of the same natural whole with it, and the image of the face 'implies' the name.

This also helps explain why it is that similar images or memories 'interfere' with each other. Suppose there are two points in a Chopin piece which occur in completely analogous contexts, but one is different from the other. I must 'inhibit' my natural tendency to play one note which would form a natural whole with that context in order to 'remember' to play the other one instead.

We are now almost ready to understand where the memory 'engram' is 'stored.' Let's return to the example of the father teaching his son to hit the ball. Suppose the son's 'natural' tendency at first is to swing at a ball that is too high to reach. The son must learn to 'inhibit' his swing after it has already begun when he realizes that he has begun to swing at a high pitch. Over time, the tendency to inhibit the swing if the pitch is too high eventually becomes part of his 'natural tendency.' At this point, it would be unnatural for him *not* to inhibit the swing as soon as he realizes that the ball is high. He has now changed the ordered functioning of his nervous system, and to a certain extent even its chemical configuration, in such a way that what *was* 'natural' is no longer 'natural.' He has also changed his overall stance so that the principles of physics help make this more 'natural'; his front foot stands more ready to push back against the smooth flow of the swing if necessary. If he continues playing baseball, he will someday have to face pitchers who can throw curve balls — balls which appear high at first but then suddenly drop over the plate. At that point, the player must learn to *inhibit* his natural tendency to *inhibit* his swing at a high pitch if he can pick up on other cues that might indicate that the pitch is going to curve.

Human beings modify 'natural tendencies' by inhibiting the initially 'natural' response so that this response is no longer the 'natural' one. Returning to our initial example, in which the baseball player's swing was a 'natural whole' or 'natural unity' which would occur to its completion unless artificially interrupted, we might imagine what would happen if the player were to begin using a lighter bat. Then what was 'natural' would no longer be 'natural,' because the principles of physics would operate differently on a body swinging a lighter bat.

Similarly, we can change our nervous system through habitual inhibitions so that the principles of physics operate differently on the altered nervous system. Now what was 'natural' is no longer 'natural.' Psychologists would say that relatively permanent or long-term 'learning' has taken place.

To see how this role of inhibition fits into the concept of consciousness as a higher-order process, consider the following (now standard) explanation for the way theta waves in the hippocampus inhibit neural activity to facilitate memories:

> The activity of the whole individual is regulated by the reticular activating system, whose influence on the hippocampus is seen in the special form of the EEG, known as theta waves, originating in the septum. The theta waves sweep across the cells of the hippocampus, inhibiting most of them but leaving a few that are active in each phase of the wave. This means that at each moment certain cells only are open to receive excitation. . . . The generation of waves is linked to the movement of the animals (Young 1988: 164).

Psychologists are often impressed with the remarkable similarity between the learning and extinction curves in behavioral conditioning experiments and the analogous curves for acquisition and forgetting of memories. There should be no surprise here when we realize that recalling a memory is merely the execution of a behavior which forms a 'natural unity' for the organism, and that the process of inhibition which modifies what is and what is not 'natural' is the same as the acquisition of a conditioned response. The difference is that 'memory recall' is a behavior of the efferent part of the brain rather than only of the overtly observable parts of the body.

We can also relate these findings to the fact that, as organisms become more intelligent — capable of learning, memory, and complex problem solving — they exhibit a greater and greater proportion of inhibitory over excitatory neurotransmitters in their nervous systems.    The process of multiply-conditional associations requires the inhibition of responses that already had resulted from the habituation of earlier inhibitions, just as the baseball player must learn to inhibit his normal tendency to check his swing at a high pitch if he is to learn to hit a curve ball.  I daresay a monkey could never learn to hit a curve ball, any more than it could solve a complex multiple-discrimination task.    As Springer and Deutsch (1989) show, inhibition is much more concentrated in the frontal lobe than elsewhere in the brain; thus lower animals, which lack extensive frontal cortex, cannot manipulate the inhibitions of responses based on earlier inhibitions of initially natural responses with this much fluidity.

Incidentally, we can now insert this role of neural inhibition into our earlier discussions of the consciousness of negations, since Restak (1984: 10) observes that the inhibition of motor behaviors correlates with inhibitory neurotransmitters.  If the consciousness of objects results from a long process in which we learn to truncate the imagination of bodily manipulation of those objects (as we saw earlier Piaget, Tucker, Rosch, Minsky and others have argued), then it would also make sense that the consciousness of the negation of certain combinations or sequences of those same objects would result from the inhibition of those truncated motoric tendencies.

It also makes sense in this regard that memory, ease of learning, logical ability, the ability to form abstract concepts, ability to solve complex discrimination tasks, and ability to modify concepts through further discrimination all tend to correlate with each other, and that availability of the same chemicals in the brain *as a whole* (especially acetylcholine and acetylcholinesterase) largely correlates with all of these abilities (Loewi 1960). All of them involve modifying the structure of the efferent nervous system, through a process of inhibition, so that what was once a 'natural whole' of efferent behavior has now changed, and the way the system now most 'naturally' reacts to the principles of physics in a given context has changed. What persists unchanged throughout the life of a memory 'trace' is not some thing-like entity in the brain, but rather the way the principles of physics (which remain the same) affect the behavior of the nervous system.

Where, then, is the memory 'engram' (i.e., that which enables the body to re-enact an efferent behavior in roughly the same way as before) 'stored'? It is stored primarily in the principles of physics, which remain the same from one enactment of the behavior to the next. The baseball player's swing is roughly the same each time because, given the continuity of his bodily structure (height, weight, strength, and certain brain materials) he can rely on the principles of physics (for example, 'centrifugal force') to pull the swing around as a 'natural unity' in about the same way each time. This is why Karl Lashley spent his life looking for the location of memory 'engrams' and could never find them — indeed, why no one has found them yet. They are not physical things, but rather processes which are 'located' in the continuity of the principles of physics. I am not making the absurd claim that we somehow unconsciously *know* (or even 'know') the principles of physics. The point is that, given the sameness of these principles from one occasion to the next, there will be a natural-feeling way for the body to react to them each time; thus, the next time the brain reacts in a similar context, there will be a feeling of naturalness and thus familiarity. If the principles of physics had changed, the feeling of familiarity would not be there. Similarly, if the brain's holistic functioning has been 'jarred' too much (as with a blow to the head), responses that previously would have felt natural and familiar now no longer do.

One of the advantages of the imagistic over the computational approach to cognition, in fact, is that in the computational approach it is very difficult to distinguish a case of *knowing* the principles of physics (whether formally or even by non-thetically knowing how to predict things) from a case in which the body merely *responds* according to these principles without our knowledge or understanding (as manifested, for example, in an ability to make predictions). In the computational approach, it is necessary to invoke *ad hoc* stipulations according to which a jar-lid's 'knowledge' of the temperature of the water we run on it is not a 'mental' knowledge, whereas a computer's knowledge of input information is 'mental' — and according to which the jar lid's response to this input (by calculating how much to expand) is not 'mental' whereas the computer's analogous response is 'mental.' So I am by no means suggesting here that our memory functioning is based on an unconscious 'knowledge' of the principles of physics, although our bodies (and brains) do respond predictably to them.

What remains to be seen (and what we must discuss in the next section) is this: Granted that the continuity of the principles of physics enables me to enact the image of my wife's face in about the same way each time I do it, what is the substrate of the 'feeling of familiarity' associated with this image that makes me feel so sure that I *have* really seen it before — i.e., the 'feeling of recognition'? To merely *see an image twice* is not the same as to *know* that we have seen it before, as many amnesic cases prove quite clearly.

The 'implicit bodily sense' of a memory is the 'feeling of recognition' or 'feeling of familiarity' that goes with the enactment of the image, association or emotion to be remembered. And this 'feeling of familiarity' in turn arises from the feeling of 'naturalness' that we have when a given efferent behavior is a 'natural whole' or 'natural unity' in the sense we have defined in this section. In the next section, I shall try to clarify still further how this 'feeling of familiarity' functions, and answer some questions about it. We must especially try to understand how there can be 'single-trial learning' in the memorization process, why we feel so certain that a memory is the memory of something real and not the memory merely of an imaginary event we have dreamed up, and how this feeling of familiarity can sometimes be so completely mistaken.

## 4. Further Questions about Memory: Single-Trial Learning and the 'Feeling of Recognition'

We have seen that, when we memorize something, we figure out how to arrange that a certain stimulus will serve as a trigger or cue to evoke a certain conscious process as its response. This means that memorization of very simple facts (for example, where I left my car keys) involves *single-trial* learning to evoke a response (the enactment of a form of consciousness very analogous to a perceptual image of my car keys lying on the table) when presented with a trigger stimulus (for example, the enactment of the question, 'I wonder where I left my car keys?'). The image formed in reaction to this cue also involves a 'feeling of recognition' or 'feeling of familiarity'; the image of the keys on the table is not *merely* an image, but one that presents itself as something I have *really* seen before (and do not merely conjure in my mind).

Several puzzling questions immediately arise from this characterization of memorization.

(1) How can single-trial learning produce such a reliable response?

(2) If the response to the trigger-stimulus is merely a mental image (for example, of my keys lying on the table), how do I know that this image is the image of something which really occurred rather than something purely imaginary? We seldom seem to be confused about whether what we remember really occurred or not, so there must be something more going on than the mere enactment of a mental image or association of mental images.

(3) Related to the previous question is the following: Not only do we know whether the event we imagine really occurred, but we also have a sense of *when* it occurred — sometimes a quite accurate sense. Especially in comparing different memories with each other, we can often say with great confidence which one occurred earlier than the other. Yet we are also often wrong about this. Also, we commonly have the 'feeling of familiarity' in a completely illusory context when we have the familiar *deja vu* experience, which has been correlated with activity of the midbrain (Restak 1984: 12); hence it is merely a *feeling* of familiarity.

(4) How is it that, on the one hand, we have a feeling of certitude that the image our memory gives us is the image of something that really occurred, and often even certitude of the order in which these realities occurred; yet on the other hand we often stand quite ready to be corrected on these points and will abandon the feeling that the images in our memory are realities if there is strong evidence that they never really occurred?

It might prove fruitful to begin with an example of question (4). Suppose I have a memory that my favorite baseball team lost last night's game, which I saw. And suppose someone tells me he read a newspaper article which clearly indicates that the team won last night. At first I insist on my opinion, reinforcing it with a recounting of the details of the game. How could I remember all these details unless they were true? But other people who saw the game all insist that the details of the game were completely different. At first I feel perplexed, but at length I feel certain they must be right. I must have confused last night's game with an earlier game. I confused the two situations in my memory because certain details of the two games were so similar. In this case, I conclude not that the images in my mind *never occurred,* but merely that they occurred in a different order from the way my memory had called them up for me. Here again, to a great extent I am again piecing together images in a way that seems to *make sense* in order to *construct* my memories, as we saw in the first section; and I am using my whole bodily felt sense to help fit together these sensible elements.

But, before jumping to any quick conclusions from this example, let's consider a couple of others that are different in certain respects. We are all familiar with the phenomenon of thinking that we remember an event from our childhood only because it has been told and retold by relatives over the years, then we discover that the event never even occurred at all. In this case we have no difficulty admitting to ourselves that what we felt was a memory is actually only a vivid but imaginary scene of which we had constructed a visual and perhaps auditory mental picture. Yet it passed for a memory until we learned otherwise.

Now consider a third example: In a softball game I ran into the shortstop as he was trying to tag second base, and was knocked out. For hours after regaining consciousness, I could remember nothing of the events leading up to the injury. When I asked someone what had occurred, she said that I had hit a ground ball to the shortstop, and then he had collided with me as I reached second base at the same time as he did. (Anyone who knows the way baseball works knows that this scenario would be virtually impossible, since the batter must fist run to first base, and if he headed toward second base the defensive player would have to tag *him,* not the base.) At first, the image I formed of this narrative seemed to 'ring a bell.' I thought I was beginning to remember it. But then I realized that this was impossible. In order for the situation to be one in which he would tag the base, I would have to have *already* been on first base, and *someone else* would have to have hit the ground ball to the shortstop. So the image that this person's narrative had conjured for me could not have been a memory. At this moment the image of what had really happened occurred to me in a spontaneous flash: I had just hit the ball, an outside pitch (I could tell by the 'felt bodily sense' of the memory), the ball was going over the second baseman's head, and he was leaping for it but missing. Then (after a gap in memory that was never filled in) the shortstop was fielding a ground ball hit by the next batter (I never remembered who) and I was running desperately to second base. The image of the shortstop fielding the ball was the same as in the illusory memory conjured by my wife's confused account. But now both that image and the image of the second baseman lunging for the ball were as if in tunnel vision — a round patch of visual imagery surrounded by a field of darkness, just as images often occur in dreams.

In all three of these examples of faulty memory, we can observe a common element. An image can easily be mistaken for a memory, and the way we resolve the mistake involves a process in which (1) we consider whether it would *make sense* for things to have occurred as our images envision them, followed by (2) a flash of insight in which the image of how things *really* occurred suddenly appears to us, resulting in (3) a 'feeling of recognition' associated with the images we now seem to remember as what really occurred. The process of figuring out what would *make sense* to have occurred is not by itself sufficient to produce an actual *memory* of what occurred, but it is a necessary element. Beyond this, there must be an unconscious, holistic 'fitting together' of the various elements, resulting in a new combination which not only produces a new image, but also 'makes sense' in terms of the way the various elements 'fit together,' and also produces the 'feeling of recognition' in our bodily sense as we entertain the images.

This process very much resembles the process of creative insight into the solution to a problem (Watson 1969; Harlow 1959; May 1976; Hunt 1985). Winson (1985: 210) also emphasizes the similarity here. We try very hard to make elements fit together in ways they cannot quite fit, and then in a moment of mental relaxation the elements suddenly come together for us in a new way, seemingly without any conscious effort. At that point we feel that we have hit on a new possibility which just might turn out to be the solution to our problem. Then as we live with this possibility, we rapidly feel more and more certain that it is the solution. It 'makes sense.' This feeling that a solution 'makes sense' is very similar to the feeling that an image 'rings a bell' and therefore must be the memory of something real, not just a mental image. There is the feeling that it 'fits.'

Both these processes relate to Gendlin's felt sense. Suppose we return to his example of remembering what I meant to do but forgot. Different possible answers occur to us, but somehow they fail to 'fit.' The way we know we have hit on the right answer is that we get a sudden bodily sense of relief. Somehow our body 'knew' the answer before our consciousness knew. How does this happen?

Again, Gendlin notes the similarity of this 'Aha!' to the experience of realizing that we have accurately identified the way we feel about a situation. In both cases, there is a bodily feeling of 'naturalness,' which tells us that the efferent parts of our brain, by forming a certain combination of mental images, are reacting to the principles of physics just as they would have in the situation we remember, and at the same time just as it would *make sense* that they would have in the given situation. Just as the ball player 'remembers' to complete his swing because it feels more natural to complete it than to interrupt it, given the principles of physics, so also we 'remember' to re-enact the combination of images along with the 'feeling of familiarity' (or 'feeling of naturalness') that goes with them, precisely because this combination *is* the most natural one for the entire body (and nervous system) to execute, given the way the principles of physics affect the body with its exact history of functional modification through a series of inhibitions which have become habitual, and inhibitions of responses that had been based on the habituation of earlier inhibitions.

A memory differs phenomenologically from a mere imagination in that it is accompanied by the particular kind of bodily felt shift that yields the feeling of familiarity, although this does not mean that a memory cannot be mistaken. During the entire time since the event which was to be remembered occurred, the body has been holding certain of its elements in a condition of preparedness to perceive or to act in relation to that event. But, in cases of long-term memory, this condition of preparedness is not dependent on holding the condition of 'looking for' the particular object continually in the limbic system, prefrontal cortex and parietal lobe in their entirety. It is based, rather, on the fact that, when things come together very similarly to the way they did on an earlier occasion, a feeling of naturalness will result from the similarity of the brain's response. What is held in the body continually is only a preparedness to enact Gendlin's 'bodily felt shift' when an image, feeling or thought recurs in a similar context.

The bodily shift — the sense of relief when everything feels as though it 'fits together,' and thus our 'implicit preparedness' can be discharged — this constellation of feelings is also a necessary part of the 'feeling of recognition' that must accompany an image in order for it to qualify as a memory.

We are now prepared to answer the questions with which we began this section:

(1) How can single-trial learning produce such a reliable response? The answer is that the 'feeling of recognition' is a feeling of 'naturalness' in the sense developed in the last section. We know that an efferent re-enactment (which is executed by diverse areas of the brain working together) is 'right' because it 'feels right.' And the reason it feels right is that it feels like a 'natural whole' or 'natural unity' of functioning. This means that the elements of the substratum are flowing naturally in accordance with the way the principles of physics impact them in their present configuration of excitation and inhibition. We know it just in the way that the son knows where his own natural swing leaves off and his father's external 'push' toward a not-yet-natural follow-through begins. When the boy's body and brain readjust so that the new, improved swing feels 'natural,' there is no way the old, awkward swing could any longer feel natural to him. He has changed permanently, and the principles of physics now affect his body differently.

How is it possible that this can occur in a single trial? In the same way that a batter who picks up a lighter bat instantaneously changes what is and what is not 'natural' in his swing. In this case, the way the principles of physics operate on his body changes *instantaneously*. The same thing would happen if he were to change his initial 'stance' by bending his knees more, or spreading his feet wider in the batter's box, or holding the bat further off his shoulder. In each case, the way physics affects the body changes, and what does and does not feel 'natural' changes accordingly.

The way the brain changes which efferent activities do and do not feel 'natural' (and thus produce a 'feeling of familiarity') is by spreading inhibitory and excitatory neurotransmitters around in various patterns. This also explains why new learning sometimes tends to erase old learning, especially when the topics involved are very similar. When the neurotransmitters are distributed in different patterns, some efferent activities that used to feel 'familiar' (because they felt 'natural') now no longer do.

But remember that when I speak of 'configurations' and 'patterns' of neurotransmitters, I am speaking of *temporal,* not just *spacial* patterns. And a pattern need not be *continually enacted* in order for the body's *tendency* to behave in that pattern to persist. A baseball player need not continually be swinging a bat in order for his body's natural tendency to swing in a certain way to persist. Nor must his tendency to swing in that way be 'stored' in some particular place in his body. Similarly, neurotransmitters need not be *continually distributed* in a certain way in order for the body's *tendency* to distribute them in that way to persist. This is why Lashley could never find the memory 'engrams.' They are not something permanently located in a place; what is permanent is the way the principles of physics would affect the body in certain contexts when they should arise. So, when connectionists and others emphasize, with Winson (1985: 179) that "Passage of a signal along a particular circuit via particular synapses makes a later passage of a signal along the same circuit easier," they are also referring to a broader fact about nature — that the more organized a pattern becomes, the more it will tend to perpetuate itself through recurrences of similar patterns, unless changed or disrupted by some external force.

In answering question (1), we have also answered question (2). How do I know that the mental image is the image of something that really occurred rather than of something merely imagined? The answer is that the 'naturalness' of the way this efferent behavior is affected by the principles of physics produces a 'feeling of naturalness' and thus a 'feeling of familiarity.'

(3) How do we know so precisely *when* the event occurred? We know this in relation to our felt sense of when other related events occurred. The reason for this is that the original image, although now more or less truncated, contained implicit interconnections with a multi-sensory and meaningful *context* of which it was only a part. The implicit bodily sense gives us the whole situation, not just the specific image we are trying to recall. And this whole situation is spatio-temporally situated in other, larger contexts, as Husserl describes extensively in his *Phenomenology of Internal Time Consciousness.* There develops in my memory system an interrelated matrix of overlapping 'natural sequences,' so that no one sequence completely comes to closure before another has begun. For example, I have conditioned myself to play the

first seven seconds of a piece of music as a 'natural unity,' but I have also conditioned myself to play the second through the eighth seconds as another 'natural unity.' Eventually, I build up this series of natural unities to the point where I can play a sequence of 450 million notes without error (if I am Claudio Arrau).

(4) How can the feeling of familiarity be mistaken? Because it is only a feeling. Sometimes the interpretation of the meaning of a feeling can be problematic. We assume normal background conditions when we interpret a feeling. For example, when an astronaut walks on the moon, he walks in a way that feels like his normal walk. But what he may forget is that the normal background conditions he usually assumes for the way his normal walk would feel have now changed (i.e., the moon's gravity is different). So what feels like his normal walk is in fact a ridiculous prancing movement. The same thing happens to ballerinas making delicate balancing movements when their bodies are unusually tired or suffering from mineral imbalances or differences in the comparative rate of development of coordinating muscles.

Similarly, what feels like our usual efferent response may in fact be different when our brains are suffering from fatigue or mineral imbalance or a hard blow to the head or any number of other unexpected alterations in the background conditions presupposed by 'what feels natural' and thus the 'feeling of familiarity.' What is remarkable is not how error can occur here, but rather how a mere feeling can function in such a reliable and consistent way that we are usually correct in our feelings of recognition.

When we remember an image, we re-enact all the neurophysiological substrata that subserved the original image, accompanied by a feeling of familiarity associated with the re-enactment. The ability to have this feeling of familiarity associated with that image is not stored in some specific place during the interim. It results from the feeling of naturalness in executing something in the same way as before.

# CONCLUSION

## The Centrality of Subjunctives

We saw in Chapter 1 that what happens in my consciousness when I imagine (form a mental image of) a pink wall as blue is that, for just an instant, I look at the wall 'as if' it were blue — i.e., in such a way as to look *for* blue in the wall, though I know in advance that I will not find it there. The fact is available to phenomenological reflection that, when I imagine the pink wall at which I am looking as a blue wall, I perform a certain type of 'looking-for-blue' which is the same in certain respects as the looking-for-blue I would perform if I were to focus on a wall fully expecting it to be blue. Dennett and other cognitive theorists are thus correct in assuming that the perceptual consciousness of a physical object occurs in the efferent activity which the afferent input from the object evokes (or as Dennet 1969: 74 says, "No afferent can be said to have a significance 'A' until it is 'taken' to have the significance 'A' by the efferent side of the brain"); then the 'looking-for' phenomenon just mentioned enables us to formulate a coherent accounting of the utterly *different* physiological correlates of the perceptual and the imaginative consciousness of the *same* cognitive 'content' ('blue wall,' for example). A mental image differs from a perception in that the perception not only involves an efferent pattern of activity which 'looks *for*' the object in question, but at the same time the afferent system delivers to the relevant efferent brain areas a pattern of activity which fulfills the efferent looking-for, so that the organism senses itself as 'looking *at*' the object. In the mental image, on the other hand, such an efferent looking-for pattern is set up —

identical in certain neurophysiological parameters to the one which would be present if we were to 'look *at*' the object in question — but the afferent system fails to deliver the corresponding message, so that the organism senses itself only as 'looking for' the object, not *at* the object (as discussed also in Ellis 1990). Every looking-at must be accompanied by a corresponding looking-for. As Merleau-Ponty (1962) says, "We must look in order to see (232)"; or, as Luria (1973) says, "The stationary eye is virtually incapable of the stable perception of complex objects and . . . such perception is always based on the use of active, searching movements of the eyes, picking out the essential clues (100)." Thus we cannot consciously 'look-at' something without having already 'looked-for' the object. But the reverse is not true: I.e., when the relevant efferent brain structures look-for the object *without* being accompanied by the sensation of a corresponding looking-at, a mere mental image of the non-present object occurs.

These phenomenological observations are consistent with the finding of Aurell (1989) and Posner and Rothbart (1992) that, when sensory input activates the primary projection area in the brain, no *consciousness* of the object is yet present. Consciousness occurs only with the activation of the prefrontal and parietal areas, which are associated with the *imagination* of an object (Richardson 1991). Activation of these areas in the *absence* of any corresponding sensory input results in a mere imagination of the object; in this case, efferent activity occurs in the parietal, secondary-sensory, and prefrontal areas, but no matching afferent signals are found in the primary projection area. Phenomenologically, what is happening is that the efferent system has geared itself up to look *for* a certain image, but this image is not found in the pattern of input from the environment. Thus Logan (1980), Corbetta (1990), Pardo *et al* (1990), Hanze and Hesse (1993), Legrenzi *et al* (1993), Rhodes and Tremewan (1993), and other cognitive psychologists find that, when we hold in our imagination the image of a certain object, we are more likely to see that object when flashed on a screen. By imagining the object, we gear ourselves up to look for it.

It is important to be clear about the central concept of 'looking-for' in this context. I 'look for' something when I put myself into a frame of mind such that I will be as likely as possible to perceive the object if it should be presented. For example, if I am told to count the number of triangles that are flashed sequentially on a screen, interspersed with other figures, I prepare myself to see triangles and to ignore other geometrical figures. This preparedness to focus on triangles when they occur is the mental act of 'looking for triangles,' which is subjectively barely distinguishable from the act of simply holding in consciousness the image of a triangle on the screen, except that the image I must hold in mind may be a fuzzy or generic one, not the image of a particular type and size of triangle. In either case, to look for something essentially involves holding a mental image or a concept of the object in consciousness. If it is a concept rather than an image that I hold in mind, then the neurophysiology involved is a little more complex, as Chapters 2 and 3 discussed. The imageless concept of a simple, imageable object such as a triangle is essentially a condition of preparedness or readiness to entertain the images which *would* be needed to ostensively define the concept if called upon to do so, and each step in this process in turn would be an act of 'looking-for.'

The act of 'looking for triangles' is also subjectively experienced as part of the act of attending to a triangle when it is presented unexpectedly. But in this case what happens is that the afferent pattern of a triangle first stimulates the thalamus, which directs the efferent system to 'look for' successively more accurate approximations to the activity of the primary projection area, until the efferent and afferent activities finally resonate by means of this cybernetic feedback loop. In this sense, we could say that the afferent signal corresponding to 'triangle' evokes the corresponding efferent pattern when it passes through the thalamus, at which point a decision is made to continue paying attention to the triangle, at which point I 'look for' the triangle which is already there so as to maintain consciousness of it (by means of the efferent system); it is precisely the act of 'looking for' an object already present which is called 'attending to' the object in such contexts. The act of looking-for may thus be preceded by an afferent delivery of the corresponding signals, but the signals do not become an attentive consciousness of the object until the 'looking-for' act is executed. Only then can it be said that I consciously 'look at' the object presented.

As we have seen, this explains the perplexing empirical finding by Aurell (1984), Runeson (1974: 14), McHugh and Bahill (1985), Srebro (1985: 233-246) and others, of the time delay of a third of a second between activation of the primary projection area and of the parietal area, even though the neurophysiological impulse should travel much faster than this. The reason is that other parts of the brain, involved in the motivated attentional process, remembering ideas associated with the given image, etc, must be awakened in order for the 'looking-for' process to motivate a *conscious image* of the object. This mental focusing of attention takes much longer than would a merely passive response to a stimulus input. An active process of search, selective attention, interpretation, and even value judgment (i.e., whether the object is important for the organism) — all of this goes into the formation of the simplest perceptual consciousness.

Normally, during waking consciousness, to merely imagine an object is also (as Sartre suggested in *The Psychology of the Imagination*) to sense that this object *is not present*. In the present context, we can say that in negation, as in imaginative consciousness, the looking-for is not met with the corresponding looking-at. Thus the doxic modalities of imagination and negation can be accounted for in a way that explains why the *imagined* or *negated* object enacts such a closely related but structurally dissimilar brain event to the one that would be enacted by the *perception* of the corresponding object. To think momentarily 'The wall is not blue' is to momentarily look for blue in the wall without finding it. To *imagine* a blue wall is to *continue* looking for a blue wall during the entire time that one is imagining the blue wall.

Thus the reason for the perceived difficulty of consciously imagining a blue wall while consciously looking at (i.e., seeing) a pink wall is that the efferent pattern corresponding to looking-for the blue wall is *incompatible* with the efferent pattern corresponding to looking-for the pink wall, yet the latter must be done if one is to *see* the pink wall. Since attending to an imagined object and attending to a perceptual object which differs from it *conflict* with each other in this way due to the conflict between the corresponding efferent event-patterns, the phenomenon of 'attention' can also be accounted for as an efferent looking-for (where 'attention' in this context means the attention to a specific object or idea in which frontal lobe activity is crucial, not the mere 'orienting reflex' or general increase of arousal that results from reticular formation functions — see Posner and Rothbart 1992; Hebb 1949).

In Chapter 2, I argued that this subjunctive act of forming mental images constitutes the basis from which abstract concepts are constructed. When we use a concept in context, we usually let its meaning remain 'implicit' (Gendlin, 1992), which means that we feel confident that the small chunk of imagery that is in our consciousness (such as the image of the name of the concept, or some image associated with the concept) *could* serve, if we wanted it to, as a starting point from which we could elaborate a long and complicated story, involving many interrelated images, which would suffice to give a directly or indirectly ostensive definition of what we mean by the concept; we would do this by citing observations which would be empirical and thus imageable in some modality (sensory, sensorimotor or proprioceptive). This is the process we would go through if we were to make the concept's meaning 'explicit,' but normally we do not actually go through this process. Yet, to the extent that we think we know what the concept means, we feel that we could go through it if needed.

Chapter 3 explored the way in which logical inferential abilities develop out of more elementary sensory, sensorimotor and proprioceptive images as well as out of abstract concepts which in turn are based themselves on the ability to use all these types of images in certain patterns. Because of such emphasis on the role of images, this was called an 'imagist' approach. 'Imagists' hold that inferential thinking is built up from combinations of mental images in various patterns and modalities, and that the images are a more basic mental and neurophysiological operation than the logical thinking and conceptualization that are built up from them. 'Computationalists' hold just the opposite view — that images result from previous inferential processing which is more basic than the images. But suppose we define inference as the kind of thought process that we actually undergo when we do logical thinking, and not in the trivial sense in which any natural phenomenon which receives an 'input' from another then 'responds' to this 'input' — as for example when a ball responds to being hit by flying off at a certain angle. And suppose, following Newton (1980, 1993), we define an 'image' as any instance of imagining what it would be like to entertain some conscious state which we are not undergoing at the time — as for example when we imagine what it would be like to see something, to ride a roller coaster or to have a headache. I.e., 'images' can be kinaesthetic and proprioceptive as well as sensory. Then it can be shown that all inferential thinking is completely built up from patterns of images, especially the imaging of rhythm patterns corresponding to logical syntax. Furthermore, the acquisition of these inference rules can also be traced to a process of trying to imagine scenarios which might serve as counterexamples to the rules, and this kind of 'imagining' can also be explained in terms of both sensory and proprioceptive images. The reason for this is that even the apparently 'imageless' concepts used to imagine such scenarios (e.g., 'if I were president') consist in each case of a feeling of preparedness to entertain a pattern of images which would be appropriate to provide a directly or indirectly ostensive definition of the concept in question, and this feeling of preparedness can be sensed proprioceptively.

Since we have thematized the role of consciousness in cognition, it is important to be clear about the ontological status of consciousness, and not to be misled by a simplistic epiphenomenalism or psychophysical identity theory into thinking that there is no need to understand and investigate the subjective side of consciousness. We saw in Chapter 4 that there are irresolvable problems with traditional approaches to the mind-body problem, including interactionism (or dualism), psychophysical identity, epiphenomenalism, and even the 'nomic equivalence' approach. A different alternative was then proposed: Consciousness has the ontological status of a process which takes the functioning of the brain as its substratum. This process-substratum model explains how conscious and physiological events can be inseparable (thus regularly correlated) without being identical, yet there is no need to propose the breaks in neurophysiological causal chains that would be necessary for interactionism, or to reduce conscious events to mere causal epiphenomena lacking explanatory value. We can explain conscious events in either physical or mental terms, just as we can explain wave phenomena through the movement of particles or through the pattern of the wave itself, which causes subsequent particles to conform to the pattern. But one or the other approach may be more feasible given available information. Moreover, in the case of organic phenomena (which conscious processes presuppose, according to the argument of Chapter 5), the process often appropriates, replaces and reproduces the substratum elements needed to facilitate the enactment of the process. This 'enactive' view is in substantial agreement with the argument of Varela *et al* (1992), who in fact used the same term to describe this aspect of conscious phenomena.

A process-substratum view of consciousness then helped toward an exploration, in Chapter 6, of issues in memory and emotion — the latter constituting, as I have argued, the key difference between conscious and non-conscious information processors. Since states of consciousness are processes which are enacted on specific occasions, and not spatially-extended, thing-like entities, they are not 'stored' as in computer storage. Memories are widely distributed re-enactments of earlier conscious processes, as evoked by cues, accompanied by a 'feeling of familiarity.' The feeling of familiarity stems from the fact that the pattern in question, having been enacted before in a similar context, 'feels natural' in the way that a baseball player's unique way of swinging the bat feels natural. A new way of swinging can instantaneously change what feels natural if it arises from a change in the way we situate ourselves in order to execute the response — for example, by switching to a lighter bat, or by changing our overall stance. In the same way, a single exposure to a new stimulus can render future executions of the image of that stimulus 'natural-feeling,' and thus 'familiar-feeling,' because it changes the overall orientation of the brain with respect to its environment. Now certain enactments feel 'natural' that previously would not have.

In the case of emotions, we saw that part of what the emotion 'desires' is to find an opportunity to 'symbolize' itself — i.e., to find substratum elements (such as words, images or actions) capable of subserving the process of the emotion or complex of emotions in an 'amplified' and 'equalized' enough way that the emotion can discover what it is 'about' by imaginatively representing the missing elements of its own needed substratum. I argued that the intersection of desire with representations is always needed in order for something to qualify as a conscious event. This always requires an imaginative and thus (again) a subjunctive process.

All the cognitive processes we have considered, including imaging, perception, concept formation, rule-governed logical thought, and memory, intimately involve the use of subjunctives and counterfactuals. We have seen, first of all, that even the formation of the simplest mental image (let alone concept) is already a process which involves counterfactuals. The activity of the prefrontal and parietal areas leads to a vague, low-level consciousness of purely *imaginary* mental contents before this imaging process is finally coordinated with what is occuring in the primary projection area to see whether there is a match between the rough image that has already been hypothesized and the incoming data from the senses. The parietal/secondary-sensory images are thus first of all subjunctive or counterfactual ones. And these images play several extremely key roles in the enactment of memories, both as remembered images *per se,* and in the image component of the sounds or visualizations that are used in the symbolization process which helps us to retrieve memories. Moreover, the process of 'making sense' out of our memories is a conceptual operation and therefore, as we have already seen, one which involves subjunctives.

In the case of each type of consciousness, then, we find that subjunctive propositions are the basis of the most elementary building blocks of human cognition. This is equally applicable to the knowledge of deductive logic, causal statements, moral statements, physical concepts, and the principles of probability. In each of these realms of discouse, complex combinations of subjunctive statements are often mistaken for straightforward, declarative statements. The attempt to analyse such statements as declarative ones then leads to inevitable philosophical confusion. Once the statements are understood as fundamentally subjunctive in form, the confusion disappears. At the same time, it becomes possible to understand the relation between intentional and extensional processes in the mind/brain complex. When we imagine an object which is not there (a 'negation' in Sartre's much misunderstood and overly-romanticized conceptualization), our brain is merely doing something whose pattern is similar in certain general efferent contours to what the brain *would* be doing *if* we were to actually perceive the corresponding physical object. Such acts of imagination then form the physiological basis for abstractions and deductive inferences.

In the film *Nicolas and Alexandra,* an old soldier has been assigned to guard the Czar while the latter awaits the decision to execute him. The old guard reveals that, until he met the Czar, he had always regarded him as a vicious, cruel monster devoid of any human sensibility. Now, he says, he realizes that Czar Nicolas is none of those things; he is merely 'a man with no imagination.' A person with no imagination, in this sense, is one who is lacking in the ability to imagine what might happen if circumstances were different from the way they are, which is the very essence of human intellectual capability. Essentially the same defect characterizes the mentally retarded, people who have trouble grasping abstractions independently of their concrete instantiations, the brain-damaged soldiers in Goldstein's studies who could not think abstractly or ask themselves questions, those who are incapable of genuine moral reflection, many types of neurotics, the completely uncreative, and those introductory logic students who cannot understand why it is important to be able to distinguish between a valid and an invalid argument even in those instances where the premises and/or conclusions are already known to be false (or true). In short, the inability to imagine what would happen if things were different from the way they are — the inability to conceptualize and manipulate subjunctive propositions — is one of the most ubiquitous of all human shortcomings, and is the first result of brain damage and of persistent understimulation of the intellect. To put the same point more positively, the ability to conceptualize and manipulate subjunctives is one of the most essential cornerstones — perhaps *the* most essential — of human intellectual ability, and thus of what it means to be 'fully conscious' in the human style.

# REFERENCES

Ahern, G.L. and G.E. Schwartz. 1985. "Differential lateralization for positive and negative emotion in the human brain: EEG spectral analysis". *Neuropsychologia* 23: 745-755.

Ahn, Woo-Kyoung and Doublas Medin. 1992. "A two-stage model of category construction". *Cognitive Science* 16: 81-121.

Anderson, John. 1983. *The Architecture of Cognition*. Cambridge: Harvard University Press.

Annis, David and Linda Annis. 1979. "Does philosophy improve critical thinking?" *Teaching Philosophy* 3: 2.

Aristotle. 1993. *De Anima*. D.W. Hamlyn trans. Oxford: Clarendon Press.

Aserinsky, Eugene, and Nathaniel Kleitman. 1953. "Regularly occurring periods of eye motility and concomitant phenomena during sleep". *Science* 118: 273.

Asimov, Isaac. 1965. *The Human Brain*. New York: Mentor.

Aston-Jones, G. and F.E. Bloom. 1981. "Norepinephrine-containing locus coerulens neurons in behaving rats exhibit pronounced response to non-noxious environmental stimuli". *Journal of Neuroscience* 1: 887.

Aurell, Carl G. 1983. "Perception: A model comprising two modes of consciousness. Addendum: Evidence based on event-related potentials and brain lesions". *Perceptual and Motor Skills* 56: 211-220.

Aurell, Carl G. 1984. "Perception: A model comprising two modes of consciousness. Addendum II: Emotion incorporated". *Perceptual and Motor Skills* 59: 180-182.

Aurell, Carl G. 1989. "Man's triune conscious mind". *Perceptual and Motor Skills* 68: 747-754.

Ausubel, David. 1963. *The Psychology of Meaningful Verbal Learning*. New York: Grune and Stratton.

Baars, Bernard. 1988. *A Cognitive Theory of Consciousness*. New York: Cambridge University Press.

Barsalou, Lawrence. 1987. "The instability of graded structure: Implications for the nature of concepts". In Ulric Neisser (ed), *Concepts and Conceptual Development: Ecological and Intellectual Factors in Categorization*. New York: Cambridge University Press, 101-140.

Bartlett, Frederic C. 1932. *Remembering: A Study in Experimental and Social Psychology*. Cambridge: Cambridge University Press.

Bechtel, William. 1986. Lecture at Southern Society for Philosophy and Psychology.

Bechtel, William. 1987. "Connectionism and the philosophy of mind: An overview". *Southern Journal of Philosophy* 26: 17-41.

Becker, Angela and Thomas Ward. 1991. "Children's use of shape in extending novel labels to animate objects: Identity versus postural change". *Cognitive Development* 6: 3-16.

Berlin, Brent and Paul Kay. 1969. *Basic Color Terms: Their Univerality and Evolution*. Berkeley: University of California Press.

Bickle, John. 1992. "Multiple realizability and psychophysical reduction". *Behavior and Philosophy* 20: 47-58.

Bickle, John. 1993. "Philosophy neuralized: A critical notice of P.M. Churchland's *Neurocomputational Perspective*". *Behavior and Philosophy* 20: 75-88.

Bisiach, Edoardo. 1992. "Understanding consciousness: Clues from unilateral neglect and related disorders". In A.D. Milner and M.D. Rugg (eds). *The Neuropsychology of Consciousness*. London: Academic Press, 113-138.

Blakemore, Colin and G.F. Cooper. 1970. "Development of the brain depends on the visual environment". *Nature* 228: 477.

Boden, Margaret. 1982. "Implications of language studies for human nature". In T.W. Simon and R.J. Scholes (eds), *Language, Mind and Brain*. Hillsdale, NJ: Lawrence Erlbaum, 129-143.

Bonatti, Luca. 1994. "Why should we abandon the mental logic hypothesis?" *Cognition* 50: 17-39.

Broadbent, Donald E. 1958. *Perception and Communication*. London: Pergamon Press.

Broadbent, Donald E. 1977. "The hidden pre-attentive process". *American Psychologist* 32: 109-118.

Brown, Charles. 1965. "Fallacies in Taylor's 'Fatalism'". *The Journal of Philosophy* 62: 349-353.

Bruner, Jerome S. 1961. *Contemporary Approaches to Cognition*. Cambridge: Harvard University Press.

Buchwald, Jennifer, Donald Guthrie, Judith Schwafel, R. Erwin and Diana Van Laniker. 1994. "Influence of language structure on brain-behavior development". *Brain and Language* 46: 607-619.

Buck, Ross. 1988. *Human Motivation and Emotion*. New York: Wiley.

Bullemer, P. and Nissen, M.J. 1990. "Attentional orienting in the expression of procedural knowledge". Paper presented at meeting of the Psychonomic Society, New Orleans, April 1990.

Burgess, Curt and Simpson, Greg. 1988. "Cerebral hemispheric mechanisms in the retrieval of ambiguous word meanings". *Brain and Language* 33: 86-103.

Butler, Keith. 1993. "Connectionism, classical cognitivism and the relation between cognitive and implementational levels of analysis". *Philosophical Psychology* 6: 321-330.

Calder, Nigel. 1979. *Einstein's Universe*. New York: Penguin.

Carr, David. 1991. *Time, Narrative and History*. Bloomington: Indiana University Press.

Cassirer, Ernst. 1923-1953. *Substance and Function*. New York: Dover.

Churchland, Patricia S. 1986. *Neurophilosophy*. Cambridge: The MIT Press.

Churchland, Paul M. 1979. *Scientific Realism and the Plasticity of Mind*. Cambridge: Cambridge University Press.

Churchland, Paul M. 1989. *A Neurocomputational Perspective: The Nature of Mind and the Structure of Science*. Cambridge: MIT Press.

Cohen, Asher, Richard Ivry, and Steven Keele. 1990. "Attention and structure in sequence learning". *Journal of Experimental Psychology: Learning, Memory and Cognition* 16: 17-30.

Cohen, R.M., W.E. Semple, M. Gross, H.J. Holcomb, S.M. Dowling, and T.E. Nordahl. 1988. "Functional localization of sustained attention". *Neuropsychiatry, Neuropsychology and Behavioral Neurology* 1: 3-20.

Corbetta, M., F.M. Meizen, S. Dobmeyer, G.L. Schulman, and S.E. Petersen. 1990. "Selective attention modulates neural processing of shape, color and velocity in humans". *Science* 248: 1556-1559.

Cornaldi, Cesare and Mark McDaniel (eds). 1991. *Imagery and Cognition*. New York: Springer-Verlag.

Coulter, Jeff. 1983. *Rethinking Cognitive Theory*. London: Macmillan.

Cutler, Anne. 1994. "The perception of rhythm in language". *Cognition* 50: 79-81.

Dahl, P., W.H. Bailey, and T. Winson. 1983. "Effect of norepinephrine depletion of hippocampus on neuronal transmission from perforant pathway through dentate gyrus". *Journal of Neurophysiology* 49: 123.

Damasio, Antonio. 1989. "Time-locked multiregional retroactivation: A systems level proposal for the neural substrate of recall and recognition". *Cognition* 33: 25-62.

Damasio, Antonio, and G.W. Van Hoesen. 1983. "Emotional disturbances associated with focal lesions of the limbic frontal lobe". In Kenneth Heilman and Paul Satz (eds), *Neuropsychology of Human Emotion*. New York: Guilford Press.

Damasio, Antonio, P.J. Eslinger, H. Damasio, G.W. Van Hoesen, and S. Cornell. 1985. "Multimodal amnesic syndrome following bilateral temporal and basal forebrain damage". *Archives of Neurology* 42: 252-259.

Dascal, Marcelo. 1987. "Language and reasoning: Sorting out sociopragmatic and psychopragmatic factors". In J.C. Boudreaux, B. W. Hamill, and R. Jernigan (eds), *The Role of Language in Problem Solving 2*. Elsevier: North-Holland, 183-197.

Davidson, Donald. 1970. "Mental events". In Lawrence Foster and Joe W. Swanson (eds), *Experience and Theory*. Amherst: University of Massachusetts Press, 79-102.

Dement, William. 1958. "The occurrence of low voltage, fast electroencephalogram patterns during behavioral sleep in cats". *Electroencephalography and Clinical Neurophysiology* 10: 291-293.

Dement, William, and Nathaniel Kleitman. 1957. "Cyclic variations in EEG during sleep and their relation of eye movements, body motility and dreaming," *Electroencephalography and Clinical Neurophysiology* 49: 673-676.

Denis, Michel. 1991. "Imagery and thinking". In Cesare Cornoldi and Mark McCaniel (eds), *Imagery and Cognition*. New York: Springer-Verlag, 103-131.

Dennett, Daniel. 1969. *Content and Consciousness*. London: Routledge & Kegan Paul.

Dennett, Daniel. 1991. *Consciousness Explained*. Boston: Little, Brown and Co.

Dewan, Edmond M. 1976. "Consciousness as an emergent causal agent in the context of control system theory". In Gordon Globus, Grover Maxwell and Irwin Savodnik (eds), *Consciousness and the Brain*. New York: Plenum Press, 179-198.

Dimond, Stuart. 1980. *Neuropsychology: A Textbook of Systems and Psychological Functions of the Human Brain*. London: Butterworth.

Dore, John, Margery Franklin, Robert Miller, and Andrya Ramer. 1976. "Transitional phenomena in early language acquisition". *Journal of Child Language* 3: 13-27.

Dreyfus, Hebert. 1979. *What Computers Can't Do*. New York: Harper & Row.

Edelman, Gerald. 1989. *The Remembered Present*. New York: Basic Books.

Edwards, Betty. 1979. *Drawing on the Left Side of the Brain*. Boston: Houghton Mifflin.

Einstein, Albert. 1922-1956. *The Meaning of Relativity*. Princeton: Princeton University Press.

Ellis, Ralph D. 1980. "Prereflective consciousness and the process of symbolization". *Man and World* 13: 173-191.

Ellis, Ralph D. 1983. "Agent causation, chance, and determinism". *Philosophical Inquiry* 5: 29-42.

Ellis, Ralph D. 1986. *An Ontology of Consciousness*. Dordrecht: Kluwer/Martinus Nijhoff.

Ellis, Ralph. 1990. "Afferent-efferent connections and 'neutrality-modifications' in imaginative and perceptual consciousness". *Man and World* 23: 23-33.

Ellis, Ralph D. 1991. "A critique of concepts of non-sufficient causation," *Philosophical Inquiry* 13: 22-42.

Ellis, Ralph D. 1992. *Coherence and Verification in Ethics*. Lanham: University Press of America.

Ellis, Ralph D. 1992b. "A thought experiment concerning universal expansion". *Philosophia* 21: 257-275.

Elman, Jeffrey. 1993. "Learning and development in neural networks: the importance of starting small". *Cognition* 48: 71-99.

Eslinger, Paul J. and Antonio R. Damasio. 1985. "Severe disturbance of higher cognition after bilateral frontal lobe ablation: Patient EVR". *Neurology* 35: 1731-1741.

Evans, Jonathan. 1993. "The mental model theory of conditional reasoning: critical appraisal and revision". *Cognition* 48: 1-20.

Farah, Martha. 1989. "The neural basis of mental imagery". *Trends in Neuroscience* 12: 395-399.

Feigl, Herbert. 1958. "The 'mental' and the 'physical'". In Herbert Feigl (ed), *Minnesota Studies in the Philosophy of Science*, II. Minneapolis: University of Minnesota Press, 370-497.

Feuerbach, Ludwig. 1966. *Principles of the Philosophy of the Future*. Indianapolis: Bobbs-Merrill.

Flor-Henry, Pierre, L.T. Yeudall, Z.T. Koles, and B.G. Howarth. 1979. "Neuropsychological and power spectral EEG investigations of the obsessive-compulsive syndrome". *Biological Psychiatry* 14: 119-129.

Fodor, Jerry. 1975. *The Language of Thought*. Cambridge: Harvard University Press.

Fodor, Jerry. 1981. In Jerry Fodor (ed), *RePresentations: Philosophical Essays on the Foundations of Cognitive Science*. Cambridge: The MIT Press.

Fodor, Jerry. 1981b. "The mind-body problem". *Scientific American* 244: 114-123.

Fodor, Jerry. 1983. *The Modularity of Mind*. Cambridge: The MIT Press.

Fodor, Jerry and Zenon Pylyshyn. 1988. "Connectionism and cognitive architecture: critical analysis". *Cognition* 28: 3-71.

Foulkes, William D. 1985. *Dreaming: A Cognitive-psychological Analysis*. Hillsdale, N.J.: Erlbaum.

Fox, Elaine. 1994. "Attentional bias in anxiety: A defective inhibition hypothesis". *Cognition and Emotion* 8: 165-195.

Freud, Sigmund. 1959. *Beyond the Pleasure Principle.* New York: Bantam.

Fuchs, W. 1922. "Eine Pseudofovea bei Hemianopikern," *Psychologische Forschung.*

Fuster, Joaquim. 1980. *The Prefrontal Cortex.* New York: Raven Press.

Gainotti, Guido, Carlo Caltagirone, and P. Zoccolotti. 1993. "Left/right and cortical/subcortical dichotomies in the neurophychological study of human emotions". *Cognition and Emotion* 7: 71-93.

Gazzaniga, Michael. 1986. *Mind Matters.* Boston: The MIT Press.

Gendlin, Eugene. 1962. *Experiencing and the Creation of Meaning.* Toronto: Collier-Macmillan.

Gendlin, Eugene. 1971. "A theory of personality change". In Alvin R. Mahrer (ed), *Creative Developments in Psychotherapy.* Cleveland: Case Western Reserve University Press, 439-489.

Gendlin, Eugene. 1973. "Experiential phenomenology". In Maurice Natanson (ed), *Phenomenology and the Social Sciences.* Evanston: Northwestern University Press, 281-322.

Gendlin, Eugene. 1981. *Focusing.* Toronto: Bantam.

Gendlin, Eugene. 1992. "Thinking beyond patterns". In B. den Ouden and M. Moen (eds), *The Presence of Feeling in Thought.* New York: Peter Lang.

Gendlin, Eugene. Unpublished. "The Primacy of the Body, Not the Primacy of Perception."

Gelman, Rochel. 1990. "First principles organize attention to and learning about relevant data: Number and the animate-inanimate distinction". *Cognitive Science* 14: 79-106.

Genesee, Fred, J. Hamers, W.E. Lambert, M. Seitz, and R. Stark. 1978. "Language processing in bilinguals". *Brain and Language* 5: 1-12.

Georgalis, Nicholas. 1994. "Asymmetry of Access to Intentional States". *Erkenntnis* 40: 185-211.

Gerow, Josh. 1986. *Psychology: An Introduction.* Glenview, Ill.: Scott, Foresman and Co.

Gibson, J.G., and W.A. Kennedy. 1960. "A clinical-EEG study in a case of obsessional neurosis". *Electroencephalography and Clinical Neurology* 12: 198-201.

Giorgi, Amedeo. 1973. "Phenomenology and experimental psychology". In Amedeo Giorgi, William Fischer and Rolf von Eckartsberg (eds), *Duquesne Studies in Phenomenological Psychology, Vol. I.* Pittsburgh: Duquesne University Press/Humanities Press, 6-29.

Glasgow, Janice and Dimitri Papadias. 1992. "Computational imagery". *Cognitive Science* 16: 355-394.

Gleick, James 1987. *Chaos: The Making of a New Science.* New York: Viking Press.

Globus, Gordon. 1987. *Dream Life, Wake Life.* New York: State University of New York Press.

Globus, Gordon and Stephen Franklin. 1982. "Prospects for the scientific observer of perceptual consciousness". In Davidson, Julian and Richard Davidson (eds), *The Psychobiology of Consciousness.* New York: Plenum, 465-482.

Goldman, Alvin. 1969. "The compatibility of mechanism and purpose". *Philosophical Review* 78: 468-482.

Goldman, Alvin. 1970. *A Theory of Human Action.* Englewood Cliffs: Prentice-Hall.

Goldstein, Irwin. 1994. "Identifying mental states: a celebrated hypothesis refuted". *Australasian Journal of Philosophy* 72: 46-62.

Goldstein, Kurt. 1938. *The Organism.* New York: American Books.

Gordon, Peter, Jennifer Eberhardt, and Jay Rueckl. 1993. "Attentional modulation of the phonetic significance of acoustic cues". *Cognitive Psychology* 25: 1-42.

Granit, Ragnor. 1922. *The Purposive Brain.* Cambridge: The MIT Press.

Gray, Jeffrey. 1990. "Brain systems that mediate both emotion and cognition". *Cognition and Emotion* 4: 269-288.

Gurwitsch, Aron. 1964. *The Field of Consciousness.* Pittsburgh: Duquesne University Press.

Hanze, Martin and Friedrich Hesse. 1993. "Emotional influences on semantic priming". *Cognition and Emotion* 7: 195-205.

Harlow, Harry. 1959. "Learning set and error factor theory". In Sigmund Koch (ed), *Psychology: A Study of a Science, Vol. 2.* New York: McGraw-Hill, 492-537.

Hebb, Donald. 1961. *The Organization of Behavior.* New York: John Wiley.

Held, Richard and Alan Hein. 1958. "Adaptation of disarranged hand-eye coordination contingent upon re-afferent stimulation". *Perceptual and Motor Skills* 8: 87-90.

Helmholtz, Hermann. 1962. *Helmholtz's Treatise on Physiological Optics*, J.P.C. Southall (trans). New York: Dover.

Hernandez-Peon, Raul, G. Chavez-Iberra, and E. Aguilar-Figuera. 1963. "Somatic evoked potentials in one case of hysteric anesthesia". *Electroencephalography and Clinical Neurophysiology* 15: 889-896.

Hernandez-Peon, Raul, Harold Scherrer, and Michel Jouvet. 1956. "Modification of electrical activity in cochlear nucleus during attention in unanesthetized cats". *Science* 123: 331.

Higgins, E.Tory and G. King. 1981. "Accessibility of social constructs: Information-processing consequences of individual and contextual variability". In Nancy Cantor and John Kihlstrom (eds), *Personality, Cognition, and Social Interaction*. Hillsdale, N.J.: Erlbaum.

Hillis, A. and A. Caramazza. 1990. "The effects of attentional deficits on reading and spelling". In A. Caramazza (ed), *Cognitive Neuropsychology and Neurolinguistics: Advances in Models of Cognitive Function and Impairment*. Hillsdale, N.J.: Erlbaum.

Hirsch, H.V.B., and D.N. Spinelli. 1970. "Visual experience modifies distribution of horizontally and vertically oriented receptive fields in cats". *Science* 168: 869.

Hoppe, Klaus. 1977. "Split brains and psychoanalysis". *The Psychoanalytic Quarterly* 46: 220-224.

Horgan, Terrence. 1992. "Nonreductive materialism and the explanatory autonomy of psychology". In S. Wagner and R. Warner (eds), *Beyond Materialism and Physicalism*. Notre Dame: University of Notre Dame Press.

Hubel, David H. and Torsten N. Wiesel. 1959. "Receptive fields of single neurons in the cat's striate cortex," *Journal of Physiology* 148: 574-591.

Hunt, Harry T. 1985. "Cognition and states of consciousness: The necessity for empirical study of ordinary and non-ordinary consciousness for contemporary cognitive psychology". *Perceptual and Motor Skills* 60: 239-282.

Husserl, Edmund. 1913. *Logical Investigations*. J.N. Findlay (trans). New York: Humanities Press.

Husserl, Edmund. 1931-1969. *Ideas*. W.R. Boyce Gibson (trans). London: Collier; from "Ideen zu einer reinen Phänomenologie und phänomenologischen Philosophie," 1913.

Husserl, Edmund. 1962. *Phänomenologische Psychologie*. Den Haag: Martinus Nijhoff.

Husserl, Edmund. 1966. *The Phenomenology of Internal Time Consciousness*. James Churchill (trans). Bloomington: Indiana University Press; based on lectures delivered in 1905.

Jackendoff, Ray. 1987. *Consciousness and the Computational Mind*. Cambridge: The MIT Press.

Jackson, Frank. 1986. "What Mary didn't know". *Journal of Philosophy* 83: 291-295.

Jacoby, Larry, and Colleen Kelley. 1992. "Unconscious influences of memory: Dissociations and automaticity". In A.D. Milner and M.D. Rugg (eds), *The Neuropsychology of Consciousness*. London: Academic Press, 235-62.

James, William. 1968. "Does 'consciousness' exist". John McDermott (ed), *The Writings of William James*. New York: Random House, 169-170.

Johnson, Mark. 1987. *The Body in the Mind*. Chicago: University of Chicago Press.

Johnson-Laird, Philip N. 1972. "The three-term series problem". *Cognition* 1: 57-82.

Johnson-Laird, Philip N. 1993. *Human and Machine Thinking*. Hillsdale, N.J.: Erlbaum.

Johnson-Laird, Philip N. 1994. "Mental models and probabilistic thinking". *Cognition* 50: 189-209.

Johnson-Laird, Philip N., and R.M.J. Byrne. 1989. "*Only* reasoning". *Journal of Memory and Language* 28: 313-330.

Johnson-Laird, Philip N., and R.M.J. Byrne. 1991. *Deduction*. Hillsdale, N.J.: Erlbaum.

Jorgensen, Julia, and Rachel J. Falmagne. 1992. "Aspects of the meaning of *if...then* for older preschoolers: Hypotheticality, entailment, and suppositional processes". *Cognitive Development* 7: 189-212.

Joseph, Rhawn. 1982. "The neuropsychology of development: hemispheric laterality, limbic language and the origin of thought". *Journal of Clinical Psychology* 38: 4-33.

Jouvet, Michel. 1967. "Neurophysiology of the states of sleep". *Physiological Review* 47: 117-127.

Kahneman, E. 1973. *Attention and Effort*. Englewood Cliffs: Prentice Hall.

Kandel, Eric, and James Schwartz. 1981. *Principles of Neural Science*. New York: Elsevier-North Holland.

Kaufman, G. 1980. *Imagery, Language and Cognition: Toward a Theory of Symbolic Activity in Human Problem-Solving*. Berlin: Universitetsforlaget.

Kimura, Doreen, and Y. Archibald. 1974. "Motor functions of the left hemisphere," *Brain* 97: 337-350.

Komisaruk, Barry. 1977. "The role of rhythmical brain activity in sensorimotor integration". In James Sprague and Alan Epstein (eds), *Progress in Psychology and Physiological Integration*. New York: Academic Press, v. 7.

Koriat, A., Lichtenstein, S. and Fischhoff, B. 1980. "Reasons for confidence". *Journal of Experimental Psychology: Human Learning and Memory* 6: 539-541.

Kosslyn, Stephen M. 1983. *Ghosts in the Mind's Machine: Creating and Using Images in the Brain*. New York: W.W. Norton.

Kretch, David, M. Rosenzweig, and E. Bennett. 1962. "Relations between brain chemistry and problem-solving among rats raised in enriched and impoverished environments". *Journal of Comparative and Physiological Psychology* 55: 801-807.

Kretch, David, M. Rosenzweig, and E. Bennett. 1966. "Effects of environmental complexity and training on brain chemistry". *Journal of Comparative and Physiological Psychology* 53: 509-519.

Kuhn, Thomas. 1962. *The Structure of Scientific Revolutions.* Chicago: University of Chicago Press.

Lakoff, George 1987. *Women, Fire, and Dangerous Things: What Categories Reveal about the Mind.* Chicago: University of Chicago Press.

Lashley, Karl. 1950. "In search of the engram". In *Symposium of the Society for Experimental Biology, No. 4.* London: Cambridge University Press.

Lavy, Edith and Marcel van den Hout. 1994. "Cognitive avoidance and attentional bias: Causal relationships". *Cognitive Therapy and Research* 18: 179-194.

Legrenzi, P., V. Girotto, and P.N. Johnson-Laird. 1993. "Focussing in reasoning and decision making". *Cognition* 49: 37-66.

Lenneberg, Eric. 1967. *Biological Foundations of Language.* New York: Wiley.

Leyhausen, Paul. 1979. *Cat Behavior* New York: Garland Press.

Lewis, David. 1973. *Counterfactuals.* Cambridge: Harvard University Press.

Liberman, A.M., F.S. Cooper, D. Shankweiler, and M. Studdert-Kennedy. 1967. "Perceptions of the speech code". *Psychological Review* 74: 431-461.

Libet, Benjamin, A.G. Curtis, E.W. Wright, and D.K. Pearl. 1983. "Time of conscious intention to act in relation to onset of cerebral activity (readiness-potential). The unconscious initiation of a freely voluntary act". *Brain* 106: 640.

Loewi, Otto. 1960. *Perspectives in Biology and Medicine, Vol. 4.* Chicago: University of Chicago Press.

Logan, G.D. 1980. "Attention and automaticity in stroop and priming tasks: Theory and data". *Cognitive Psychology* 12: 523-553.

Ludwig, Arnold. 1972. "Hysteria: A neurobiological theory". *Archives of General Psychiatry* 27: 771-777.

Lukacs, Georg. 1966. "Existentialism or Marxism". In *Existentialism versus Marxism,* G. Novak, ed. New York: Delta Press, 134-153.

Luria, Alexander R. 1968. *The Mind of a Mnemonist.* Chicago: Henry Regenery Co.

Luria, Alexander R. 1973. *The Working Brain.* New York: Basic Books.

Luria, Alexander R. 1980. *Higher Cortical Functions in Man,* 2nd ed. New York: Basic Books.

Lyons, William. 1983. "The transformation of introspection". *British Journal of Social Psychology* 22: 327-342.

Lyons, William. 1984. "Dennett, functionalism, and introspection". *Canadian Journal of Philosophy* 11: 55-83.

Lyons, William. 1986. *The Disappearance of Introspection.* Cambridge: The MIT Press.

MacKay, Donald. 1984. "Mind talk and brain talk". In Michael Gazzaniga (ed), *Handbook of Cognitive Neuroscience.* New York: Plenum Press, 293-318.

Mackie, John L. 1974. *The Cement of the Universe.* Oxford: Oxford University Press.

Macrides, Foteos, H.B. Eichenbaum, and W.B. Forbes. 1982. "Temporal relationship between sniffing and the limbic theta rhythm during odor discrimination reversal learning". *Journal of Neuroscience* 2: 1705.

Malcolm, Norman. 1967. "Explaining behavior". *Philosophical Review* 76: 97-104.

Mandler, Jean. 1992. "The foundations of conceptual thought in infancy". *Cognitive Development* 7: 273-285.

Margolis, Eric. 1994. "A reassessment of the shift from the classical theory of concepts to prototype theory". *Cognition* 51: 73-89.

Marks, Lawrence. 1978. *The Unity of the Senses: Interrelations Among the Modalities.* New York: Academic Press.

May, Rollo. 1976. *The Courage to Create.* New York: Bantam.

Mayes, A.R. 1992. "Automatic memory processes in amnesia: How are they mediated?" In A.D. Milner and M.D. Rugg (eds). *The Neuropsychology of Consciousness.* London: Academic Press.

McCauley, Robert. 1994. "On Choosing a Metaphor for Thinking". Lecture at Southern Society for Philosophy and Psychology.

McHugh, D.E. and A.T. Bahill. 1985. "Learning to track predictable target waveforms without a time delay". *Investigative Ophthalmology and Visual Science* 26: 932-937.

Mele, Alfred. 1993. "Motivated belief". *Behavior and Philosophy* 21: 19-27.

Merleau-Ponty, Maurice. 1962. *Phenomenology of Perception.* Colin Smith (trans). New York: Humanities Press.

Merleau-Ponty, Maurice. 1963. *The Structure of Behavior.* A. Fischer (trans). Boston: Beacon; original French edition 1942.

Metcalfe, Janet. 1993. "Novelty monitoring, metacognition, and control in a composite holographic associative recall model: Implications for Korsakoff amnesia". *Psychological Review* 100: 3-22.

Metcalfe, Janet. 1994. *Metacognition: Knowing about Knowing.* Cambridge: MIT Press.

Miller, Lawrence. 1984. "Neuropsychological concepts of somatoform disorders". *International Journal of Psychiatry in Medicine* 14: 31-46.

Miller, Lawrence. 1990. *Inner Natures: Brain, Self and Personality.* New York: Ballantine.

Miller, Robert. 1981. *Meaning and Purpose in the Intact Brain.* Oxford: Clarendon Press.

Miner, A.C. and Reder, L.M. 1994. "A New look at feeling of knowing: Its metacognitive role in regulating question answering". In J. Metcalfe (ed), *Metacognition.* Cambridge: MIT Press, 1994.

Minsky, Marvin. 1986. *The Society of the Mind.* New York: Simon and Schuster.

Mitchell, D.E., R.D. Freeman, M. Millodot, and G. Haegerstrom. 1973. "Meridional amblyopia: Evidence for modification of the human visual system by early visual experience". *Vision Research* 13: 535.

Moray, Neville. 1970. *Attention: Selective Processes in Vision and Hearing.* New York: Academic Press.

Morrison, Adrian. 1979. "Brain-stem regulation of behavior during sleep and wakefulness". In James Sprague and Alan Epstein (eds), *Progress in Psychobiology and Physiological Psychology, Vol. 8.* New York: Academic Press, 91-93.

Morrison, Adrian. 1983. "A window on the sleeping brain," *Scientific American,* 248: 94-103.

Natsoulas, Thomas. 1993. "What is wrong with appendage theory of consciousness". *Philosophical Psychology* 6: 137-154.

Nauta, Walle J. 1971. "The problem of the frontal lobe: A reinterpretation," *Journal of Psychiatric Research* 8: 167-187.

Needleman, Jacob. 1968. *Being in the World: Selected Papers of Ludwig Binswanger.* New York: Harper & Row.

Neely, J.H. 1977. "Semantic priming and retrieval from lexical memory: Roles of inhibitionless spreading activation and limited-category attention". *Journal of Experimental Psychology: General* 106: 226-254.

Neisser, Ulric. 1967. *Cognitive Psychology.* Englewood Cliffs, N.J.: Prentice-Hall.

Neisser, Ulric. 1976. *Cognition and Reality.* San Francisco: Freeman.

Neisser, Ulric. 1994. "Ecological Psychology". Lecture at Southern Society for Philosophy and Psychology.

Newton, Natika. 1982. "Experience and imagery". *Southern Journal of Philosophy* 20: 475-487.

Newton, Natika. 1989. "Visualizing *is* imagining seeing: a reply to White". *Analysis* 49: 77-81.

Newton, Natika. 1991. "Consciousness, qualia, and reentrant signalling". *Behavior and Philosophy* 19: 21-41.

Newton, Natika. 1992. "Dennett on intrinsic intentionality". *Analysis* 52: 18-23.

Newton, Natika. 1993. "The sensorimotor theory of cognition". *Pragmatics and Cognition* 1: 267-305.

Noren, Stephen. 1979. "Anomalous monism, events and 'the mental'". *Philosophy and Phenomenological Research* 40: 64-70.

Olds, James. 1977. *Drives and Reinforcement: Behavioral Studies of Hypothalamic Functions*. New York: Raven.

Ornstein, Robert and Richard Thompson. 1984. *The Amazing Brain*. Boston: Houghton Mifflin.

Paivio, Allan 1986. *Mental Representations: A Dual Coding Approach*. New York: Oxford University Press.

Pardo, J.V, P.J. Pardo, K.W. Janer, and M.E. Raichle. 1990. "The anterior cingulate cortex mediates processing selection in the stroop attentional conflict paradigm". *Proceedings of the National Academy of Sciences* 87: 256-259.

Pauli, Wolfgang. 1958. *Theory of Relativity*. G. Field (trans). New York: Dover.

Petersen, S.E., P.T. Fox, M.I. Posner, M. Mintum, and M.E. Raichle. 1989. "Positron emission tomographic studies of the processing of single words". *Journal of Cognitive Neuroscience* 1: 153-170.

Petersen, S.E., P.T. Fox, A.Z. Snyder, and M.E. Raichle. 1990. "Activation of extrastriate and frontal cortical areas by visual words and word like stimuli". *Science* 249: 1041-1044.

Piaget, Jean. 1928-1965. *Judgment and Reasoning in the Child*. Marjorie Warden (trans). London: Routledge & Kegan Paul.

Piaget, Jean, and Barbel Inhelder. 1969. *The Early Growth of Logic in the Child*, E.A. Lunzer and D. Papert (trans). New York: W.W. Norton.

Place, U.T. 1956. "Is consciousness a brain process?" *British Journal of Psychology* 47: 44-50.

Place, U.T. 1993. "A radical behaviorist methodology for the empirical investigation of private events". *Behavior and Philosophy* 20: 25-35.

Plato. 1976. George M. Grube, trans. *Meno*. Indianapolis: Hackett.

Poggio, Tomaso and Christof Koch. 1985. "Ill-posed problems in early vision from computational theory to analogue networks". *Proceedings of the Royal Society of London*. B226: 303-323.

Popper, Karl and John Eccles. 1977. *The Self and Its Brain*. Berlin: Springer-Verlag.

Posner, Michael I. 1980. "Orienting of attention". *Quarterly Journal of Experimental Psychology* 32: 3-25.

Posner, Michael I. 1990. "Hierarchical distributed networks in the neuropsychology of selective attention". In A. Caramazza (ed). *Cognitive Neuropsychology and Neurolinguistics: Advances in Models of Cognitive Function and Impairment.* New York: Plenum, 187-210.

Posner, Michael I. and Mary K. Rothbart. 1992. "Attentional mechanisms and conscious experience". In A.D. Milner and M.D. Rugg (eds), *The Neuropsychology of Consciousness.* London: Academic Press.

Posner, Michael I., and Petersen, S.E. 1990. "The attention system of the human brain". *Annual Review of Neuroscience* 13: 25-42.

Premack, David. 1988. "Minds with and without language". In L. Weiskrantz (ed). *Thought Without Language.* Oxford: Oxford University Press, 46-65.

Pribram, Karl. 1980. "Mind, brain, and consciousness: the organization of competence and conduct". In Julian Davidson and Richard Davidson (eds), *The Psychobiology of Consciousness.* New York: Plenum Press, 47-64.

Pribram, Karl. 1971. *Languages of the Brain.* New York: Prentice Hall.

Pribram, Karl, M. Nuwer, and R. Baron. 1974. "The holographic hypothesis of memory structure in brain function and perception". In R.C. Atkinson, D.H. Krantz, R.C. Luce and P. Suppes (eds), *Contemporary Developments in Mathematical Psychology, vol. 2.* New York: W.H. Freeman, 416-454.

Putnam, Hilary. 1993. "Functionalism". Paper presented at a meeting of the American Philosophical Association, December 28, 1993.

Pylyshyn, Zenon. 1973. "What the mind's eye tells the mind's brain". *Psychological Bulletin* 80: 11-25.

Reder, L.M. and Ritter, E.E. 1992. "What determines initial feeling of knowing? Familiarity with question terms, not with the answer". *Journal of Experimental Psychology: Learning, Memory, and Cognition* 9: 55-72.

Restak, Richard. 1984. *The Brain.* New York: Bantam.

Rhodes, Gillian and Tanya Tremewan. 1993. "The Simon then Garfunkel effect: Semantic priming, sensitivity, and the modularity of face recognition". *Cognitive Psychology* 25: 147-87.

Richardson, John. 1991. "Imagery and the brain". In Cesare Cornoldi and Mark McDaniel (eds), *Imagery and Cognition.* New York: Springer-Verlag, 1-46.

Roffwarg, Howard, J.N. Muzzio, and W.C. Dement. 1966. "Ontogenetic development of the human sleep-dream cycle". *Science* 152: 604.

Rogers, Carl. 1959. "A theory of therapy, personality, and interpersonal relationships". In Sigmund Koch (ed), *Psychology: A Study of a Science, Vol. 3.* New York: McGraw-Hill, 184-256.

Rorty, Richard. 1966. "Mind-body identity, privacy, and categories". *Review of Metaphysics* 19: 24-54.

Rosch, Eleanor. 1975. "Cognitive representations of semantic categories". *Journal of Experimental Psychology: General* 104: 192-253.

Rosch, Eleanor. 1981. "Prototype classification and logical classification: the two systems". In Ellin Scholnick (ed), *New Trends in Conceptual Representation.* Hillsdale, N.J.: Erlbaum, 73-85.

Rosch, Eleanor, C.B. Mervis, W.D. Gray, D.M. Johnson, and P. Boyes-Braem. 1976. "Basic objects in natural categories". *Cognitive Psychology* 8: 382-349.

Runeson, Sverker. 1974. "Constant velocity -- not perceived as such". *Psychological Research* 37: 3-23.

Ryle, Gilbert. 1949. *The Concept of Mind.* New York: Barnes and Noble.

Sartre, Jean Paul. 1957. *The Transcendence of the Ego.* F. Williams and R. Kirkpatrick trans. New York: Noonday.

Sartre, Jean Paul. 1966. *The Psychology of the Imagination.* New York: Washington Square Press.

Sartre, Jean Paul. 1971. *Sketch for a Theory of Emotions.* London: Methuen.

Scheler, Max. 1928-1968. *Man's Place in Nature.* Hans Meyerhoff (trans). New York: Nonday Press.

Schopenhauer, Arthur. 1962. *The World As Will and Idea* New York: Modern Library.

Schües, Christina. 1994. "The anonymous powers of the habitus". *Study Project in the Phenomenology of the Body Newsletter* 7: 12-25.

Schyns, Philippe. 1991. "A modular neural network model of concept acquisition". *Cognitive Science* 15: 461-508.

Searle, John. 1984. *Minds, Brains and Science.* Cambridge: Harvard University Press.

Sedikides, Constantine. 1992. "Mood as a determinant of attentional focus". *Cognition and Emotion* 6: 129-148.

Segal, Sydney. 1971. *Imagery: Current Cognitive Approaches.* New York, Academic Press.

Sellars, Wilfrid. 1965. "The identity approach to the mind-body problem". *Review of Metaphysics* 18: 430-451.

Sharvy, Richard. 1963. "A logical error in Taylor's 'Fatalism'". *Analysis* 23: 96.

Shaver, Phillip, Lee Pierson, and Stephen Lang. 1974-1975. "Converging evidence for the functional significance of imagery in problem solving". *Cognition* 3: 359-375.

Simon, Michael. 1979. "Action and dialictics". *Philosophy and Phenomenological Research* 39: 468-69.

Slomianko, Joshua. 1987. "Learning to learn". Seminar presented at Atlanta University, August 1987.

Smart, J.J.C. 1963. "Materialism". *Journal of Philosophy* 60: 651-662.

Smart, J.J.C. 1970. "Sensations and brain processes". *Philosophical Review* 68: Reprinted in C.V. Borst (ed). *The Mind-Brain Identity Theory.* London: Macmillan, 1970, 141-156.

Smith, Edward, Christopher Langston, and Richard Nisbett. 1992. "The case for rules in reasoning". *Cognitive Science* 16: 1-40.

Smith, Peter, and O.R. Jones. 1986. *The Philosophy of Mind.* London: Cambridge University Press.

Sperry, R.W.. 1966. "The great cerebral commissure". In Stanley Coopersmith (ed), *Frontiers of Psychological Research.* San Francisco: W.H. Freeman, 60-70.

Springer, Sally, and Georg Deutsch. 1989. *Left Brain, Right Brain.* New York: W.H. Freeman.

Srebro, Richard. 1985. "Localization of visually evoked cortical activity in humans". *Journal of Physiology* 360: 233-246.

Stich, Steven. 1983. *From Folk Psychology to Cognitive Science: The Case Against Belief.* Cambridge: The MIT Press.

Streri, Arlette, Elizabeth Spelke, and E. Rameix. 1993. "Modality-specific and amodal aspects of object perception in infancy: The case of active touch". *Cognition* 47: 251-279.

Studdert-Kennedy, M. and D. Shankweiler. 1970. "Hemispheric specialization for speech perception". *Journal of the Acoustical Society of America* 48: 579-594.

Symons, Donald. 1993. "The stuff that dreams aren't made of: Why wake-state and dream-state sensory experiences differ". *Cognition* 47: 181-217.

Taylor, Richard. 1962. "Fatalism". *The Philosophical Review* 71: 55-66.

Taylor, Richard. 1963. *Metaphysics.* Englewood Cliffs.

Taylor, Richard. 1963. "A note on fatalism". *The Philosophical Review* 72: 497-99.

Taylor, Richard. 1964. "Comment". *The Journal of Philosophy* 61: 305-307.

Taylor, Richard. 1964. "Fatalism and ability". *Analysis* 24: 25-27.

Thompson, Richard F. 1975. *Introduction to Physiological Psychology.* New York: Harper & Row.

Titchener, Edward B. 1912. "Descriptions vs. statement of meaning". *American Journal of Psychology* 23: 165-182.

Tienson, John. 1987. "An introduction to connectionism". *Southern Journal of Philosophy* 26: 1-16.

Treisman, A.M. 1964. "Selective attention in man". *British Medical Bulletin* 20: 12-16.

Tucker, Don. 1981. "Lateral brain function, emotion and conceptualization". *Psychological Bulletin* 89: 19-43.

Umilta, Carlo. 1988. "The control operations of consciousness". In A.J. Marcel and E. Bisiach (eds), *Consciousness in Contemporary Science*. Oxford: Clarendon Press, 334-356.

Vaid, Jyotsha and Fred Genessee. 1980. "Neuropsychological approaches to bilingualism: A critical review". *Canadian Journal of Psychology* 34: 419-447.

Varela, Francisco, Evan Thompson, and Eleanor Rosch. 1991-1993. *The Embodied Mind*. Cambridge: The MIT Press.

Vygotsky, Lev. 1962. *Thought and Language*. Cambridge: The MIT Press.

Warrington, E.K. 1985. "Visual deficits associated with occipital lobe lesions in man". *Pontificiae Academiae Scientiarum Scripta Varia* 54: 247-261.

Wason, P.C. and Johnson-Laird, P.N. 1972. *Psychology of Reasoning: Structure and Content*. Cambridge, MA: Harvard University Press.

Watson, James. 1969. *The Double Helix*. New York: Signet.

Watson, John. 1900-1930. *Behaviorism*. Chicago: University of Chicago Press.

Watson, John. 1913. "Psychology as the behaviorist views it". *Psychological Review* 20: 157-158.

Weil, Vivian. 1979. "Intentional and mechanistic explanation". *Philosophy and Phenomenological Research* 40: 459-473.

Weiskrantz, Lawrence. 1986. *Blindsight: A Case Study and Implications*. Oxford: Oxford University Press.

White, Alan. 1987. "Visualizing and imagining seeing". *Analysis* 47: 221-224.

Whitehead, Alfred N. 1925. *An Enquiry Concerning the Principles of Natural Knowledge*. New York: Dover.

Williams, Bernard. 1966. "Imagination and the self". *Proceedings of the British Academy, vol. 52*, 105-124.

Winson, Jonathan. 1986. *Brain and Psyche*. New York: Random House.

Winson, Jonathon and Charles Abzug. 1977. "Gating of neuronal transmission in the hippocampus: Efficacy of transmission varies with behavioral state". *Science* 196: 1223.

Winson, Jonathon and Charles Abzug. 1978a. "Neuronal transmission through hippocampal pathways dependent on behavior". *Journal of Neurophysiology* 41: 716.

Winson, Jonathon and Charles Abzug. 1978b. "Dependence upon behavior of neuronal transmission from perforant pathway through entorhinal cortex". *Brain Research* 147: 422.

Wittgenstein, Ludwig. 1953. *Philosophical Investigations.* New York: MacMillan.

Woodward, Steven H. 1988. "An anatomical model of hemispheric asymmetry". *Journal of Clinical and Experimental Neuropsychology* 10: 68.

Wyer, Robert S. and Thomas K. Srull. 1981. "Category accessibility: Some theoretical and empirical issues concerning the processing of social stimulus information". In E.T. Higgins, C.P. Herman, and M.P. Zanna (eds), *Social Cognition: The Ontario Symposium, Vol. I.* Hillsdale, N.J.: Erlbaum, 161-198.

Yarbus, Alfred L. 1967. *Eye Movement and Vision.* New York: Plenum.

Young, John Z. 1988. *Philosophy and the Brain.* Oxford: Oxford University Press.

# Index